# THE

# HITLER
# YOUTH

# THE
# HITLER
# YOUTH

## HOW GERMANY INDOCTRINATED
## A NEW GENERATION

JULIAN FLANDERS

## Picture credits

**Alamy:** 40, 61, 63, 71, 80, 90, 96, 100, 102, 124, 135, 138, 165, 176, 192, 192, 213, 219, 231.

**Bundesarchhiv:** 150.

**Library of Congress:** 112.

**Public domain:** 19, 23, 51, 77, 83, 92, 102, 114, 133, 150, 208, 224, 233.

This edition published in 2024 by Arcturus Publishing Limited
26/27 Bickels Yard, 151–153 Bermondsey Street,
London SE1 3HA

AD010542UK

Printed in the UK

# Contents

## Introduction

# The Illusion of Hope

One of the most memorable representations of the rise of Nazism in 1930s Germany can be found in the 1972 film *Cabaret*. In a scene set in a Berlin beer garden on a warm and gentle summer's afternoon in 1931, two men settle an argument and toast a joyful future. In the background, a sweet boy's voice begins to sing about nature: 'The sun on the meadow is summery warm, The stag in the forest runs free.' The men turn to listen, as do other drinkers as the band takes up the tune. The camera pans back and reveals the boy wearing a Hitler Youth uniform. At that moment, the music becomes more rousing, the lyrics more nationalistic. Swept up by the song, by its lyrics and the rousing melody, people rise from their chairs and more voices join in the fervent chorus, 'Tomorrow belongs to me!', as the boy gives a vigorous Nazi salute. The scene is hugely effective in revealing how self-delusional many Germans were at the time about the Nazis.

When the song first appeared in stage performances of the play *Cabaret* in 1966, it was met with outrage. People were shocked that a genuine Nazi anthem could feature in a Broadway musical. The song has since been adopted by right-wing groups in the USA, the UK,

Sweden, Italy, Austria and even by neo-Nazi groups in Germany. Although the song was inspired by traditional patriotic music of the 1930s and even borrowed a few lyrical phrases from an authentic Nazi song, in fact it was written in the mid-1960s by John Kander and Fred Ebb, two Jewish songwriters working on Broadway. Appropriately, the song was an illusion, a deception – a technique the leaders of the Hitler Youth employed to shape the thinking and actions of millions of young Germans after its official formation in 1926.

Among the many common questions about the rise of the Nazis is how such a civilized, highly educated society as Germany could elect a group of violent thugs to government who, in five years, would turn a 'continent into a charnel house'?[1] Why did the German people put themselves in the hands of a murderous dictator? Why did the world allow a man described by author William Shirer as a 'vagabond', whose 1923 Beer Hall Putsch was a 'comic fiasco', to become a genocidal *Führer* whose regime threatened to last a thousand years? The answer is multi-faceted – as the number of books, articles, talks, interviews and documentary films that are still produced on the subject today attest. But much is revealed by examining Germany's history since its unification in 1871 – the subject of the first two chapters of this book – and in a study of the extraordinary success of the Hitler Youth movement.

## The Aryans take power

In January 1919, shortly after the armistice that ended the First World War and six months before the punitive terms of the Treaty of Versailles were agreed, a small political party, the *Deutsche Arbeiterpartei* (DAP or German Workers' Party), was formed. In September that year, a new recruit was welcomed into its ranks, one Adolf Hitler. In February 1920, he announced the party's 25-point programme, which promised campaigns including the removal of the 'disgrace of the armistice', overturning the Treaty of Versailles, the unification of all German-speaking peoples into one Reich and the restoration of the army to make Germany 'strong' again.

Initially a matter of little interest to the by-then renamed *National-sozialistische Deutsche Arbeiterpartei* (NSDAP or Nationalist Socialist German Workers' Party), as the Nazi Party was called, because under-18s were voteless, the youth only became interesting to them following Hitler's incarceration in Landsberg Prison in 1924 for his part in a failed putsch. During his short jail sentence, he wrote his political manifesto *Mein Kampf*, in which he outlined his racist worldview. Hitler explained that he believed in a hierarchy of different races, with the German Aryan[2] race at the top and Jews, Black people, the disabled, homosexuals, Gypsies and other minorities at the bottom. He identified Judaism and communism as the world's two greatest evils, hinted at genocide by destroying the weak to make room for the strong and outlined his plans for expansion in the east. To help him accomplish these aims, which he knew would take time, and to secure his party's future existence, Hitler needed to create a generation of young Aryans with Nordic[3] features who were racially pure, loyal to him, steeped in Nazi ideology, physically fit and ready to fight and die for Germany, and who could secure the future of the Reich.

## Baldur von Schirach

Like many Nazi ideas, the formation of a youth group was not an original one; there had been a history of youth groups in Germany dating back to the 16th century. In its first iteration, boys recruited into the *Jungsturm Adolf Hitler* in the early 1920s acted as the youth counterpart to the militant Nazis, the *Sturmabteilung* (SA or Storm Troopers), who regularly used vandalism and street brawling to voice their angry nationalism and discontent with the Weimar government. When Hitler was imprisoned, the *Jungsturm's* activities had to go underground for a few years until they could be formally recognized as the Hitler Youth in 1926.

# Introduction

Following Hitler's appointment as the chancellor of Germany on 30 January 1933, the Nazis took power. Germany quickly became a military dictatorship as the party began a campaign of propaganda, terror, coercion and intimidation to take control of all aspects of public life including politics, the economy, education, law and culture. For Germans born between 1925 and 1933 – the so-called Hitler Youth Cohort – life was changed forever. The movement was a slow starter, but the appointment in 1931 of Baldur von Schirach as Reich Youth Leader turned its fortunes around. Having played a full part in the spate of elections in 1932, the movement had approximately 50,000 members – boys and girls – when Hitler took control the following year. By the end of 1933, that number had increased to more than 2 million (30 per cent of German youths aged 10–18). By 1937, with all other youth groups banned, the number stood at 5.4 million and by 1940 membership reached 8.8 million – over 90 per cent of German children.

Between 1933 and the outbreak of the Second World War in 1939, the Hitler Youth movement – by then wielding a powerful influence on German children from the age of six to 18 – drove a wedge between youth, the educational system and even their own dissenting families, producing a generation of anti-intellectuals indoctrinated with Nazi ideology, believing in a sense of national unity and ready for military service. For the boys, it meant military training. For the girls, it meant learning the values of obedience, duty, self-sacrifice, discipline and physical self-control. Their role was to be good Nazi women – prepared for motherhood and to raise children in the ways of National Socialism.

On the eve of war, the Hitler Youth constituted the single most successful mass movement in the Third Reich and comprised many of its most committed Nazis.

# Chapter 1

# End of Empire

At 5.20 am on Monday 11 November 1918, representatives from Britain, France and Germany met aboard the Supreme Allied Commander's private train parked in a railway siding in the Forest of Compiègne, near Paris. After hasty negotiations, Germany, bereft of manpower and supplies and in danger of imminent invasion, had little choice but to sign the armistice, which was to come into effect at 11 am that day, bringing the First World War to an end. After four years of fighting – with more than 9 million soldiers dead, 21 million wounded and a further 6 million civilians dead from disease, starvation or exposure – the guns fell silent. It was a watershed moment for the German nation and its people.

## 'Deutschland, Deutschland über alles'

Four years earlier, buoyed by the so-called 'spirit of 1914', a sense of euphoria among many Germans greeted cross-party agreement in the *Reichstag* on 1 August 1914 in support of joining the nascent European conflict. Many were craving war, including Chancellor Bethmann Hollweg; the nobility; the military, led by Helmuth von Moltke, who had the Kaiser's approval; industrialists; imperialists; and nationalists, all of whom believed it was time for Germany to confirm its position in the ranks of world powers – its so-called 'place in the sun'. The German establishment believed that the people would unite behind the monarchy, and they were right. The German army peacetime conscription system stated that all able-bodied German men aged 17 to 45 were liable for military service and in August 1914, it required only 12 days to expand its numbers from 800,000 to 3.5 million soldiers, the majority of whom were under the age of 20. Young men, particularly from the middle and upper classes, enlisted in their thousands and marched off to war with the cheers of the population ringing in their ears.

Despite the promise of some early victories on the battlefield, disorganization and disillusionment soon set in and by November 1914 the opposing forces on the Western Front had dug in, signalling the end of mobile warfare and the start of a war of attrition in the trenches – a deadly stalemate that would last for four more years. Ultimately, the conflict would prove to be a catastrophe for Germany.

In September 1914, four new German army corps (made up of approximately 48,000 men) were formed. Some 40,000 of them were young volunteers, aged between 17 and 19. On 19 October, having been incorporated into the German Fourth Army, where they became known as the 'Kinderkorps' because of their youth, they marched towards Ypres. With no experience and little training, they faced the well-trained soldiers of the British Expeditionary Force (BEF). Ordered to attack and break through the British positions at Langemarck, they fought bravely, some reportedly singing 'Deutschland, Deutschland über alles' as they moved forward, and died in their thousands under the fire of the British machine guns. It was a military blunder of epic proportions. Estimates say that some units lost 70 per cent of their soldiers. It did not get better. During the next four years of unending carnage, one-third of all German men aged between 19 and 22 were slaughtered and the war ended in catastrophic defeat. With them died the optimism and idealism of 'the flower of German youth'.[4]

## The Black Hand

Of course, it wasn't supposed to have been like that. In the summer of 1914, following the assassination of Archduke Franz Ferdinand, heir to the throne of Austria-Hungary, and his wife in Sarajevo, Bosnia, when the First World War began the mood among the European nationals involved was one of optimism. In Germany, the coming war inspired a wave of patriotism buoyed by the massive growth in the economy since the turn of the century, with victory expected, probably in a relatively short time. There was less optimism among some army generals, but these views were not seen as helpful by the politicians or the major newspaper editors. Germany entered the conflict by declaring war on Russia but sending its armies through Belgium with the aim of taking Paris from the north. In response to the German invasion of Belgium, Britain declared war on Germany.

While the catalyst of the conflict was the assassination of the archduke, the reasons behind what became known as the Great War are more complex. In 1914, Austria and Hungary made up the Austro-Hungarian Empire, ruled by the Habsburgs, and had been one of Europe's major powers since it was formed in 1867. The archduke was in Sarajevo to inspect the imperial armed forces in Bosnia and Herzegovina, which had been annexed by Austria-Hungary in 1908. He and his wife were shot by Gavrilo Princip, said to be a Serbian nationalist and a member of a secret organization known as the Black Hand, who believed that the territories should be part of Serbia.[5]

A rapid chain of events unfolded. Austria-Hungary immediately blamed the Serbian government for the attack and, having sought assurances from its ally Germany that it would step in in case of an escalation, declared war on Serbia. Russia, already in alliance with

Serbia, began mobilization, prompting Germany to declare war on Russia. Fear of Germany's growing strength had encouraged Russia and France to enter into an alliance in 1893. In 1904, Britain had negotiated agreements with both for the same reasons, so when Germany invaded France, intending to achieve a swift victory before the slow-moving Russian army was organized, Britain was pulled into the conflict. In terms of alignments in 1914, Germany, Austria-Hungary, Turkey and Bulgaria formed the Central Powers. Arrayed against them were the Allies: Russia, France and Britain, along with Japan. Italy, which had been allied with the Central Powers before the start of the war, declared neutrality in 1914 and joined the Allies in 1915, and the USA joined in 1917.

## Root causes of the conflict

While historians agree on the significance of the events in Sarajevo, there has been much debate over the actual root causes of the conflict that followed, which involved not only the alliances previously mentioned, which had already prompted hostility and even war in the previous four decades, but also imperialism, militarism and nationalism, all of which stoked old tensions beyond the Balkans.

At the beginning of the 19th century, France was the leading power in Europe. The French Revolution, which began in 1789, saw the end of the monarchy, the creation of a new constitution and a new bicameral legislature. In 1799, a young general named Napoleon Bonaparte staged a *coup d'état* and appointed himself 'first consul', which put an end to the revolution and began the Napoleonic era. Over the next 15 years, the French hero led his nation to great military victories over Italy, Austria, Russia, Prussia, Belgium, the Netherlands, Switzerland and Germany. In doing so, he is credited with overthrowing feudal remains and setting up new, more modern codes of law in much of Western Europe. Historian Andrew Roberts claims that Napoleon was responsible for some of the key ideas of the modern world, in that 'meritocracy, equality before the law, property rights, religious toleration, modern secular education, sound finances and so on were protected, consolidated, codified and geographically extended.'[6] This meant glory for France on the one hand and the creation of many enemies on the other. The Revolutionary and Napoleonic wars, which came to an end with Napoleon's defeat by the British at Waterloo in 1815, had caused some 4 million deaths.

At this point, competition for places at the top table of European countries was fierce, with France, Britain, Russia, Prussia and Austria jostling for position along with the USA and later Italy and Japan. The middle years of the 19th century were marked by rapid industrialization, economic development and the growing power of Great Britain, the USA and Prussia, then Italy and Japan. In turn, this led to imperialist and colonialist competition for influence and power throughout the world, most notably in the 'Scramble for Africa' in the 1880s and 1890s. Britain led the way with a wide network of colonies and the unchallenged hegemony of its Royal Navy.

By the second half of the 19th century, politics and military power had become inseparable in the minds of the leaders of the major powers, all of which were preparing for a large-scale war. After all, a powerful state needed a powerful military to protect its interests. In effect, such thinking led to an arms race among the world's leading powers and a growing belief that war was coming.

At this point, Germany was still a loose federation of states, known as the First Reich, although often referred to by historians as German Central Europe, in which the states of Prussia – with its capital Berlin – Bavaria, Saxony and Austria were dominant. Prussia, in particular, had the most powerful army in Europe. Led by Field Marshal von Moltke, its battlefield strategies, training, advanced weaponry and command and control systems were second to none. Its crushing defeat of France in 1871 proved it to be the most dangerous and effective military force in Europe. Following Unification (see Chapter 2), the new supreme commander, Kaiser Wilhelm II, insisted on employing Prussian commanders, personnel and methodology for the new German imperial army, which by then included conscription. German ambitions to build a battle fleet also initiated a naval arms race with Britain.

Britain – confident that its navy, which was essential to maintain its imperial and trade interests, still 'ruled the world' and that its army, particularly following victory in the Crimean War (1853–56), was strong enough not to need conscription – was more restrained in its military build-up. However, driven by public interest and the press, who suggested that Britain was 'unprepared for war', the army was expanded and there was increased expenditure on new weapons and equipment. In the early 1900s, the navy developed a new type of battleship, the Dreadnought ('fear nothing'). These were fast, with serious armour plating, high-quality rangefinders and ten long-range big guns. 'We want eight [Dreadnoughts] and we won't wait' was one popular slogan at the time.

There were developments too in heavy artillery, which could fire bigger shells much further and with greater accuracy; in machine guns, which were smaller and lighter and capable of firing 600 rounds per minute; in small arms; and in the use of barbed wire as an anti-personnel device. As the historian Zara Steiner said of Britain, 'The belief in war as a test of national power and a proof of national superiority added a scientific base to the cult of patriotism … In Britain, a real effort was made to teach boys that success in war depended upon the patriotism and military spirit of the nation, and that preparation for war would strengthen "manly virtue" and "patriotic ardour".'[7]

In 1870, the combined military expenditure of the six major European powers (Britain, France, Germany, Austria-Hungary, Russia and Italy) totalled the equivalent of £94 million. By 1914, the total was £398 million, with an increase in Germany's spending of 73 per cent during the period, dwarfing those of all the other nations. Fear of Germany's growing strength after Unification had indeed prompted the Franco-Russian alliance of 1893. In 1904, Britain's negotiated agreements with Russia and France indicated that the battle lines were being drawn.

## Colonial expansion and growing nationalism

Following the end of the Franco-Prussian War, marked by the signing of the Treaty of Frankfurt, the Unification of Germany and the establishment of the German Empire under Otto von Bismarck, and the *Risorgimento* (Unification of Italy), which were all completed by 1871, Europe entered into a period of relative peace. However, the jostling for influence and financial advantage in the colonies continued: with the French in Asia and Africa, the English in Egypt, Russia in Central Asia along with Portugal, and Italy and Japan in the mix. The Kaiser, Wilhelm II, meddled in it too, supporting the Boers in South Africa and in the process souring relations with Britain.

But there was greater interest for Germany in the Balkans, which centred on the possible disintegration of the Ottoman Empire and the rise of nationalism among its Christian population, a matter keenly supported by Serbia. Germany feared confrontations between its ally, Austria-Hungary, and Russia, as well as between Russia and Britain. In the 1870s and 1880s, Chancellor Bismarck's foreign policy for the region was one of containment based on the balance of power. As Germany had the strongest economy in Continental Europe, he did not want to rock the boat. However, there were some influential German politicians alarmed at France's quick recovery from defeat in 1871 and by its rapid rearmament programme, which prompted talk of a pre-emptive war to keep it in its place. This angered the British and the Russians and forced Bismarck to understand the fear and alarm that Germany's fast-growing power was causing its neighbours. Indeed, when he was ousted by the Kaiser in 1890, a new, more aggressive position was taken, providing further justification for the Franco-Russian Alliance.

After 1900, the situation grew markedly worse in the Balkans with the rise of Muslim Turkish nationalists, hostile to all nationalities and all non-Muslims. The Ottoman Empire began to break up, resulting in the setting-up of nation states in Greece, Serbia, Montenegro, Bulgaria, Romania, Bosnia and Albania. Treaties and agreements that had been made in the previous 25 years, particularly the Treaty of Berlin (1878), were seen as advantageous by some and unacceptable by others, particularly since many of them had been made with the idea of keeping ethnic groups together, creating new, local grievances. In October 1908, Austria-Hungary announced the annexation of Bosnia and Herzegovina, having been awarded custody by the 1878 treaty. Russia, Italy and, in particular, Serbia were outraged – and this sentiment eventually led to the assassination of Franz Ferdinand in 1914.

Ethnic divisions among the new nation states of the former Ottoman Empire continued to cause unrest. In 1912, ethnic nationalists in Bulgaria, Greece and Montenegro formed the Balkan League to deal with the issues that they perceived the Great Powers could not. In October that year, the League's armies attacked Turkish positions in the Balkan Peninsula in what became known as the First Balkan War. Within seven months, Constantinople asked for terms. These were drawn up by the Treaty of London in May 1913, which took away almost all the Ottoman Empire's possessions in the Balkans. However, the terms of the treaty, imposed by the Great Powers, were unsatisfactory for some of the Balkan states, particularly Bulgaria, unhappy that territory in Macedonia had been divided up between Serbia and Greece. In June, a second war began when Bulgaria attacked Macedonia in order to force its former allies out. However, within a month, the Bulgarian offensive was stopped, and the Serbian and Greek armies launched a counter-attack. Romania, already in territorial dispute with Bulgaria, attacked as well, as did Turkey, keen to regain some of its territories. The Second Balkan War lasted a little over a month and terms were agreed in August at the

Treaty of Bucharest. However, tensions in the Balkans and among the major powers remained high with Austria, Serbia, Russia, Germany, Bulgaria and Turkey all remaining vigilant.

## War commences

On 28 June 1914, the archduke was assassinated. A month later, on 28 July, with German encouragement Austria-Hungary declared war on Serbia. Russia's support of Serbia brought France into the mix. Germany declared war on Russia on 1 August and France on 3 August. At 2 pm on 4 August, Britain issued an ultimatum demanding that Germany withdraw its troops, which were massed on the Belgian border ready for the invasion of France. At 11 pm that deadline passed without reply and Britain declared war on Germany.

Historians differ in their opinions of why Germany joined the First World War. The most persistent argument is that the government saw

*By the end of World War I more than two million German soldiers had been killed, including one-third of all men between the ages of 19 and 22.*

itself surrounded by increasingly powerful enemies – Russia, France and Britain – who would crush them if they did not act first. Others claimed that Germany had no choice but to act because of the dizzying events in the chain of long-standing alliances, conflicts, colonization and military build-ups that had occurred since 1871. A third theory, put forward by German historian Fritz Fischer in the 1960s, claimed that Germany simply wanted to dominate Europe and took advantage of the events of July 1914 to start the war.

While having the luxury of choice in joining the conflict, Germany had few options when it came to ending it. Following the failure of their spring offensive in May 1918 and the fact that American troops were soon to arrive on the Western Front, it was clear that Germany was going to lose the war. When the Allies launched the Hundred Days Offensive on 8 August, German defences faltered. Conditions at home continued to deteriorate, with severe shortages of food and coal. For many, the food supply consisted of bread and potatoes, with a hugely reduced supply of cheese, butter, rice, cereals and eggs. The harsh winter of 1917 was known as the 'turnip winter', as the potato supply ran short. Morale on the battlefield and at home was at an all-time low.

## The 'Wandering Birds'

In 1895, all of this was still to come for Herman Hoffmann, a law student at the grammar school in Steglitz, a firmly middle-class suburb of Berlin. In the autumn of that year, Hoffmann asked for permission to organize stenography classes to relieve the boredom of what he felt was the 'bourgeois complacency' of his life. The following year, the classes evolved to include weekend walks around Steglitz without parental supervision and, in 1897, a two-week hike in the Harz highlands. Other youngsters joined the group and, as they walked, with their backpacks, water bottles and guitars, they discussed their lives in a rapidly changing world.

Although Hoffmann had no particular purpose for his scheme, he was alarmed at the effects of industrialism and commerce on young lives like his and felt that the 'youth had to rediscover nature, the fields, woods, brooks, lakes, and meadows from which the city dweller had been alienated.'[8] Breaking with convention, they dressed informally in shorts, casual shirts, hats, hobnail boots and rain gear when necessary. They also carried their own supplies, slept in barns and haylofts, and cooked for themselves. The emphasis in the early days was on independence, a frugal way of life, an absence of authority, a disdain for marked paths and contempt for the comforts of home. Such a group was not a unique concept but what was new was that they were led by other youths and not by adults, as they wanted something greater to believe in than the strict and unadventurous values of their parents. This outlook was directly in line with the conditions experienced by lower- and middle-class youths at a time when the repressive and authoritarian values dominant in Germany made young people feel superfluous.

In 1898, they began to meet weekly in a rented room where they told folk stories and sang old folk songs, accompanied by guitar and mouth organ. The popularity of the back-to-nature group grew rapidly and, at a meeting in the cellar of Steglitz town hall on 4 November 1901, it became an official association, named the *Wandervögel* – a word apparently discovered on a gravestone as a description of the person buried there – meaning 'wandering bird'. Before moving from Berlin to Magdeburg in 1898, Hoffmann handed leadership of the group over to another law student, Karl Fischer, who had realized that becoming 'official' in Wilhelmine Germany was necessary to get the group accepted among schools and parents and so attract new members. Fischer and his friend Wolfgang Kirchback, also the group's president, drew up a constitution and began to circulate pamphlets and eventually a series of magazines to advertise themselves and their causes.

By this time, the group had consciously withdrawn from the school and set up its own hierarchy. They put in place a military-style ranking system, with a new recruit known as a *Scholar*; after passing some tests and completing some tasks, a member could become a *Bursche* (student) and then a *Bachant* (fellow). A new and more specific style of dress was adopted. The 'uniform' included shorts; blue, white, brown, green or grey shirts with neckties; and marching boots. They greeted each other by raising the right arm and using the greeting '*Heil*'. They also had membership badges and pins to mark their achievements. New groups set up in their own *Heim* (nest), a meeting room that was decorated with flags and banners and the movement's emblem. Along with the singing, marching and communing with nature in mountains and woods, they were anti-materialism and set against the burgeoning industrial life. Their goal was to revive romantic Teutonic idealism through German folklore and national heroes. They wanted to create a *Jugendkultur*, a culture of youth led by youth, in which they would be truly valued as individuals – in many ways becoming a model for a more sinister German youth group of the future.

Over the next ten years, the *Wandervögel* quickly developed into a nationwide movement and by 1914 there were over 800 local branches, made up of some 25,000 members. At the centre of their self-proclaimed core mission, they encouraged 'self-responsibility, true comradeship, a primitive healthful life and new forms of recreational activity'.[9] They also developed an anti-capitalist worldview and voiced criticism about the moral and social implications of 'modern' civilization and the drive for progress that had accompanied Germany's Industrial Revolution.[10] Members expressed their opposition to the restrictive urban society through a return to nature, abstinence from alcohol and tobacco, communal living, modest dress and the call for freedom. Such views attracted the attention and even grudging admiration of the mainstream political parties and religious establishments, some of whom borrowed their ideas to set up their own groups.

Of course, the movement was not without its problems. It had started as an all-male group, but under pressure to expand its numbers, girls were invited to join in 1907. Given the strict moral code of the day, 'officially' boys' and girls' groups had to be kept separate, a rule that was, of course, doomed to failure. In its early days the movement had, in its romantic innocence, been strictly neutral on political, religious and racial matters, but as the war approached, anti-establishment nationalism and anti-Semitism began to show itself among its members. In 1913, the *Wandervögel* no longer accepted Slavs or Jews into its ranks. Later that year, a meeting of 25,000 members at the Hoher Meissner mountain, south-east of Kassel, witnessed the first political cracks appearing in the movement, leading to a crisis that divided the leadership into 'conservative' Right and 'progressive' Left.

*A Scout-like troop of* Wandervögel *take a hike in the Berlin countryside dressed in uniform with guitars and flags in the early 1930s.*

# From patriotism to disillusionment

In January 1913, the so-called 'Festive Year', the Kaiser announced a series of patriotic festivities, mostly parades, military ceremonies and speeches. They took place from March to October to celebrate the centennial of the Wars of Liberation against France and 25 years of Wilhelm II's reign. Those years had seen the development of contrasting visions of the German nation. On the one hand were the aristocratic conservative elite who regarded the monarch and the machinery of the 'state' to be the basis of political sovereignty; on the other were the majority of the German people, the '*Volk*', who felt that they 'were the site of the nation and the culture.'[11]

Some historians argue that the festivities were part of an 'imperial offensive' to boost the waning popularity of the monarchy. In fact, they threatened to do the opposite, by bringing to the surface 'the tenuous relationship between the imperial monarchy and the German public'[12]. There was progress in this area, as the Kaiser recognized the need to connect with the people more effectively and acknowledge the importance of public opinion. But, in reality, the celebrations were elitist and harked back to a monarchical period long past. Though there was criticism from growing voices on the socialist left and the nationalist right, who were conspicuously absent from the official festivities, the 'offensive' worked. The masses that turned up at the Kaiser's public appearances, the parades and the grandiose ceremonies were easily aroused to patriotism. The 'festive year' was very effective as a tool to aid mass mobilization the following year, when millions blindly and enthusiastically followed their leaders to war.

At the start of 1918, still optimistic that Germany would win the war, General Erich Ludendorff, who along with Paul von Hindenburg were in de facto charge of both military and civilian matters, launched his spring offensive intended to break through the Allied lines and force the French to seek armistice terms before the expected arrival of American troops. By late 1918, following the operation's failure, Germany was on the brink of military defeat and economic collapse. Almost a million German soldiers had died in the first six months of the year and the troops were now in retreat. Supply lines did not work well enough to keep up with demands for food, ammunition and reinforcements. On top of this, the people left at home were starving. The Allied naval blockade had severely reduced food imports and there were labour shortages caused by enlistment and conscription. That summer, the harvest had failed and there had been a deadly influenza infection that spread through Europe in August, killing millions. Morale in Germany was low.

On 29 September, following a 56-hour-long bombardment, Allied forces broke through German positions along the Hindenburg Line, which at that point marked the last line of German defences on the Western Front. In the final hour of the offensive, the Allies' 1,637 guns fired 945,052 shells at the 10,000-yard (9 km)-long front before the German troops left their positions.[13] General Ludendorff finally admitted that 'the German army have reached the end ... the troops can no longer be relied on'.[14] The fate of the empire and the army was thus sealed.

Ludendorff demanded that Germany seek an immediate armistice based on the terms suggested by US President Wilson in his 'Fourteen Points' address in January that year. On 1 October, alarmed by Ludendorff's unwelcome and unexpected news, Chancellor Georg von Hertling resigned and was replaced by Prince Max von Baden, son of Prince Wilhelm of Baden. His first move was to reject any idea of admitting defeat in the hope of retaining some powers of negotiation with the Allies. But, with further rumblings from the Supreme Command about the war zone and from his cabinet about the growing anti-war sentiment on the home front, on 4 October von Baden telegraphed a request for a ceasefire to Washington. Despite a reorganization of the new government, which declared the chancellor and his government answerable to the Reichstag – a move intended to convince the American president to accept the offer of peace – the request was refused. The public were shocked when they were informed of these events the next day.

In the following days, fighting continued in France, Belgium and Italy, while across Europe empires collapsed and new nations emerged. At the insistence of President Wilson, peace negotiations were conducted by civilian members of the German government rather than the military. Ludendorff was outraged at the prospect of what he saw as 'unconditional surrender' and was forced to resign by the Kaiser.

Amid rumours of an army mutiny and of negotiations for Germany's surrender, on 29 October war-weary sailors at the navy port at Wilhelmshaven refused orders to prepare for a final battle with the British navy. The unrest spread to Kiel, where 40,000 sailors joined dock workers in setting up a Workers' and Soldiers' Council to take over the dockyard. Unrest spread quickly; by 7 November 'revolutionaries', calling for the replacement of the undemocratic rule of the Kaiser, had seized cities including Hanover, Brunswick, Frankfurt am Main and Munich, where the King of Bavaria, Ludwig III, was forced to abdicate. Other federal princes soon followed.

On Saturday 9 November, crowds gathered in Berlin demanding the total abolition of the monarchy. In response, Chancellor von Baden announced the abdication of Wilhelm II, although he had not yet agreed to it but was, in fact, already on his way to the Netherlands for reasons of safety. Von Baden then announced that he had passed the chancellorship to Friedrich Ebert, leader of the Majority Social Democratic Party of Germany (MSPD), the biggest party in the government of the day.

Shortly after 2 pm that day, Social Democrat Philipp Scheidemann proclaimed Germany a republic from the balcony of the Reichstag in Berlin, even though he'd not been authorized to do so. 'The people have triumphed,' he said to the throng of cheering people below. At 4 pm, an equally large crowd gathered at the Imperial Palace in Berlin. There, Karl Liebknecht also proclaimed a republic. His speech culminated in the proclamation of a 'free socialist Republic of Germany' that would bring an end to the Hohenzollern dynasty. Instead of the hated Imperial standard, the 'red flag of the free Republic of Germany' would fly from now on. Two days later the armistice was signed, ending the war in Western Europe – but, for Germany, that did not mean the return of peace. From its first day on, the newly proclaimed republic had a heavy burden to bear.

The young republic was trapped in a dilemma, because the people were divided. For some, the Russian Revolution in November 1917 was an enlightening model of a socialist society based on equality and they wanted the same for Germany. For others, it was a portentous omen of a coming downfall. Between these two positions there was no common ground. Both left- and right-wing parties supported armed gangs that fought openly in the streets. The attempt to introduce a new era after the ravages of the First World War was a total failure. Soldiers returning from the front were confronted with sheer chaos in which it was impossible for them to find their bearings. Many of them joined the right-wing Freikorps movement or the left-wing Spartacists.

Of course, they were the lucky ones. The end of the First World War had a profound effect on the youth of Germany. Since eagerly following the Kaiser into battle in 1914, millions of German boys and men had been slaughtered in senseless battles in places such as Ypres, Verdun, Sedan, Galicia, the Ukraine, Palestine, Windhoek and the Bay of Bengal. Fewer than half of the 14,000 members of the *Wandervögel* who saw active service returned home. Those who made it back were shell-shocked, disillusioned and had little left to believe in. They found the country in the chaos of revolution.

# Chapter 2

# Blood and Iron

---

Of course, the *Wandervögel* was not the first organized youth group in Germany; in fact, similar 'protest' groups had been recorded since the 16th century. However, as historian H.W. Koch points out, "'youth" as a social group, in Germany and elsewhere, was not an organized body or a force in its own right until the end of the nineteenth century."[15] What links such groups as the Hutterites in the 1500s, the Romantics in the 1700s and the *Burschenschaft* (fraternity) in the 1800s is that they all critiqued society – whether for non-conformity, a dislike of industrialization or political ire – and withdrew from it.[16] These movements and others swept through Germany on the tide of history, infecting its youth, usually the upper and middle classes, with thoughts and ideas that they carried into adulthood, adding credence to a 19th-century description of Germany as 'the land of poets and thinkers'.

## German youth and the French Revolution

Youthful rebellion is not a new phenomenon. Its ideals and political leanings depend on particular historical, sociocultural and geopolitical situations and traditionally involves the rejection of the sociocultural systems of their parents. There were rich pickings for rebellious German youths, particularly between the end of the 18th and 19th centuries. The French Revolution of 1789 with its promise of greater human liberties was greeted with enthusiasm by youngsters with romantic and utopian daydreams of being themselves and not copies of 'a fossilized parent-generation which was only the product of a fossilized social system'[17], which is how they saw the rationalist thinking of the Enlightenment period. Where once like-minded youths would have got together to discuss the issues of the day in local student organizations, called *Landsmannschaften*, they now began to gather in 'fraternities' called *Studentenverbindung*. Some discussions were highbrow, concerned with the writings of Immanuel Kant or Johann Gottlieb Fichte, while others were centred around a future utopia in which between 'citizens of the world' there would be universal brotherhood and peace.

However, these illusions were quickly replaced with delusions and fear of a newly aggressive French nationalism and horror at the news of executions of the revolution's opponents. During the French monarchy's death throes, a new constitutional monarchy was declared. Louis XVI had been forced to accept a new constitution but was still nominally in charge. Due to his situation, relations between France and its neighbouring monarchies quickly deteriorated. In August 1891, Austria and Prussia released the Declaration of Pillnitz, which urged European powers to unite and restore the monarchy in France. In April 1792, following a vote in the revolutionary-led government and with Louis' reluctant consent, France declared war on Austria and Prussia. French troops defeated imperial forces at the Battle of Valmy on 20 September 1792 and secured control of the Rhineland, which it was to retain for 20 years. Meanwhile, in August, the monarchy in France was suspended. In September, it was abolished, and France was declared a republic. On 21 January 1793, Louis XVI was executed by guillotine.

## Napoleon Bonaparte

Over the next few chaotic years of political unrest, France was ruled by a series of governments: first the National Assembly, then the Legislative Assembly, then the National Convention and finally the Directory in 1795. By 1799, the government was bankrupt, while inflation, taxation and unemployment were soaring. There were widespread fears of a Jacobin resurgence and a royalist restoration. By 10 November, the regime had lost control and unrest in Paris had reached a critical point. A young general, Napoleon Bonaparte, in charge of all the troops in the capital, lost patience with the politicians who were arguing about what to do next and declared, along with his brother Lucien and others, a *coup d'état*. Over the next few days, a new constitution was agreed and formally proclaimed on 13 December with Napoleon as First Consul with full executive power. Five years later, in May 1804, Napoleon was given the title Emperor of the French and so began the Napoleonic era.

In the ensuing years, the French Empire achieved military supremacy across mainland Europe. In 1805, Napoleon crossed the Rhine and defeated the Fourth Coalition, including the Prussian army at Jena and Auerstädt, before capturing Berlin. Following the Battle of Austerlitz the previous year, Napoleon had formed the Confederation of the Rhine, which comprised 16 of the 39 German states that he had reorganized (approximately 300 states had existed in 1789), and dissolved the Holy Roman Empire – an event marked by the abdication of the last Holy Roman Emperor, Francis II of Austria.

Before the Napoleonic era, Germany was a loose group of Germanic states united by a common language and vague cultural similarities overseen by an elective monarch or emperor. An institution that had lasted for over a thousand years, its full name was the Holy Roman Empire of the German Nation and it was once regarded by the Roman Catholic Church as the only legal successor of the Roman Empire. But there was scant evidence of a national identity. In reality, its government had little power other than the religious authority of the emperor and, beyond that, of the Pope.

However, the dissolution of the empire was met with shock and fear by the general public in the states not included in Napoleon's new confederation, such as Prussia and Austria, as well as those that were, such as Bavaria, Baden and Württemberg. Many were uncertain and fearful for the future and for Germany itself. This treatment at the hands of an unwanted invader forced a rethink among fraternity members, whose ideas of brotherhood and world peace were quickly replaced with thoughts of individual and national survival.

German patriotism did show its head under threat of Napoleon's invasion, but resistance was fairly feeble. Of course, young Germans had been enthusiastic about some aspects of revolutionary France, and now they envied the power and patriotism of the French army and the strong national consciousness and cultural identity they brought with them. However, as historian Franz Schnabel explains, growing dissatisfaction with French occupation began to generate a militant German nationalism. 'Suddenly the realization dawned that it was the absence of a powerful united state which had allowed France to deal with Germany piecemeal; that Germany needed not only unity but an ideological *raison d'être* with which to oppose French revolutionary ideology.'[18]

Two types of nationalism developed: one more conservative and wanting a return to the old ways before French occupation; the other more liberal and including greater civil liberties and true self-government. For the former, it was the state, the *Reich* – the Holy Roman Empire, the German nation – that was the focus and driving force of patriotism. For the latter, the heart of the nation and its culture was to be found in its people, the *Volk*, a concept first developed by rationalist philosopher Johann Gottfried Herder. His views, as published in *Ideas for the Philosophy of the History of Mankind* (1784), opposed those of

Enlightenment thinking. For the rationalists, society was the sum of its members. For the more emotional Herder, the community was a natural organism and the only place in which the individual could fully realize his or her potential. Without his *Volk*, the individual is nothing; just as the state is nothing without its *Volk*. Herder also believed that every nation was different and had its own unique specialities, culture and identity, for example, in its language, history, folklore and way of life (*Volksgeist*). As H.W. Koch explains, '... in Herder's view the realization of the *Volk* could in many instances only be achieved in opposition to the existing state – supposing the state did not correspond with the true interests of the *Volk* – and especially when that state was occupied and dominated by a foreign power.'

In his stance against the rationalist thinking of the establishment and foreign invaders, Herder's religiously inspired nationalism was a potent brew and particularly persuasive for young people. Indeed, students were among the first to take up arms against the occupiers, believing that Germany could be liberated from the French. In 1808, there were a number of unsuccessful attempts to assassinate Napoleon. The next few years saw an increasing number of uprisings in the Tyrol, Austria and Westphalia as hatred for the oppressors began to fester and grow.

## Increasing Prussian influence

After the national humiliation of its defeats at Jena and Auerstädt, Prussia had undertaken a serious programme of social and military reform. Gerhard von Scharnhorst, the Prussian army's chief-of-staff, and Major von Gneisenau were responsible for the military reforms. Ironically following the French model, they called for changes that would increase competition for positions, opening them up to everyone based on talent, rather than birth. They stressed to their soldiers the importance of moral incentives, personal courage and individual responsibility. As a result of this and also recognizing its courage in standing up to Napoleon in the first place, German nationalists began to look favourably in Prussia's direction, looking for leadership and a way out from Napoleonic dominance.

The social reforms taking place in Prussia at the time also had lofty aims, such as abolishing serfdom, lessening the restrictions of opportunity for the lower classes, paving the way for a modern free-market economy and generally modernizing the state. In 1810, Chancellor Hardenberg confiscated Church property, ended the monopoly of trade guilds and gave Jews equal rights. He even persuaded the Prussian king, Frederick William III, to discuss the possibility of constitutional monarchy. Prussia was on the move, its citizens excited and unified. National pride soared, the prospect of war against Napoleon was welcomed and the state became the focus of a new German nationalism.

At its height, the First French Empire ruled lands in Italy, Spain, the Netherlands, Poland, Switzerland, Germany and elsewhere and included more than 90 million subjects. But in 1812, Napoleon made a major mistake. Convinced that the Tsar was conspiring with his British enemies, he assembled an army of 600,000 soldiers and invaded Russia. He defeated the Russian army at Borodino and marched on to Moscow. As the Russians retreated from Moscow, they applied a 'scorched earth' policy, destroying or carrying off anything that might be useful, and then setting the city on fire. Napoleon had counted on billeting his troops there during the long Russian winter, but no shelter was left standing. As a result, the French army suffered terribly from starvation and cold as they made the long trip back to France.

Seizing its opportunity, Prussia declared war on France and the king issued a call to arms to the population of all parts of the German lands. More than 50,000 volunteers joined up and were soon wearing the black, red and gold uniforms of the Prussian army.

Smarting from his retreat from Moscow as well as French defeats in the Peninsular War, Napoleon retreated to Paris and raised another army with the intent of re-establishing his position in Germany. In October 1813, Napoleon organized his forces around Leipzig to protect his supply lines. Ranged against him were the Coalition armies of Austria, Sweden, Russia and 90,000 Prussian soldiers, comprising young middle-class students, farmers, peasants and labourers from both Prussia and other German states. Led skilfully by Commander von Blücher, Prussian soldiers fought bravely on the northern front. The Battle of Leipzig, the bloodiest of the Napoleonic Wars with some 100,000 dead, wounded or missing, ended in a comprehensive victory for the Coalition as Napoleon and his *Grande Armée* were forced to retreat back over the Rhine.

Forced to abdicate in 1814, Napoleon returned to power in March 1815. Still obsessed with a desire to impose a single state in Europe with him at its head, Napoleon decided to plan a pre-emptive strike against his former enemies. The Coalition countries, Britain, Belgium, the Netherlands, Prussia and some other German states, mobilized their armies immediately. The two sides met at Waterloo, in Belgium, in June 1815. Napoleon planned to drive a wedge between the British and Prussian armies and defeat the Prussians first. But Blücher's soldiers held firm, regrouped and reinforced British army positions, turning the tide of battle. After fierce fighting, the now-outnumbered French troops retreated in chaos.

Defeat at the Battle of Waterloo marked the end of the Napoleonic Wars, which cost the lives of some 5 million people, and marked the end of the First French Empire. Napoleon returned to Paris to find that he had lost the support of the army and the French people. In response, he abdicated for a second time and was exiled to the British-held island of Saint Helena, where he died in 1821. For France, events meant a return to monarchy, as Louis XVIII was restored to the throne. For Prussia, their contribution to the defeat of the French Army at Waterloo entered into the mythology of the Prussian state, creating a strong sense of nationalism, which would in time play a big part in the formation of the new German Empire in 1871.

## Peace at last

With peace in Europe secured after 23 years of war, the Great Powers – Britain, Prussia, Russia and Austria along with representatives from France – started planning for the post-war world in a series of meetings between September 1814 and June 1815 known as the Congress of Vienna. They faced a difficult task. After a revolution and more than 20 years of war, the borders of many states had been arbitrarily changed, and some had even disappeared altogether. As a result, the continent, and particularly Germany, was in a state of political chaos. Europe had a pressing need for peace.

The congress began with Napoleon exiled in Elba. Delegates were most concerned about a strong France, whose borders were restored to how they were in 1792, before Napoleon took power. They also created strong border states in the Netherlands and northern Italy. Prussia was awarded the left bank of the Rhine; the monarchy was restored in Spain; and Bavaria, Württemberg and Saxony remained as they were while some of the remaining German states formed a confederation. Poland's sovereignty remained a problem. The delegates met again after the hiatus at Waterloo to put the finishing touches to their work. Despite the fact that each nation had its own list of wants, complicated negotiations were skilfully conducted by Europe's finest diplomats. Potentially explosive issues, such as the future of Poland, were dealt with and the balance of power restored within what they believed was a political landscape in which no one power could dominate.

Vienna was a success for a number of reasons. Most importantly, it gave birth to the Congress System, by which the Great Powers met regularly to talk about and solve specific issues between European states, thus marking the beginnings of conference diplomacy in internal relations'. It also marked the beginning of 40 years of relative peace in Europe, known as the Concert of Europe, which was broken in 1853 by the outbreak of the Crimean War. The Congress of Vienna settlement formed the framework for European international politics until the outbreak of the First World War and, for some, served as a model for the League of Nations in 1919 and the United Nations in 1945.

## The spread of republican liberalism

However, the congress had its critics. The settlement had ignored the principles of liberalism and nationalism, which had been sacrificed in favour of the restoration of the old order of previous ruling aristocracies. Known as the Conservative Order, this was the result of a conscious programme that was put in place by statesmen such as Prince Klemens von Metternich of Austria and Lord Castlereagh of Britain to contain revolution and revolutionary forces by restoring ruling families such as the Bourbons and the House of Orange-Nassau. Such a reactionary move is said to have stifled politics in Europe, suppressing the development of democracy and civil rights associated with the American and French Revolutions. It also failed the check the spread of revolutionary movements that were to cross the continent 30 years later.

In Prussia, there was nationalist outrage at the settlement, particularly among students, some of whom had fought against Napoleon and were unhappy at the restoration of the attitudes of the *ancien régime* and the rejection of any notions of a nation state. In October 1817, the first meeting of the newly formed, mostly Protestant *Burschenschaft* was held at the Wartburg Festival. About 500 students from universities across Germany met to discuss and further the cause of liberty and the 'independence of the fatherland'. It was the first national event of the movement for national unification. The movement spread quickly, with its members adopting a black, red and gold flag, which soon came to be recognized as a symbol of unity against the old Conservative Order.

The movement's rise in popularity heralded surveillance and repression from Austria's ultra-conservative foreign minister, von Metternich, still the political master of the predominant German state following the Congress of Vienna. The movement was banned by the Carlsbad Decrees in 1819, which also introduced censorship of the press.

However, as Protestant theologian Karl von Hase said in 1820, 'Laws such as the Carlsbad Decrees try to stop us being German, but there are things that cannot die. We are all Germans, joined by the same language, customs and ancestors. They cannot be taken from us.' While the movement had been wounded, it was not dead. Worsening economic conditions, increasing taxation and political repression provoked violent reactions in Paris, Poland and a number of German states in the early 1830s. By this time, the middle-class students had been joined by members of the workers' associations and more than 20,000 of them met at Hambach Castle in May 1832 for a major rally to demand the creation of a German nation state.

Though censored by the authorities, the spirit of nationalism was kept alive in Germany and other European countries by the political idealism of youth. Quiet activism for liberal reform eventually broke free of its chains in Paris in February 1848. Unrest spread quickly to Vienna in Austria, Berlin in Prussia, Baden, Saxony, the Rhineland, Bavaria and Italy. Students, workers and artisans, fed up with famine, unemployment and the dying embers of the feudal system, demanded a constitution, freedom of assembly, freedom of the press and government by elected assembly. Troops were used against them, and hundreds of demonstrators were killed. Ultimately, however, the revolts failed. In Prussia, demonstrators had been promised a democratically elected government and the Frankfurt Assembly began working out ways to unite the German states and produce a written constitution. Though it lays claim as the first freely elected parliament for all of Germany, it only lasted a year, had no power and simply declined into debate. By the end of the year, it was clear that the revolutions of 1848, in Germany and elsewhere, had come to nothing.

## Bismarck and the birth of the new Germany

Austria and Prussia had been the leading states in Germany since the Congress of Vienna but between 1815 and 1860 Prussia had developed rapidly. The Congress had awarded it valuable land in the Rhineland that was rich in coal, iron and steel resources. The state's population grew, and it developed road and rail transport systems, which broke down provincial barriers. The home of German nationalism was on the rise. In 1818, Prussia had set up a free-trading customs union that got rid of tariffs and customs duties on all goods traded. By 1936, 25 German states had joined the so-called Zollverein, though Austria was excluded. With access to 26 million people, Prussia's growing wealth strengthened its challenge to Austria for control of the German states. It also illustrated the financial benefits of co-operation and hinted at the possible achievements of a united German state.

During the climate of fear and violence that swept through Berlin in 1848, a 33-year-old aristocratic former civil servant named Otto von Bismarck spoke out in favour of the Prussian King Frederick Wilhelm IV. The following year, he stood and was elected to the Prussian Chamber of Deputies. A confirmed monarchist, the young politician was then opposed to unification because he felt that Prussia would lose its independence in the process. However, he was also imbued with a sense of 'political realism' and, when elected to the Diet of the German Confederation in Frankfurt in 1851, quickly realized that Prussia's real enemy was Austria. As a result of this, he became convinced that Prussia would have to ally itself with other German states to maintain its position.

In 1862, Bismarck was appointed prime minister of Prussia, known then as 'an army with a state rather than a state with an army'. By now determined to unite Germany, Bismarck made a famous speech in which he said that the nation would achieve its goals only by the use of 'blood and iron'. He planned to use Austrian support to capture the German-speaking provinces of Schleswig and Holstein from Denmark. He then engineered a quarrel with Austria over the administration of the provinces. This led to a war in which the modernized and powerful Prussian army was victorious. He announced the formation of the North German Confederation in 1867, comprising Prussia and 21 other states of northern Germany. Military success brought Bismarck increasing political popularity in Prussia. Aware that France would not be happy at Prussia's victory over Austria upsetting the balance of power and believing that 'a Franco-German war must take place before the construction of a united Germany could be realized', Bismarck engineered one.[19]

In 1870, Bismarck lured Napoleon III into conflict with Prussia by suggesting that King Wilhelm I supported the German Prince Leopold's claim to the vacant Spanish throne. The French declared war on 19 July and mobilized its army. Seeing France as the aggressor, the German states, swept up by nationalistic fervour, agreed to send troops in support of Prussia. After battles at Sedan and Metz, Prussia was victorious, and Napoleon was deposed. Bismarck was quick to take advantage of the patriotic sentiment of victory. He negotiated with the south German states, offering concessions if they agreed to unification. Events moved quickly after an agreement was reached. On 18 January 1871, Kaiser Wilhelm I of Prussia was declared Emperor of Germany in the Hall of Mirrors at Versailles. Bismarck was appointed imperial chancellor and Prussia assumed leadership of the second German Empire. The Unification of Germany was officially declared.

## Political stagnation, social upheaval

The new Germany continued to establish itself as a leading world industrial and military power with rapid industrialization, urbanization

*For different reasons Kaiser Wilhelm II (left) and Chancellor Bismarck (in white uniform) – pictured opening the Reichstag in June 1888 – maintained the dominance of the aristocratic elite, ignoring the changing economic and social demands of the German people.*

and the accompanying social upheaval. But, historians argue, it differed in its development as a modern, liberal democracy from other major industrialized states, such as France and Britain. Although nationalists had achieved their aim of a united nation, the authoritarian political system it imposed ensured the continuing dominance of the traditional ruling elites and failed to embrace liberalism and democracy. One German historian explained that 'the proud citadel of the new German Empire was built in opposition to the spirit of the age.'[20]

Despite unification and the declaration of a constitutional monarchy, for the next few decades Germany remained a federal state with local rulers and local government, albeit with Prussia firmly in control of political power, state bureaucracy and the army. The king of Prussia was automatically appointed German Kaiser and the Prussian prime minister became the German chancellor. However, the state's political structure was one of the most undemocratic of the German states, and run by the landowning and industrial elites. The Reichstag (parliament) included 400 elected deputies from parties on the right (Conservatives), the centre (Liberals and Progressives) and the left (Social Democrats). It had little power and was separate from the government, which was appointed by the Kaiser with the chancellor as his 'agent'. This top-heavy system was dominated by the Kaiser, who controlled foreign policy and the armed forces and could appoint and dismiss his chancellor. In other words, political power remained in the hands of the aristocratic elite, with a middle class who saw no need for reform and with no voice for the vast majority of the population.

The lack of development of German political structures was in stark contrast to the rapid and dramatic changes that took place in the economy and society during the second half of the 19th century. In the 1850s, the German economy was still agrarian; by 1907, industry had become its greatest employer. This dramatic change, on a population that increased from some 40 million in 1871 to almost 70 million in 1914, saw villages grow into towns and towns into cities, transforming both rural and urban life all over the country. The ever-expanding economy required an ever-expanding workforce, which, inevitably, grew ever-more heterogeneous. Migrants began to arrive – from Poland, Denmark, Alsace-Lorraine and elsewhere. Catholics worked side by side with Protestants, peasants worked with skilled artisans, men alongside women. These huge social changes, along with improvements in transport, technology, wages and universal manhood suffrage, resulted in better education and the inevitable politicization of the lower-middle and working classes. Despite these shifts, Bismarck continued to pursue his reactionary, conservative politics.

The financial crash of 1873 put an end to a long period of expansion for the German economy and marked the beginning of a depression that did not ease until 1879. Because the Prussian political system had not adapted to the demands of a modern industrial economy, it was unable to react to the downturn effectively. Working conditions deteriorated, with long hours and frequent overtime shifts, real wages began to fall, and unemployment began to bite. Bismarck acted to shore up the ruling elites and attempted to close ranks against the dissenting voices of the middle and lower classes. Catholics, ethnic minorities like Poles and Danes, Jews and socialists were all labelled *Reichsfeinde* (enemies of the state) and faced discrimination, repression and blame. Jews, in particular, became targets of resentment for Germany's economic ills. While these policies were effective at the time, in the long term these minority groups continued to survive and organize.

For Bismarck, then, protests were unwelcome. Consolidation of the values of the new Germany required adherence to a nationalist, monarchist and conservative ideology – values imparted in particular by the Protestant Church. As the Kaiser was head of the Church, in turn the Church used its considerable influence to instill, via the sermon and the classroom, the values of obedience, discipline and order in the German people. 'The Protestant Church undoubtedly preached allegiance to the German state and it upheld the conservative hierarchy, reinforcing the authoritarian role of the father within the family, the employer in the factory and the Kaiser in the nation.'[21] In contrast, the minority Catholic Church maintained local links, often with the new generation of industrial workers for whom it provided welfare.

For German youth at this time, there seemed to be no reason to protest. Unification had been achieved, the Industrial Revolution was in full swing and middle-class families were benefitting from the profits. As for the national cause, Bismarck was doing it all. For those still at school, Protestant values were much in evidence, encouraging loyalty to the monarchy and obedience to the state. The history of the Fatherland, the language and the culture of Germany were emphasized. National victories and state occasions were celebrated regularly. In contrast, socialist ideas and even social mobility were discouraged. Education functioned to keep everyone in their place. For most, school ended at the age of 14. Only those who could afford it went on to secondary level. Some historians describe this process as the 'feudalization of the bourgeoisie'.

The army also played a prominent part in maintaining the interests of the ruling elite. Having been very involved in Unification, the military had popularity, prestige and power. Through conscription, the army more than doubled in size from 400,000 to almost 900,000 between 1870 and 1913. Ranking soldiers were left in no doubt as to their obligations to defend Germany against external aggressors and internal enemies, such as socialists. Many ex-soldiers joined the police, further extending the notion that imperial Germany was a militarized society. The officer corps were, of course, predominantly made up of men from aristocratic families. This ensured their determination to support Germany's aggressive and expansionist foreign policy and so assert Germany's position in the world.

## All roads lead to war

In 1890, Bismarck's confrontational domestic policies, designed to shore up the interests of the ruling elite, were no longer regarded as relevant. He offered his resignation to the new Kaiser, Wilhelm II, who accepted it without hesitation. With such a huge personality gone, a vacuum remained into which stepped a number of unresolved domestic problems that Bismarck had swept under the carpet during his years in office.

In 1890, Germany entered into a period of mass politics. As new social classes established themselves, peasantry, the working class, the lower-middle class, women and the bourgeoisie all wanted to make their way into a political system dominated by the elite. However, though voter turnout in the various Reichstag elections was high, it still wielded little power. As historian Lynn Abrams puts it, 'Votes cast may have reflected the mood of the country, but they did not affect the way the country was run.' Political movements began to take place outside of party politics. Trade unions, for example, expanded, as did the women's movement, temperance campaigners, pacifists and the labour movement. In the Reichstag, the Social Democratic Party went from strength to strength. The party, however, did not represent the entire workforce; many young people, for example, did not want to support them and unskilled workers, the so-called *Lumpenproletariat*, were not invited to join. With little or no representation, industrial unrest, in the form of strikes and riots, escalated during these years.

Of course, political pressure groups were not confined to the left and a number of nationalist groups drew extensive support. These populist groups, offering clear and simple messages in stark contrast to the complicated party politics under Wilhelm II, were very effective in furthering the causes of the ruling classes and government policies, for example, in foreign policy and the development of a large navy. There was also a marked increase in the number of anti-Semitic pressure groups during the 1890s, which achieved some success in the *Reichstag* elections of 1893.

Mistakes and bad advice on foreign policy decisions during the 1890s undid many of the alliances forged by Bismarck. Germany rejected their alliances with Russia and Britain, who both developed more cordial relationships with France. Suddenly surrounded by potentially hostile enemies and with only Austria for support, Admiral von Tirpitz, encouraged by the Kaiser, began to rebuild the German navy with a view to challenging the British.

On the eve of war, the opposing political opinions present in Germany seemed to coalesce: socialists, liberals and conservatives; Protestants and Catholics, middle and lower classes, now unified, were all faced with the same problems. For some, war seemed the best option to solve Wilhelmine Germany's political instability; for others, the threat from Russia justified joining in with an imperialist war.

Exactly why Germany started the war has already been debated (*see* Chapter 1). But whether it was thought that 'attack is the best form of defence', or because it was the only way by which the ruling elite could maintain its power, one thing is certain: Germany was not prepared for the war that was to follow.

# Chapter 3

# Hitler and the Piano Polisher

Among others infused with the 'spirit of 1914' was a 25-year-old failed artist, loner and drop-out named Adolf Hitler. For him, the onset of war was a godsend. In his biography of Hitler, historian Ian Kershaw explains that '... it gave him for the first time in his life a cause, a commitment, comradeship, an external discipline, a sort of regular employment, a sense of well-being, and – more than that – a sense of belonging.'[22] Hitler volunteered for military service immediately with the First Bavarian Infantry Regiment and in October, after a period of training, left his adopted city of Munich on a troop train bound for the battlefields of Flanders.

He was assigned as a dispatch runner, carrying messages among the trenches on foot or by bicycle. On the front line at Ypres, he showed courage and was soon promoted to corporal. Despite being extremely thin, taciturn and without any semblance of a sense of humour, his colleagues liked him but found him rather odd; his seriousness and fanatical support of the war made him the butt of regular jokes. In their recollections, soldiers who served with him reported that he revealed little of his political opinions and prejudices, apart from being critical of the Social Democrats. In October 1916, he was injured in the thigh at the Somme and was sent to hospital near Berlin. He found Berlin and Munich much changed since he had last visited, and the people dispirited and angry, so he was keen to return to the front line. Two years later, in October 1918, his unit was caught in a gas attack near Ypres that left most of the troops with temporary blindness. Once again, Hitler returned to Germany for treatment in Pasewalk. It was there he heard of Germany's defeat, the armistice and the revolution.

## Revolution

There was unrest in Germany as a consequence of military failure. Many Germans were shocked they had lost the war, because 'good news' propaganda had been coming from the High Command up until October 1918. In reality, German society was shattered and the mood at home was explosive. Politically, the two-fold proclamation of the republic on 9 November that year reflected the conflict that underlay the revolution. Splits were evident everywhere: monarchists against republicans, Bavarians against Prussians, warmongers against pacifists, townspeople against farmers, left against right. Perhaps most importantly, with the Kaiser gone, there was a split too in the country's most popular political party, the Social Democrats, who were given the task of taking power in the most difficult of circumstances. The party had split into two in 1917, when the anti-war members left the party to form the USPD (Independent Social Democratic Party of Germany). To avoid confusion, the original party was renamed the MSPD (Majority Social Democratic Party of Germany). For the USPD, whose supporters were mainly from the lower-middle classes, the time was right for the adoption of socialist ideals in the form of Soviet-style councils. But the MSPD went the other way. Despite the fact that there was little support for the newly established parliamentary democracy among the armed forces, the police, the judiciary and the civil service, they opted to work with the old power brokers of the empire to restore order.

Despite the differences, on the same day as the proclamation of the republic, a Council of People's Representatives was formed, comprising three MSPD and three USPD representatives, and ratified as the provisional government. Military co-operation was secured on 10 November and on 12 November the government passed some new laws, including the introduction of votes for women, and announced that elections to a new German National Assembly would take place on 19 January 1919.

In the meantime, the alliance in the provisional government broke down. A group of extreme leftists, led by Karl Liebknecht and Rosa Luxemburg, broke away from the USPD to form a Communist Party (KPD), known as the Spartacists. They launched a poorly planned 'second revolution' in Berlin in mid-January, which was savagely put down by the right-wing *Freikorps* with the full support of the MSPD. The group's leaders were brutally murdered. Similar protests led by the so-called Red Army of workers around the country were attacked by *Freikorps* groups and members of the regular army. In all, more than a thousand people were murdered.

Despite the continuing unrest, the government pressed ahead with elections, the first in which women were allowed to vote and from which the MSPD emerged as the strongest party. The elected members took their seats in the city of Weimar on 6 February. On 11 February, Friedrich Ebert was elected president of the Reich, the first German government to be accountable to parliament. Its members, including politicians from the MSPD, the Centre Party and the German Democratic Party (DDP), took office the following day.

## Hitler's ideology foments

For historian and Hitler biographer Ian Kershaw: 'The last two years of the war, between his convalescence in Beelitz in October 1916 and his hospitalization in Pasewalk in October 1918, can probably be seen as a vital staging-post in Hitler's ideological development.'[23] Born in German-speaking Austria, he was brought up in Linz. As a youth, he was interested in art and architecture and wanted to use these skills in his future career. He moved to Vienna, taking with him the prejudices and phobias of his early years. His political ideas were based on those of Georg Ritter von Schönerer, an extreme Pan-German who loathed the Habsburgs, Christianity, socialists and Jews and claimed that 'he longed for the day when a German army would march into Austria and destroy it.'[24] Schönerer demanded that the German-speaking parts of Austria be absorbed into the German Empire to preserve the racial purity of the Germanic race.

Hitler spent five years in Vienna. Failing to secure a place in the city's Academy of Art, he lived in a cheap men's home, existing on handouts from his aunt and by selling a few paintings. Embittered by his failings, he looked for things to blame: the establishment that was rejecting him, rules and regulations, the law, Jews, the state, the Social Democrats. Even the things he appeared to love – the music of Richard Wagner, for example, whose rabid anti-Semitism was well known – added fuel to his bitter fire.

Having received some money from his father's estate, Hitler moved to Munich in April 1913, delighted to have escaped the 'racial cosmopolitanism' of the Austrian capital. He continued his bohemian lifestyle until 15 August the following year, when he was swept up by the 'spirit of 1914' and volunteered for the Bavarian army. Despite being an Austrian citizen, and most likely due to the confusion of the first days of the war, he was accepted. In truth, Adolf Hitler was rescued by the outbreak of war. As a soldier, Hitler was fanatical; victory for

Germany was essential. He hated the fact that British and German troops had met in no man's land at Christmas in 1914 to play football and sing songs together. He met any defeatist talk with fury. But defeat and surrender were to follow. In *Mein Kampf*, Hitler described his feelings on 10 November 1918 when the local pastor brought the news, to the hospital in Pasewalk where he was recovering from the gas attack, that the conflict had been lost: 'It was impossible for me to stay in the room. Everything went black before my eyes again and I staggered and stumbled my way back to the dormitory ... and buried my burning head in the blanket and pillow.

'I had not cried since the day I stood beside my mother's grave ... It had all been in vain. All the sacrifices and starvation were in vain ... Was all of this so a mob of miserable criminals could dare to lay hands on the Fatherland?

'These are immoral and miserable criminals! The more I tried to understand this outrageous event, the more my cheeks burned with indignation and shame. The pain of my eyes was nothing compared to this wretchedness. Awful days and worse nights followed ... During those nights, hatred grew – hatred for the perpetrators of this deed.'[25]

This rather fanciful account of the incident ended with Hitler claiming that that was when he resolved to become a politician.

## 'Stab in the back' myth

The situation on the streets of German cities in the spring of 1919 was dangerous and underlined by bitter hatred between left and right. Although the violent suppression of the Communists had been supported by the moderate Social Democrats, the *Freikorps* and other armed nationalist right-wing gangs that roamed the streets had no love for democrats or socialists and hatred for those that they felt had caused the revolution. Many of the *Freikorps'* leaders were former soldiers, who believed the army had been 'stabbed in the back' by the politicians when they agreed to the armistice and overthrew the Kaiser in November 1918. Now dubbed the 'November Criminals', these politicians – including Democrat Walther Rathenau, who had signed the armistice; the Social Democratic Party's Philipp Scheidemann, who had proclaimed the Weimar Republic; Hugo Haase and the Centre Party's Matthias Erzberger – were regarded as traitors to the nation.

Of course, the idea that they had stabbed the army in the back was a myth. In reality, when the military commanders realized that they were going to lose the war, they did not want the army or its high-powered allies to take the blame. They also knew that if the Allies invaded Germany, then it would have peace imposed on it. General Erich Ludendorff, effectively in control of the army and so the state in late 1918, pressed the Kaiser for a rapid change of government and

*This right-wing political cartoon from 1924 shows Philipp Scheidemann and Matthias Erzberger in the act of stabbing the German army in the back. Two rich Jews are portrayed as the instigators of this 'betrayal', said to have been a conspiracy to allow social democratic politicians to take power.*

the establishment of a constitutional monarchy in Germany, keeping the Kaiser but bringing in a new level of government. His reason was twofold: first, to appease the US President Woodrow Wilson and so secure a better peace deal; and second, to create a new civilian government and make them surrender and negotiate the peace, so they would be blamed for defeat. The success of the 'stab-in-the-back' myth would bring disaster to the Weimar Republic and help ensure the success of the Nazi regime to come.

## Hitler joins the DAP

Still employed by the army, in June 1919, with Munich in a ferment of nationalist, counter-revolutionary sentiment, Hitler was ordered to attend some 'anti-Bolshevik' courses designed to do away with any remaining socialist ideas from ranking Bavarian soldiers. He was fascinated by the lectures, on history, economics, politics and the 'Jewish Question', from the perspective of the far right. So impressed were his superiors, not only by his interest but also his ability to speak out and make comments to the large audiences during group discussions, that he was selected to be an instructor at further courses that year.

By now firmly present in the minds of his superiors, Hitler was also assigned the task of monitoring the work of extreme left- and right-wing groups in Munich. On 12 September, he attended a meeting of the right-wing German Workers' Party (DAP). Unable to contain his ire during a discussion in favour of Bavarian separatism, Hitler spoke out vehemently and drove the speaker off the stage. Party chairman Anton Drexler was impressed with his words, Hitler less so with the party's shabby organization. However, within a fortnight he had joined the DAP with a view to making his mark rather than helping the party grow. He made his first speech to the party's members on 16 October 1919 at Munich's Hofbräukeller. He had plenty to say.

## Universal outrage at Versailles

For the German people during the winter of 1918–19, everything seemed on the verge of collapse. The war had been lost; the terms of the armistice were shocking. The Allied blockade continued and so did the shortages of food and fuel, and a flu epidemic continued its cruel progress across the country. Soldiers returning from the fronts in their hundreds of thousands were left stranded, poor, jobless, hungry and bitter. There was brutal violence in the streets as the revolution raged. During the elections of January 1919, three-quarters of the voters had given their support to the idea of Germany as a democracy. The new assembly had high hopes for the peace settlement with the Allied powers, which they wanted to be based on US President Woodrow Wilson's 'Fourteen Points', including a seat at the negotiation table, self-determination and support for the new democratic republic. The treaty that emerged following the Paris Peace Conference, which met in January 1919, was very different.

The defeated powers – Germany, Austria-Hungary, Bulgaria and Turkey – were not represented in the French capital. Russia, one of the Allied powers until the Russian Revolution in 1917, was also absent and negotiated its own treaty with Germany. Woodrow Wilson had set out a wide-ranging vision for peace, which recognized the importance of self-determination for Europe's various ethnic populations and a reduction in the armed forces of all nations, and proposed the formation of a 'general association of nations' to mediate any future disputes and so avoid other large-scale conflicts in the future. This was later established as the League of Nations. But Lloyd George, representing Britain, and particularly George Clemenceau of France had other, more direct concerns. Vittorio Orlando, the Italian prime minister, was looking to secure the territorial gains in the Balkans, which had been guaranteed by the Allies in 1915 in return for abandoning the Triple Alliance with

Germany and Austria-Hungary and remaining neutral until joining the conflict on the other side. Orlando's claims were firmly rejected by Woodrow Wilson. For Britain, Lloyd George personally agreed with Wilson's ideas. He wanted Germany to be given the ability to stand on its own two feet and face up to the Bolshevik threat from the east, but bowed to public opinion, which sided with France. Clemenceau, determined to protect France from another attack from Germany, was adamant that it had to pay – in terms of its land, its industry, its armed forces and colossal reparations.

The resulting compromise was harsh: Germany was to lose 13 per cent of its land (including a corridor to the sea for Poland, which cut Germany in two), 12 per cent of its people, 48 per cent of its iron resources, 15 per cent of its agricultural production and 10 per cent of its coal. In addition, its army was to be reduced to 100,000 men, the navy to 36 ships and no submarines, and it was to lose its entire air force. The country was to accept total blame for the war and pay £6.6 billion in compensation. It was not offered a place in the newly established League of Nations. Importantly, the union of Germany and German-speaking Austria was forbidden. Germany was not allowed to make changes to the treaty's provisions and was only given 15 days to respond. Faced with the revolutionary atmosphere at home and the deteriorating conditions of war, on 28 June 1919, the German delegation signed the treaty at the Palace of Versailles, outside Paris.

There was universal outrage across Germany at the harshness and injustice of the terms. People felt that Germany had lost its place at the table of the Great Powers and been denied the right to defend itself. The signing of this dictated peace was seen as a national disgrace. Blame for this outrage soon spread from the victors to those politicians who had agreed to it and signed it off.

If ordinary Germans were horrified about the treaty, extreme right-wing nationalist groups such as the Pan-Germans and the newly formed Fatherland Party were galvanized by their devotion to the German nation. In reality, these groups were mainly made up of men from the middle classes; the working class remained committed to the Social Democrats and the new republic. Other groups formed, particularly ones made up of soldiers returning from the front. Most prominent among these were the 'Steel Helmets', who were unashamed of their wish to restore the values of the Bismarckian Reich and not averse to using violence to promote their views. Violence on the streets of German cities had been legitimized by the First World War, during which organized gangs of armed thugs representing differing political views fought battles that ended in injury and often in death.

## The piano polisher

The end of the war had a profound effect on the youth of Germany. Nearly everything they had believed in 1914 had essentially been destroyed by 1918. The task of rebuilding was a daunting one. Following the example of the *Wandervögel* and other youth groups before them, post-war youths reached out to new groups in search of social and political stabilities they now found lacking. There was the *Bündische Jugend* for more liberal-minded individuals, Catholic and other Church-sponsored groups, communist and socialist-sponsored groups, and the *Völkische* movement, sponsored by the National Socialists. Other, smaller groups were formed representing parties right across the political spectrum. One such party was the DAP who, despite claiming to be the party of the youth of Germany, virtually ignored the youth in its early days, since they did not represent votes.

In September 1921, however, a 17-year-old named Gustav Lenk and his father attended a meeting of the newly named Nationalist Socialist German Workers' Party (NSDAP, but soon to be shortened to Nazi) at the Höfbrauhaus tavern in Munich to hear a speech by new party leader Adolf Hitler. It was not the first time they had heard him speak, having listened to his message from the steps of the city's Feldherrnhalle and the Hofbräuhaus in the preceding months.

Lenk, born in Munich in 1903, was a piano polisher by trade. In 1919, during the tumultuous months of revolution following Germany's defeat in the war, the mutiny of the navy, the abdication of the Kaiser and the signing of the armistice, he had joined the German Youth Movement.[26] Having grown up in Germany during the war, he had faced the reality of poverty, hunger and unemployment. Fearful that the new regime would be similar to the old one and resenting the politicians he held responsible for the misery inflicted on Germany, he looked elsewhere for help, rejecting the movement's middle-class bias.

He was energized by Hitler's words and by his ideas, since they offered some form of hope for the future of the working classes. He wrote to the party headquarters and asked them if he could join but his application was rejected as he was not yet 18. He asked if the party had a youth organization he could join. A reply in the negative included a suggestion that he organize one himself.

However, in March 1922, a public proclamation appeared in the NSDAP's official newspaper, the anti-socialist and anti-Jewish *Völkischer Beobachter*, in which Hitler announced the organization of the party's youth movement to promote the cause of the NSDAP in Germany. Initially, there was little response, since there were numerous other well-established rivals with a similar political message already on the scene. Two months later, the Nazis held a public meeting in the Bürgerbräukeller beer hall in Munich to officially announce the founding of its *Jugendbund* (Youth League). The hall was full to capacity, but there were only 17 youths among the crowd, though the speeches and beer went down well. With no training for youth work of any kind, Lenk was appointed leader, albeit under the command of the *Sturmabteilung*, the party's private militia who protected members at mass meetings and confronted rival parties in the streets.

Lenk was no public speaker, but he was an energetic organizer and administrator. He immediately announced the make-up of the League: the *Jugendmannschaften* for boys aged 14 to 16 years and the *Jungsturm Adolf Hitler* for 16 to 18-year-olds. The aims of the League were as follows: to increase membership based on *Völkisch* (racial) principles, to support and fight for *Völkisch* ideals; to educate fellow Germans regarding their love of the *Heimatland* (homeland) and the German *Volk* (people); to maintain a high regard for moral and civilized values; and to have a strong contempt for 'Jewish Mammonist' ideals. Membership was only open to Aryan Germans and excluded all foreigners, adherents to the Jewish faith and other 'inferior' races. Those who were accepted for membership had to swear personal allegiance to Adolf Hitler. Having done so, new recruits were issued with their uniforms.

## The power of speech

With his party on the rise, Hitler's confidence grew. There were dozens of other right-wing parties, such as the anti-Semitic German Nationalist Protection and Defiance Federation League and the nationalist German-Socialist Party, but none had anyone in their ranks with the public speaking skills of Adolf Hitler. He had discovered his ability as a persuasive speaker during the army courses he had attended in Munich. On joining the NSDAP as their principal speaker, he began to speak more regularly and hone his subject matter and techniques. Although the audiences he addressed in the beer halls were ready-made for him, he never let them down. Using short sentences, trigger words and emotive slogans, he would tell those in attendance what they wanted to hear. One of his favourite techniques was the 'either-or' fallacy, which was tremendously powerful in the vengeful, ultra-nationalist atmosphere at this time. For example, 'There are only two possibilities in Germany … either the victory of the Aryan, or annihilation of the Aryan and the victory of the Jew.'

Addressing the German people as a whole rather than as a series of individuals, he would propose a problem, identify those who caused the problem – usually Jews, Marxists or pacifists – and then present the solution. As the speeches progressed, his voice would get louder, his gestures wilder, with sweat on his brow. The effect was electric; here was passion and a fighting spirit listeners could admire. He would often end speeches by reminding the audience of the 'stab-in-the-back' myth, the unfair terms of the Treaty of Versailles, which he believed treated the Germans as subhuman, and finally making clear to his audience that the blame for Germany's ills lay with its national enemies, usually communists, liberals, Jews and foreign governments. He would then leave the hall immediately, with the audience enraged and wanting more. It was populism of the highest quality and drew larger and larger crowds.

## The Battle of Coburg

The first public outing of the *Jugendbund* took place at Nuremberg in September 1922 when some 900 members attended Sedan Day, held in remembrance of the Prussian victory over Napoleon in 1870. A month later, in Coburg, they first left their mark. Hitler and 'some gentlemen of his company' were invited to this small city in northern Bavaria by the local Gauleiter (regional leader) to liven up the atmosphere of *Deutscher Tag* (German Day). He also wanted to show the local populace that there was an alternative to the local socialists and communists who had a foothold in the politics of Coburg. Sensing the opportunity for publicity, the NSDAP hired a special train, taking some 800 *Sturmabteilung* and *Jugendbund* members and a 40-piece band to the event. On arrival and against explicit instructions from the police, the Nazis unfurled their banners and swastikas and the band started up, as they marched to the town centre. Workers lined the streets, hurled insults and spat at the marchers. In return, the stormtroopers used sticks and truncheons to beat their tormentors. At one point, a pitched battle took place with locals and the police siding with the Nazis.

Fighting continued that night, following a speech from Hitler and a number of his colleagues in the city's main hall, and again the following afternoon when there were more parades and a number of anti-Semitic rallies. After that, having soundly defeated the left-wingers and won over the support of the townsfolk, Hitler and his party marched back to the railway station in triumph and took the train back to Munich. Ten years later, on the verge of taking power, Hitler ordered the striking of a medal to be presented to the original participants of this battle to memorialize the event that took place that day in northern Bavaria. The so-called Coburg Badge, with approximately 436 recipients, was the first badge recognized as a national award by the Nazi Party.

## The Nazi bandwagon rolls on

On 27 January 1923, Hitler held his first official Nazi *Parteitag* (party conference) in Munich. A few days earlier, in response to the lack of payment of reparations as laid down by the terms of the Treaty of Versailles, the French and Belgians had marched into the Ruhr and seized coal, timber and other materials. This caused uproar with strikes, demonstrations and acts of sabotage. The timing was perfect. Thousands of Nazis paraded along the streets of Munich carrying flags, banners and pennants marked with the Aryan swastika symbol. Thousands more watched and applauded. The *Jungsturm* made an appearance. They were presented with official pennants bearing the Nazi Party's swastika on a white background. Although membership numbers for the party's youth movement were still small, said to be close to 1,200, Lenk persisted. He set up groups in Nuremberg, Zeitz, Dresden, Hanau and Dortmund. Outside Germany there was interest too, among German-speaking Austrians and Sudeten Germans in Czechoslovakia. Lenk's progress was hampered somewhat by Hitler's unwillingness to consider fusion with any other groups who, in turn, did not wish to make themselves subservient to the NSDAP. Despite this, Hitler promoted Lenk from a regional position to a national one, even though he remained in a subordinate position to the SA.

In May the following year, Lenk organized the publication of a youth magazine, the *Nationale Jungsturm*. But with too few subscribers, the magazine was a failure and ended up as a supplement in the *Völkischer Beobachter*. In contrast, the popularity of Hitler's regular speeches was growing quickly. Since the early days in Munich's many beer halls, crowds of several hundred had grown to several thousand by the end of 1920, by which time Hitler had added venues in other cities, such as Stuttgart, Rosenheim, Salzburg, Vienna and elsewhere to his roster. In February the following year, he made his first speech at the Circus Krone, Munich's biggest venue, in front of 3,500 people. Entitled 'Future or Ruin', it centred on the denunciation of reparation payments to the Allies. While his speech during the first *Parteitag* had been heard by some 6,000 members, in August 1922, at a mass gathering of Bavarian nationalist associations, he spoke to a crowd of 70,000 assembled in Munich's Königsplatz. On and on he went, addressing the Jewish Question, the November Criminals, Marxism, Bolshevism, the Versailles peace, the government and why Germany should look forward to a future of National Socialism.

## The Beer Hall Putsch

Hitler's unbridled rhetoric had promised much, prompting membership of the Nazi movement to expand rapidly – up to 55,000 by mid-1923 – but apart from that, he had delivered nothing apart from rumours that he was planning a putsch. The need for action increased in the middle of the year when, as a natural result of years of war, unemployment, revolution, debt and instability, the German economy began to buckle, sparking a period of hyperinflation. Tensions rose further in the build-

*In 1923, hyperinflation rendered German banknotes virtually worthless. In November you needed 2.5 trillion marks to buy one US dollar, by December 4.2 trillion. Families used baskets or wheelbarrows to take their pay packets to the shops immediately to buy supplies before the money lost its value.*

up to 1 May, a day significant for the left as 'International Labour Day', and to the nationalist right as the anniversary of the end of Soviet-style councils of the revolution in 1919. The authorities in Munich were alarmed at the prospect of serious disturbances, since there had already been a number of street fights between communists and National Socialists in the lead-up. They had given permission for a trade's union parade to which the nationalists had objected. Hitler proposed a counter demonstration, but the police denied his request. In the event, the day passed with few incidents. However, Hitler's failure to make the most of his opportunity was seen as humiliating, and some observers expressed the view that his star was now on the wane.

That summer, other nationalist right-wing groups, such as the *Bund Oberland*, the *Reichsflagge* and the *Wikingbund*, formed a loose association of radical nationalists with former General Ludendorff as its unofficial leader. It seemed likely that the majority of Hitler's followers, the SA, would join too. However, Hitler kept up his 'relentless agitation against the "November Criminals"'[27]. His message was still potent, drawing larger and larger audiences, particularly at the Circus Krone venue. Hitler's reputation was completely restored by his speech at the *Deutscher Tag* rally in Nuremberg on 2 September. Some 100,000 members of nationalist paramilitary forces and veterans' associations attended. On the podium for the parade were General Ludendorff, Adolf Hitler and Prinz Ludwig Ferdinand of Bavaria. In the evening, Hitler took to the stage at the city's Festhalle (civic centre). What Germany needs, he proclaimed, is 'a nationalist revolution today to restore Germany's might and greatness. We can save Germany from internal and foreign foes, only through blood and sword. We need a revolution, bloodshed, and a dictatorship ... We must have a new dictatorship. We need no parliament, no government like the present. We cannot expect Germany's salvation from the present condition, but only through a dictatorship brought through the sword.'[28]

*Adolf Hitler with Alfred Rosenberg (left) and Dr Frederick Toben at the Oberland Free Corps in Munich on 1 May, 1923. He had hoped to organize a counter demonstration to the trade union parade on that day but was not permitted to do so.*

Fine words for the nationalists; but still Hitler did not act. He knew that in order for a putsch to succeed he needed the support of the army and the police. Although *Deutscher Tag* had ended with the formation of the *Deutscher Kampfbund* (German Combat League), comprising the NSDAP, the *Bund Oberland* and the *Reichsflagge*, which gave him the so-called political leadership of the right, a revolution in Bavaria was still unlikely to succeed. Meanwhile, inflation continued to soar with devastating effect, rendering pensions and insurance policies redundant and the cost of living incalculable. There were strikes and demonstrations everywhere and, in October, a state of emergency was declared in Bavaria. At Hitler's insistence, members of the *Kampfbund*, still without a guarantee of support from the police or the military, agreed to act.

On the evening of 8 November, a large crowd had assembled at the Bürgerbräukeller to hear the monarchist head of the Bavarian government, Gustav von Kahr, speak on the anniversary of the end of the November revolution. There was some excitement following a rumour that he was going to announce the restoration of the Bavarian monarchy. Some way into the speech there was a disturbance as Hitler entered the hall surrounded by steel-helmeted SA. Unable to be heard among the uproar, he drew his pistol and fired a shot in the air, then announced that the national revolution had begun: the Bavarian government was to be deposed and replaced by a new Reich government, with Hitler as chancellor, Ludendorff in charge of the army, and prominent posts for the heads of the police and the *Reichswehr* (army), and Kahr himself.

News of the coup spread rapidly across the city and was greeted by some with delirium and others with dismay. For a while, confusion reigned. Overnight, however, it became clear that the police and the army did not support the move. In desperation, at noon the following day, Hitler and Ludendorff led a march of some 2,000 putschists from the beer hall to the War Ministry in the hope of garnering popular support along the way. At one point confronted by a cordon of police, they were corralled and told to disperse. A gunfight began and ended with 14 putschists and four policemen dead and a number injured, including Hitler and Hermann Göring, at that time in command of the SA.

The following day, Hitler was arrested and taken to prison in the old fortress in Landsberg, some 64 km (40 miles) from Munich. Following a five-week trial, Hitler and the other leaders of the so-called 'Beer Hall Putsch' were found guilty. Hitler was given a five-year sentence. The NSDAP and the *Jugendbund* were disbanded and outlawed on the orders of the Weimar government.

# Chapter 4

# *Kampfzeit!*

Despite the failed coup, a shoulder injury, arrest and imprisonment, the Beer Hall Putsch was, paradoxically, a major success for Adolf Hitler. His trial was, in many ways, a stitch-up. The Bavarian authorities, many of whom had nationalist sympathies, persuaded those in Berlin to hold the trial in Munich, at the time a hotbed of right-wing extremism. It also seems likely they offered him a plea bargain in return for admitting his guilt. After all, he had lots of damning information on local politicians, senior police and army officers and the judge chosen was known to be a nationalist sympathizer.

Given that Hitler was accused of high treason against the state, that four policemen were killed and that he took full responsibility for the putsch, the five-year sentence was astonishingly lenient. The judge's reasoning was that the participants had acted with patriotic motives and should therefore be treated with clemency. During the trial, Hitler had basically taken over the courtroom, expounded his views at great length and even been allowed to interrogate witnesses. Many were outraged; others delighted. In the event, he served only nine months of his sentence.

## *Mein Kampf*

Hitler was comfortable in prison, reading newspapers, letters, telegrams from well-wishers and books from the prison library. He chatted to and heard the news from his many visitors in a large room filled with flowers and gifts. He also spent time dictating an account of his life and opinions to his colleague Rudolf Hess, who had also been imprisoned. The process of writing gave him time to think. In this text, which would be published the following year as *Mein Kampf* (*My Struggle*), he confirmed his beliefs in the revision of the Treaty of Versailles, the restoration of German borders in 1914 and the self-determination of German-speaking peoples. His 'real' vehemence was reserved for the Jews, the 'sworn enemy of the German race, whose historic mission it was, under the guidance of the Nazi Party ... to annihilate them entirely.'[29] Linking them with Bolshevism and Marxism, he also outlined his plan to find *Lebensraum* (living space) for the expanding German population in Russian lands, taken by conquest from the 'Jewish-Bolsheviks'. It was a grim read, full of 'crude prejudice, conspiracy theory, race hatred and perverted Darwinism.'[30]

He also explained what he had learned during his short time in politics and through the failure of the putsch: the need to adopt 'legal' principles to ensure political success, that he and only he should lead the struggle, that propaganda was essential to his cause and that only the army's support would guarantee victory. His blueprint for the future was helped in no small part by State Prosecutor Ludwig Stenglein in his closing speech at Hitler's trial. He said, 'It is understandable that the enthusiastic youth suffers from impatience, but youth must be disciplined and led in the right direction by mature men. Impatience must be replaced by the ability to work quietly and confidently for the future, waiting with clenched teeth until the hour is ripe.'

However, one condition of Hitler's release in December 1924 was that he was forbidden to speak in public, an act that removed his most powerful weapon. When the Nazis took power in 1933, part of the carefully crafted Nazi mythology, taught as part of the school curriculum, referred to the years between 1925 and 1933 as the *Kampfzeit* (the 'Time of Struggle').

## Nazis reorganized

While Hitler emerged from prison a changed man, the Germany he found was changed too. The Weimar Republic had stabilized, particularly since the appointment of Gustav Stresemann as foreign minister, whose negotiating skills had allowed the implementation of the Dawes Plan that successfully resolved the issue of the First World War reparations and the withdrawal of the French from the Ruhr. With the economy improving, social unrest was brought under control. In Bavaria, the state of emergency was finally ended in February 1925. At this point, refreshed and ready, confident of his popularity and his leadership qualities and clearer in his thinking, Hitler re-reorganized the Nazi Party.

During his incarceration and the banning of the NSDAP, there had been a number of splits and rivalries among the radical nationalist groups. Hitler's release stirred the pot. However, when Ludendorff resigned from the National Socialist Liberty Movement in February 1925, Hitler's greatest rival to the leadership of national reconstruction was gone. He began his party reorganization in earnest. While it was not his top priority, Hitler also revived the Youth League, though Gustav Lenk had been discarded for showing 'independent tendencies'. However, Lenk had not been idle while Hitler was in prison, having set up a number of other groups, including the Greater German Youth Movement in Plauen, Saxony, led by the Lenk-appointed former law student Kurt Gruber. There were other youth groups too, all vying for the attentions of the now-undisputed leader of the Nazi Party. Hitler used his normal tactic in these circumstances, refusing to take sides openly with any one group, allowing them to destroy themselves and then assume the leadership himself.

Another organization re-founded in 1925 was the *Schutzstaffel*, better known as the SS, which had begun life in 1923 as Hitler's personal bodyguard. As part of his 'Leadership Principle', Hitler required protection by an elite formation of soldiers who were racially pure, and offered blind obedience and loyalty to him. The first commander of the SS was a dedicated Hitler loyalist, Julius Schreck, formerly commander of the SA Assault Squad. In 1929, the group was taken over and further developed by Heinrich Himmler. By 1933, the SS consisted of 35,000 soldiers, who regarded themselves as the ultimate defenders of the Aryan race, steeped in Nazi ideology and a symbol of Nazi terror.

Reorganization continued at the Bamberg Conference in 1926. Hitler's aim was not only to reunite the Catholic-tolerant nationalists in Bavaria and the northern Protestant socialist division that had opened in his absence but also to reinvent the party as a political force, which focused on gaining power through popular support and the ballot box rather than by violence alone. Plans were laid to infiltrate existing social structures of specific professions, such as doctors and lawyers, to help in recruitment. More emphasis was to be put on the Hitler Youth, too. For those who could not be persuaded, of course, the SA and the newly formed SS were there to help.

His conference speech stressed a number of new ideas. First, that Germany's salvation would not come from an alliance with Russia, but from *Lebensraum* in the east at Russia's expense. Second, that the party would henceforward stand 'on the basis of law', so as not to allow 'a Jewish system of exploitation a legal excuse for the complete plundering of our people'. Third, he explained that the party wanted to create a *Volksgemeinschaft*, a community of true Germans, who would be bound together by national unity with Hitler as its unquestioned *Führer* (leader).

## Birth of the Hitler Youth

Although independent thinking didn't work for Gustav Lenk, it did work for Kurt Gruber. Born in 1904, he accepted that National Socialism was the only way forward for Germany and, with the financial support of a local textile firm, was able to devote his whole time to his youth work. His administrative skills were admirable, and he designed a new uniform for the group's members, which included brown shirts and armlets featuring the Nazi swastika. He was able to establish branches of his group in other parts of Germany, particularly among working-class youths from industrial districts. Despite his successes, Gruber was not Hitler's immediate choice as leader of the new Nazi Party youth movement and at first was not allowed to continue his work without party interference. But Gruber's appeal to Hitler was not only his efficiency, but also the fact that he was young and so fitted Hitler's youth-leading-youth idea. Other pros were that he was no threat, that he accepted Hitler's programme without question and that he was happy to obey his every command. On Sunday 4 July 1926, at the Nazi Party rally in Weimar, the Greater German Youth Movement was renamed the *Hitlerjugend, Bund der Deutschen Arbeiterjugend*, and the Hitler Youth was born with Kurt Gruber as its first *Reichsführer*.

By this time, Hitler's Nazi Party had set up the administrative structure devised at Bamberg. The country was divided up into *Gaue* (districts), each of which was headed up by a Gauleiter. All Gauleiters reported to the *Reichsleitung* (the leadership office of the NSDAP), which was controlled by Rudolf Hess and his successor Martin Bormann. Other important officials at this time included Gregor Strasser, Joseph Goebbels, Jew-baiter-in-chief Julius Streicher and the head of the newly reorganized SA, Pfeffer von Salomon. In terms of party membership, progress was slow. From some 27,000 in 1925 to 49,000 the following year, it was not until 1929 when 178,000 members were recorded that the Nazis took their place at the top table of German politics.

Gruber was given a place in the Nazi hierarchy, as adviser on youth questions at the party headquarters in Munich. Hitler made it clear that he wanted the youth section completely integrated into the party and that it would be answerable to the SA. Members of the *Hitlerjugend* (HJ) above the age of 18 also had to join the party. If you did not join the party, then you would lose membership of the youth section. In effect, this meant that the party had a measure of control on the levers of the HJ. In addition, the NSDAP had to be consulted on the appointment of high-ranking members and on public appearances. Orders from party leaders had to be obeyed and HJ meetings were subject to party guidance. New recruits were charged a small membership fee and issued with new armbands, with a horizontal white stripe behind the swastika, designed to avoid confusion with those of the SA. Gruber was happy to agree to these terms but was politically aware enough to keep his headquarters in Plauen rather than moving to Munich, under the noses of the party leadership.

## March of the *Hitlerjugend*

The establishment of the HJ and its new relationship with the SA had advantages and disadvantages. On the plus side, new pro-Hitler groupings in other parts of Germany and Austria were happy to join up. Gruber divided the membership into groups: for education, culture, military sport, propaganda and film, incorporating the same organizational divisions as the NSDAP. Set against this were growing fears that the HJ were vulnerable to interference from the older generation of NSDAP party members – violating the idea of youth-leading-youth. This situation was made worse in 1927 when an NSDAP order stated that all members of the HJ had to join the SA as soon as they turned 18. As the HJ already lacked trained leaders, who were often transferred over as soon as they had finished training, this turned a molehill into a mountain. Another major concern for Gruber was finances. Membership fees alone were not sufficient to run the organization, and the coffers had to be kept up by private donations and, though illegal, by private collection during propaganda marches.

Despite these petty squabbles, Gruber continued to do good work. As well as the armbands, he introduced new flags, insignia and emblems, including the S-rune of the sun and victory. He created new branches, including the Deutsches *Jungvolk*, for boys aged 10 to 14, and another for girls. He also oversaw the publication of two newspapers, *Die Junge Front* and *Hitlerjugend Zeitung*.

The pinnacle of Gruber's leadership came in 1927. On 1 May, Labour Day, the Hitler Youth organized a major rally in Plauen, which

*In his speech on the so-called 'Day of Awakening' at the third party congress, in Nuremberg in August 1927, Hitler was full of praise for the newly named Hitler Youth, 300 of whom, proudly led by Kurt Gruber, took part in the parade alongside 30,000 brown-shirted stormtroopers.*

was praised by observers as it 'differed markedly in matters of discipline from the traditional and Socialist processions.'[31] On 19 and 20 August, Gruber and 300 Hitler Youth joined with 30,000 'brownshirts', as the SA had become known, at the third Nazi Party congress. Both Hitler and Goebbels made speeches at what was billed as the 'Day of Awakening' and Hitler was at pains to praise the 'patriotism and unselfishness' of his youthful supporters. With funds still lacking, many of the youths had walked to Nuremberg from Berlin, an annual tradition that later became known as the 'Adolf Hitler March'.

For Gruber, this event marked a turning point in the development of the Hitler Youth. He felt as though his group had cast off the mantle of the SA and the movement was now developing of its own accord. The group began to create its own character and traditions, organize its own meetings and marches, and even wrote new words for stirring traditional songs to be sung during public marches.

In November 1928, the Hitler Youth's Party Day, called the *Reichsappell*, was held in Plauen. Over a few days, a number of public rallies were held, as well as meetings at which party matters were discussed. The setting up of the *Jungvolk* was confirmed, as was the creation of the *Bund Deutscher Mädel* (BDM/League of German Girls). New departments were created: a Hitler Youth news service to 'break the Jewish monopoly of news'; the *Landesjugendamt* (State Youth Welfare Office), to look after the interests of the youth in agricultural regions, and another to organize youth activities for those who lived in border regions and German-speaking areas of Czechoslovakia and Poland. Despite all these advances, recruitment numbers were still too low. Gruber thought that this might be because there was little to distinguish between the Hitler Youth and the many other nationalist groups. To counter this, he came up with some principles by which the HJ was to stand going forward, describing it as a 'new youth movement of you social-revolutionary-minded Germans.' His message was firm and left little doubt about the direction of travel for this organization. From now on, the HJ was to produce individuals who would not only fight but also be prepared to die for their country in an effort to rid it of 'the enemies of the German race'. Its stated aim was to create a new national socialist community 'over the dead bodies of capitalism and Marxism'.[32]

Party propaganda was revamped and more targeted, particularly at farmers and rural workers. Party membership grew from 100,000 in 1928 to 150,000 the following year. The party was in motion, dynamic. Hitler's charisma, in person and while speaking, was ever more effective. The greeting, 'Heil Hitler', with outstretched right arm was now mandatory, whether the man himself was present or not. A cult of personality was growing around him. With the party now dependent on him, Hitler's confidence was growing. In August 1929, some 40,000 people attended the Party rally in Nuremberg, where they put on a huge propaganda display.

## The Wall Street Crash

Between 24 and 29 October, the stock market on Wall Street in New York crashed. The German economy, which had benefitted from international loans and investments to rebuild schools, businesses and hospitals after the war, collapsed again as US investments were called in. The resulting slump led to bankruptcies, depression, unemployment, poverty and hopelessness, and destabilized the already fragile Weimar government. With a near worthless currency and facing widespread ruin, the German people, many of them uncertain and frightened for the future, looked elsewhere for help. One option, offering strong-arm action and stable leadership, was the Nazi Party. With simple but drastic solutions, aggressive nationalism, an omnipotent leader and its clearly visible uniformed youths and SA and SS troops offering help to their supporters and terror to their enemies, Nazi popularity and power was growing.

Buoyed by their increasing popularity, party members and the HJ threw themselves into campaigning for the national elections in September 1930. Coming as the country was facing the effects of the Great Depression, the elections saw a record 82 per cent voter turnout. While the Social Democrats once again emerged with a majority, the NSDAP polled over 6 million votes, earning the Nazis 107 seats in the Reichstag and making them the second largest party in the legislature.

Backed by increasingly effective propaganda, devised by Joseph Goebbels, the Nazis gave out simple messages tailored to specific groups of people, such as the working class or women, and designed to exploit their particular fears. Goebbels had been a writer and journalist before joining the Nazi Party in 1924. A key part of his methodology to communicate in the early 1930s was through poster campaigns. One such poster, released in 1932, had black text on a white background that said: '5,600,000 unemployed demand work! The need of the unemployed is the need of the whole people! On Friday evening, 15 January 1932, at 8 pm there will be sixteen mass meetings of the unemployed'. It then listed the meeting venues. Another, aimed at women, was headlined 'The Red War' and highlighted the need to fight against communism. Using the Nazis' favourite either-or rhetoric, it listed the choices: 'Mother or Comrade? Men or Machine? God or Devil? Blood or Gold? Race or Half-Breed? Folk Songs or Jazz? National Socialists or Bolsheviks?' Some posters were text only, using carefully selected colours and fonts; others used images too. Images carry impact because they attract attention, communicate information quickly and appeal to people's emotions. Hitler was fully aware of the power of propaganda. In *Mein Kampf*, he said: 'Propaganda is a truly terrible weapon in the hands of an expert ... All propaganda must be popular and its intellectual level must be adjusted to the most limited intelligence among those it is addressed to.'[33]

## Chaos and lawlessness in the streets

As the Great Depression bit deeper, Germany's industrial output started to fall rapidly, businesses began to cut back or collapse completely, and unemployment figures rose at startling speed. By 1932, one in three workers were registered as unemployed. With less money, there was less to spend on food, so unemployment spread to the countryside too. The benefits system, introduced in 1927, was based on unemployment insurance, financed by companies themselves, local authorities and central government, and designed to offer temporary relief for some 800,000 people. In 1932, the unemployment figure stood at over 6 million! As tax revenue began to tumble, benefits had to be cut; as the crisis continued, so benefits began to be stopped altogether.

The situation on the streets of German towns and cities began to deteriorate. With little else to do, gangs of men and boys would gather around in groups. Whether they were threatening or not, they appeared to be, since there was a menacing atmosphere on the streets, especially at night. And there was plenty of violence, too, particularly provoked by the Communist Party, whose popularity in those desperate days was skyrocketing. In 1929, their national membership was just over 100,000; by 1932, it had risen to 360,000, many of the new members joining because they were unemployed. There was already residual hatred between the Communists and the Social Democrats because of the 1918–19 revolution, and this threatened to boil over again. With no interest in the faux democracy peddled by what they called the 'fascist' Weimar government, the Communists were happy for chaos and lawlessness to prevail. They organized rent strikes in working-class areas, proclaimed no-go areas in Berlin and other cities in which strangers would be beaten up or threatened with guns. They adopted pubs and bars as their own, with rules that were enforced by their paramilitary organization, the Red Front-Fighters League.

For a while, the threat of a Communist revolution, led by its party leader Ernst Thälmann whose orders came directly from the Comintern[34] in Moscow, seemed a distinct possibility for millions of middle-class Germans. For them, in 1931, dinner-time conversation probably revolved around a worrying problem: if the government falls, will it be replaced by Hitler or the Communists? But the Communist Party had a number of its own problems. While they hated the government, they failed to provide any alternatives. Their future success seemed to depend on the total collapse of capitalism. Ironically, the party, whose supporters consisted largely of the unemployed, was terminally short of money. Behind the scenes, the SA and the Hitler Youth were busy in the poorer parts of the big cities meting out brutal violence and driving the Reds back to their tenement buildings in the slums. In this conflict, the sympathies of the police and the general population were with the Nazis, who were not enemies of capitalism and had no intention of replacing it with a 'Soviet State'.

## Gruber out, Schirach in

Kurt Gruber also had a fight on his hands. In a sense, he was a victim of his own success. As the Nazi Party and its youth movement became more successful, so it became more attractive and less easy for him to control. In addition, his access to Hitler had made his position at the head of the Hitler Youth an attractive one. Petty squabbles and jealousies among the Nazi Party's higher echelons was common – indeed Hitler encouraged them as it helped him choose which way to put his favours. Gruber had two main rivals. One was Ernst Röhm, a brutish, aggressive long-term soldier who had been imprisoned for his part in the Beer Hall Putsch, after which he had become a military instructor in Bolivia. The other was Baldur von Schirach. Coming from a prominent and wealthy, culturally conservative family from Berlin, Schirach had a top-class education, good looks and the 'right' Nazi worldview. He joined the

Young German League aged ten, where he developed racist views along with a hatred of his own aristocratic class. Apparently, after reading *Mein Kampf* and hearing Hitler speak in Weimar in 1925, he was converted to Nazism. The following year, the Schirach family met and began a friendship with Hitler. Hitler was flattered by the attention, particularly by the poems he received from the artistically inclined and silver-tongued Baldur. Hitler encouraged the boy to study at Munich University, where he read German folklore and art history. When he completed his studies in 1928, Hitler appointed him Leader of the Nazi Student Association with the task of promoting Nazism in the universities.

The signs for Gruber were not good when Ernst Röhm was appointed chief-of-staff of the SA, which by now had over a million members. Hitler assumed supreme command and was at pains to remind Gruber

*The son of a German theatre director and his American wife, the polished, aristocratic, artistic, well-educated and handsome Baldur von Schirach was not your run-of-the-mill Nazi. However, as leader of the Hitler Youth, he used his outstanding organizational qualities, idealism and blind devotion to the Führer succeeded in winning over millions of young Germans to the Nazi cause.*

that the Hitler Youth was still a department of the SA and that he was therefore subordinate to Röhm. A whispering campaign against Gruber began, in which both Röhm and Schirach were involved, with complaints about his poor administration, delays in getting subscription money from members to Nazi headquarters, frustration at the lack of new recruits, and other matters. His promises to improve the numbers fell on deaf ears and in October 1931 his resignation was accepted, although he had not offered it, and he was immediately replaced as Reich Youth Leader of the NSDAP by Baldur von Schirach.

Still only one of many youth organizations in Germany at the beginning of the 1930s, Schirach's HJ was essentially confined to a propaganda role, spreading Nazi ideology by handing out leaflets and pamphlets, holding up placards, marching in rallies and parades, chanting slogans and thereby displaying power, strength and unity, all to show the public that the rise of the Nazis was irresistible. Such a demonstration of Nazi strength took place over the weekend of 17 and 18 October 1931, when some 60,000 SA men and members of the HJ assembled in Brunswick for a 'central German SA meeting'. In effect taking over the town, they held a night-time procession, the consecration of a Nazi standard, a six-hour march-past and a speech by Hitler. As the event was taking place, SA troops rampaged through the working-class districts of the old town. Breaking through police lines, armed with guns and iron bars, they destroyed shops and homes at random, killing two and wounding 62. 'Thus symbolic occupation was allied with terror directed specifically at the working-class.'[35] For the Nazis, such images of unity, strength, youth and revolt were the expression of a strongly symbolic understanding of politics.

Alarmed at this display of Nazi strength, the Weimar authorities imposed a national ban on all uniformed paramilitary groups, including Nazis and Communists. But the ban had little effect as street violence, the disruption of meetings and political hooliganism continued. In terms of membership of the HJ, the ban backfired: membership stood at some 26,000 in 1930 and more than 63,000 by the time the ban was announced.

## The first National Socialist martyr

Born in 1916, Herbert Norkus was the son of a taxi driver named Ludwig. A veteran of the Great War, Ludwig had joined the SA in 1929 in protest at the failings of the Weimar Republic. The family lived in the Beusselkiez neighbourhood of Moabit, a drab, lower-class industrial section of Berlin riddled with poverty, hunger, suffering and hostility. His mother discouraged him from joining the Hitler Youth because their area was known as 'Red' due to the gangs of marauding Communists who roamed the streets there. When she died in a sanitorium in 1931, as a result of repeated assaults by Communists in the milk store that she ran on Wiclefstrasse, his father let him join.

Attracted by the Führer's guaranteed deliverance from the dark tenement world of Depression Berlin rather than any political considerations, Herbert quickly became a devoted Hitler Youth member. He loved the daily activities of the organization; meetings, rallies, propaganda work, music and weekends in the country were a welcome relief from the boredom of school and gave his life structure now that his mother was gone.

Herbert knew the streets were unsafe but was prepared to take the risk of a beating for a cause in which he believed. He had often been chased but had avoided injury because he was street smart and quick on his feet, often escaping over the bridge or hiding in the forest around the nearby cemetery.

At dawn on 24 January 1932, Herbert was sent out to post bills advertising an NSDAP rally to be held later that day at the Sport Palace where Goebbels was due to speak. He headed out with his friend Johannes Kirsch. They worked their way up and down the streets stuffing the flyers into tenement mailboxes and doorways, looking out for any signs of danger. They had no idea that a group of 30 or 40 communists were waiting in the darkness for them, apparently following a tip-off. Suddenly confronted, both boys ran for their lives. Johannes escaped but Herbert was caught. He fought back, punching and kicking, but was stabbed twice. He managed to escape and hammered on the door of a nearby house, shouting for help. The door was opened by a night watchman but when he saw the bloodied boy and not wanting any trouble, he slammed the door shut.

Cornered and stabbed again, at least four times, Herbert dragged himself away, leaving a trail of bloody handprints along Zwinglistrasse, where his assassins left him to die. His body was taken to Moabit hospital, where an autopsy revealed five stab wounds in the back and

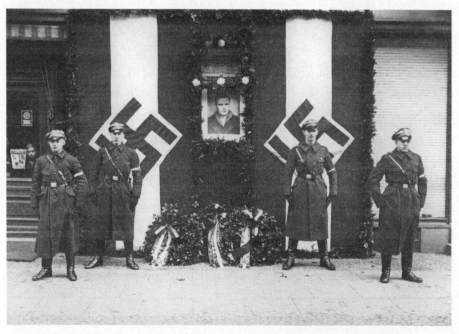

*Herbert Norkus' coffin sits beneath his portrait as it waits to be carried in procession to Johannes Cemetery for burial. His death, the subject of a hastily written novel and a film,* Hitlerjunge Quex, *soon became another cog in the Nazi propaganda machine.*

two in the chest. His face had been mutilated beyond recognition and his top lip had been completely cut off.

Later that morning, the Sport Palace was outraged at the news. Goebbels took full advantage of his opportunity to denounce the communist killers. Herbert's body, lying in an open casket in a very effective dramatization of the brutality of his death, was given a 24-hour guard of honour by his comrades.

On 27 January, his coffin, draped in the livery of the Hitler Youth, was carried through the pine forest in which Herbert had often hidden from his adversaries, and laid to rest in the Johannes Cemetery. Thousands of followers were in attendance, including members of the party elite, the Hitler Youth, the SA and the SS. Goebbels spoke of his martyrdom and his redemption, calling for revenge and atonement. In honour of 'a hero who had died for the cause of National Socialism', the Nazis declared 24 January as a national day of commemoration for all fallen Hitler Youth. Between 1931 and 1933, 23 Hitler Youths (and without question considerably more communist youths) were killed in street fights. Herbert's death (he was the youngest victim at the time) inspired thousands more young people to join the Nazi youth movement.

## Hitler becomes chancellor

In the presidential election in March 1932, which pitted the venerable Paul von Hindenburg against his new adversary, Adolf Hitler, there was no result since no one received the majority vote. A second ballot the following month was won by Hindenburg. But in the federal elections in July, the Nazis scored their biggest political victory yet, with more than 13 million votes, giving them a 37.4 per cent share and 230 seats in the Reichstag, making them the largest single party.

With conditions in Germany at rock bottom in the winter of 1932, the political instability continued. President Hindenburg had dismissed the so-called 'Grand Coalition' government led by the Social Democrat

Hermann Müller in 1930. His successor was the Centre Party's Heinrich Brüning, who did not have a majority and had to rely on Article 48, which allowed government by presidential decree, to get things done. His failure to come up with a plan for the provision of the unemployed led to his dismissal in 1932. A new election followed, and Hindenburg appointed conservative politician Franz von Papen as chancellor on the recommendation of his advisor, Defence Minister Kurt von Schleicher.

With president and chancellor in agreement with the country's conservative elite that an authoritarian leader was needed to stabilize the country, Papen called for another election in November 1932. However, the result changed nothing, apart from a small but worrying reduction in right-wing voters and a rise in support for the Communists. Following the election, Hindenburg dismissed Papen and replaced him with Schleicher, even though it was traditionally the leader of the party with the most seats in the Reichstag who was appointed as chancellor. Hindenburg was hesitant in giving Hitler the job despite his repeated demands. However, discussions were already underway behind closed doors, with leading politicians, important industrialists and other right-wing interest groups all united against a common enemy, the political left, and keen to retain their power and money. Papen, eager to return to power, suggested that Hitler be made chancellor and charged with destroying their left-wing political opponents and, in turn, the Weimar Republic itself. With Papen installed as vice-chancellor, he would control Hitler and so return power to the conservative elite.

Papen presented his plan to President Hindenburg on 23 January 1933. A week later, hoping to avoid a vote of no-confidence in the Reichstag, Schleicher asked Hindenburg to declare a state of emergency. Hindenburg declined, Schleicher resigned, and, with a heavy heart, the president tasked Papen with forming a new government that would bring in Hitler. On 29 January, Papen met Hitler and Hermann Göring to discuss the new government. At the meeting, Hitler announced his plan to dissolve the Reichstag and activate the Enabling Act, to introduce laws without the involvement of government. Papen, happy to be named as vice-chancellor, dismissed his advisors' concerns at this news, claiming that with the confidence of the president, Hitler would soon be ousted. At 11.30 the following morning and against all his instincts, Hindenburg appointed Adolf Hitler as Reich chancellor.

*This propaganda postcard shows Hitler bowing deferentially to Hindenburg in Potsdam on 31 March 1933, known later as the 'Day of Potsdam'. In what Ian Kershaw described as 'a carefully orchestrated propaganda play' the Nazis wanted to demonstrate the alleged unity of the nation through the symbolic historical continuity between the Third Reich, Prussia and the German Empire. The reality, of course, was somewhat different.*

# Chapter 5

# 'Deutschland Erwache!'

History recalls that the night of 30 January 1933 saw a torchlit parade in Berlin in celebration of Hitler's appointment. Columns of brown-shirted SA and SS men, the Hitler Youth along with Steel Helmets, and some 40,000 non-uniformed civilian supporters – all accompanied by bugles, drums and the sound of triumphant songs, carrying flaming torches and red-and-white flags with black swastikas – created 'a river of light' that flowed through the city. The stirring words of songs such as 'Deutschland Erwache!' and the 'Horst Wessel Lied' ('Horst Wessel Song'), named after the young 'martyr' of the SA who was murdered by Communist thugs in 1930, had become the anthems of the Nazi Party. Crowds lined the streets, many cheering as the uniformed paramilitaries marched by. Passing through the Brandenburg Gate, the parade made its way down Wilhelmstrasse, past the President's Palace, from where Hindenburg could be seen watching proceedings from a brightly lit window. A few yards further on, the crowds saw Hitler on a balcony in the Chancellery, saluting the marchers and the crowds below.

## Beginnings of the Nazi state

For the organizer, Joseph Goebbels, the parade was a triumph. He had arranged for a live commentary on state radio with observations from Hermann Göring, who likened the spirit to that of August 1914 in the build-up to the war. Pro-Nazi newspapers were full of praise for the event, with one putting the number of marchers at 700,000.[36] Others had different recollections. The more critical press put the number at some 60,000, and there were eyewitness reports of stormtroopers exchanging their burned-out torches for new ones and marching in wide circles to give the impression of greater numbers. Others noted the indiscipline of the brownshirts; indeed Hindenburg is said to have mistaken them for prisoners.

However, many who witnessed the Berlin march were caught up in the enthusiasm of the occasion. Fifteen-year-old Melita Maschmann, for example, was taken to watch the parade by her parents. They were conservative but they were not National Socialists. Melita, however, was entranced, all the more so as she saw boys and girls of her own age among the marchers. Years later, she remembered her feelings as she watched the parade: 'I wanted to escape from my childish, narrow life and I wanted to attach myself to something that was great and fundamental.' Later that night she told her parents that she wanted to join the Hitler Youth. They refused her request, and she stormed off to bed, accusing them of being old-fashioned and out of touch.

Others were worried by events in Berlin that night and in towns and cities in many other parts of Germany during the next few days. Communists and Jews, in particular, were fearful of reprisals. There were counter demonstrations and a number of violent clashes but no collaboration between the various opposition groups. In fact, many Germans seemed disinterested. After all, the Nazis were not in charge. The new cabinet, announced after Hitler's appointment, included only three of them: Hitler, Wilhelm Frick as Minister of the Interior and Göring as Reich Minister without Portfolio and acting Prussian Minister of the Interior. The remaining posts were taken by Von Papen and his associates, who were confident that they had matters in hand. Others were not so sure.

In reality, the Nazi ministers had full control over matters of law and order, particularly through the police. It also became clear that General Werner von Blomberg, the Minister of Defence, was sympathetic to Nazi views and had little knowledge or interest in politics. Emboldened, the Nazis almost immediately embarked on a campaign of what they termed *Gleichschaltung*, the pre-planned 'co-ordination' of all elements in German life into a functioning Nazi state. In the cause of national unity, they planned to replace the hated republic with a one-party state. The first step was to unleash a campaign of violence and terror against Social Democrats, trade unions and Communist Party members. A new auxiliary police force comprising SA, SS and Steel Helmet troops was formed that, with the approval of the Nazi ministers, was able to act lawfully in smashing up offices, collecting and destroying documents, breaking up meetings, closing down anti-Nazi newspapers, and beating up and murdering their political enemies at will. With no official state police force in place, there was little co-ordinated opposition.

In February, campaigning began for another election due to take place on 5 March. The Nazi campaign, helped in great part by a flow of new funds provided by Germany's major industries who were keen to see the Nazis elected so as to avoid civil war, presented Hitler as the man who would crush the Marxist threat and lead the reconstruction of Germany. His speeches, now held in huge halls in front of ecstatic supporters and broadcast to the entire nation on the radio, identified the same old enemies. However, the main political threat to the Nazis, that of the Communists and the possibility of an 'unstoppable proletarian revolution they had long threatened,' remained strong.[37]

## The violence begins

On the night of 27–28 February 1933, fate took a hand when the Reichstag building caught fire. A young Dutchman, Marinus van der Lubbe, was allegedly caught in the act of arson. Despite evidence that he had acted alone and was merely passing through Berlin on his way home from Poland, he was a militant communist, and his action was deemed political. Pinning the blame on the German Communist Party, and knowingly seizing the advantage that had fallen into their laps, the Nazis launched severe and ruthless reprisals across the country, arresting party leaders and tens of thousands of its members, stealing party funds and other booty from members' homes. Simultaneously, they issued the Reichstag fire decree, which suspended the protection on civil rights, free speech, the free press and the due process of the law under the German Constitution.

Having almost completely devastated the Communists, the Nazis turned on their other political opponents in the week before the election. Without explicit orders, the brown-shirted stormtroopers carried out intimidatory acts of aggression and violence in towns and cities across the country, aimed at showing who was now in charge. Election Day, Sunday 5 March, was memorable for its menacing atmosphere. All over Germany, railway stations were guarded by police, armed stormtroopers patrolled the streets looking for anyone campaigning for the 'other' parties and the main streets were festooned with black, white and red flags and swastika banners. There were few signs advertising the politics of the opposition. Marketplaces housed radio loudspeakers, which relayed Hitler's recent speeches. Transport was laid on to take voters to the polling stations.

Despite receiving more than 17 million votes, the Nazis failed to achieve their desired majority even after the high levels of intimidation they employed. Undaunted, the Nazi campaign of violence continued. In many areas, local government had ceased its work since Hitler's appointment as chancellor. Local brownshirts took advantage, raising Nazi flags on municipal buildings and installing local officials of their own choosing in all parts of Germany.

With so many arrests since the Reichstag fire – of communists, Social Democrats and other dissidents – workhouses, police cells and the state prison system could not possibly cope. On 22 March, Heinrich Himmler, who had been appointed head of the SS in 1929, announced the opening of 'a concentration camp for political prisoners' in a broken-down munitions factory in Dachau, just outside Munich. Hastily prepared, if at all, the camp facilities, such as heating, toilets and washrooms, were poor and insanitary and shared by hundreds of prisoners. Between long days of exhausting forced labour, prisoners were treated with brutality by the guards, who used their fists, whips and truncheons to beat them up at random, often inflicting serious injury. Many chose suicide rather than endure such treatment.

In June, Himmler appointed Theodor Eicke as camp commander at Dachau. He installed an electric fence around the camp with watchtowers. In training his SS camp guards, Eicke demanded they put aside any feelings of sympathy for prisoners. They underwent rigorous military training, relieved only by camp guard duty during which they were expected to witness or participate in acts of cruelty against prisoners. Eicke instilled in his men a genuine hatred for the prisoners and convinced them to treat all inmates as dangerous enemies of the state, telling them, 'There behind the barbed wire lurks the enemy and he watches everything you do. He will try to help himself by using all your weaknesses. Don't leave yourself open in any way. Show these enemies of the state your teeth. Anyone who shows even the smallest sign of compassion for [them] must disappear from our ranks. I can only use hard men who are determined to do anything. We have no use for weaklings.'[38]

In 1934, Eicke was promoted to become inspector for all the Nazi concentration camps. The system of organization and administration he developed at Dachau, including regulations for perimeter guards and the treatment of prisoners, with certain modifications, became the model for the entire Nazi concentration camp system as it expanded.

## Hitler turns dictator

On 24 March, Hitler succeeded in passing the Enabling Act, which would allow the chancellor to pass laws without consulting the Reichstag or the president. In order to secure the passage of this law, Hitler needed a two-thirds majority in parliament. In the run-up to voting day, all the Communist and a number of Social Democrat members of the government were rounded up and detained in the new camps to prevent them from voting. On the day, SA and SS troops were sent into the Kroll Opera House, used as a makeshift Reichstag since the fire, to 'encourage' the compliance of the remaining representatives. In his address to the house, Hitler offered 'friendly co-operation' with the other parties and promised 'not to threaten the Reichstag, the president, the states or the churches'[39] in return for their assent. The law, which granted these emergency powers for four years, passed easily, with only the remaining Social Democrats voting against it, effectively ending parliamentary democracy in Germany and installing Hitler as a dictator.

Another law passed that day dissolved existing state governments and permitted the appointment of a *Reichsstatthalter* (Reich governor) for each state. Reporting directly to Reich Minster of the Interior Wilhelm Frick, the governors were responsible for implementing Nazi policy within their state.

In April, Hitler targeted the civil service, enacting a law that dismissed all Jews, communists and other political opponents from every level of government administration. Those dismissed lost not only their jobs, but also their retirement benefits. The new law also covered judges, teachers, university professors and lawyers. At the time, many German civil servants were conservative and nationalistic and were supportive of the Nazis and only too keen to put the new law into practice. In May, all trade unions were abolished and replaced by the *Deutsche Arbeitsfront* (German Labour Front), a single overarching trade union, which represented all workers and employees and was designed to emphasize national economic goals rather than personal well-being. On 14 July, the Nazis passed a law against the founding of new parties, which also meant that membership of any party, apart from the National Socialist German Workers' Party, became illegal.

Though the Nazis only held three positions in the cabinet when they initially took power in January, the passage of the Enabling Act severely reduced the ability of the cabinet to make political decisions

*Dr Joseph Goebbels was one of the most powerful and cruellest of the Nazi leadership. A master propagandist and public speaker, he was able to vent his feelings of inadequacy – he was small, slight, with a club foot – through the power of his intellect and his feelings of hatred towards the world in general and the Jews in particular.*

and it stopped meeting in person. Of the original cabinet, some joined the NSDAP, some were dismissed and some resigned. To replace them, Hitler created new ministries and appointed new ministers at will. As leader, he had little interest in detail, preferring to speak his thoughts, expecting the ministries to work up draft proposals and present them to him for rejection, revision or signing. Of course, this meant jobs for the boys and over the next few years Nazi ministers, including Hermann Göring, Joseph Goebbels, Heinrich Himmler, Albert Speer, Martin Bormann and Baldur von Schirach held positions of great power.

By June 1933, virtually the only organizations not controlled by the NSDAP were the army and the churches. Within six months of taking power, the Nazis had eliminated all organized political opposition and turned Germany from a democracy into a single party state.

## *Gleichschaltung* begins to bite

But the Nazis were not content merely with political power. Their worldview also encompassed the cultural landscape, wanting to win the hearts and minds of the *Volksgemeinschaft* it wished to create in alignment with its ideals. To ensure that its cultural policy was effective, a few days after taking power Hitler had appointed Joseph Goebbels as Minister for Public Enlightenment and Propaganda with responsibility for the party's propaganda apparatus, film, radio, theatre and the press.

A noted anti-semite, Goebbels had joined the Nazi Party in 1924 and served as Gauleiter of Berlin from 1926, during which period he learned his propaganda skills. Following his appointment to the new ministry, he set to work quickly, organizing the Day of Potsdam on 21 March in celebration of the passing of power from Hindenburg to Hitler. The following week, he wrote the text of Hitler's decree in support of a one-day boycott of all Jewish businesses set to take place on 1 April. Julius Streicher, director of the Central Committee for the Defence against Jewish Atrocity and Boycott Propaganda and publisher of the anti-Semitic tabloid *Der Stürmer*, stated in the appeal for the boycott that Germans must show the Jews that they cannot 'besmirch Germany and disparage its honour without punishment.' In the event, the boycott was cancelled, possibly because the Nazi leadership feared a backlash against a boycott with no evidence of wrongdoing.[40] Historians point to this and other events to illustrate the fact that at this point ordinary Germans were not yet 'certain of the *centrality* of anti-Semitism to their ideology.'[41] *Gleichschaltung* still had more work to do.

Goebbels' next event, which took place on the night of 10 May, was a spectacle not seen in Europe since the Middle Ages. In fact, it was the climax of a month-long nationwide campaign, led by the National

*More than 25,000 volumes were hurled into the flames in Berlin's Opernplatz on the night of 10 May 1933 in an act of naked censorship. In his speech to the crowd at the event, Joseph Goebbels urged, 'No to decadence and moral corruption! Yes to decency and morality in family and state!'*

Socialist German Students' Association, of action against the 'Un-German Spirit'. The action was an affirmation of traditional German values in response to what they saw as a worldwide Jewish 'smear campaign' against Germany. University towns and cities across the country witnessed torchlit parades by students and members of the SA, SS and Hitler Youth, who marched along with bands, songs, trucks and oxcarts filled with banned books. They were piled up, doused in gasoline and burned. In Berlin, the event held in the Opernplatz was attended by some 40,000 people, who heard a speech from Goebbels. He said, 'The future German man will not just be a man of books, but a man of character. You do well, in this midnight hour, to commit to the flames the evil spirit of the past. From this wreckage the phoenix of a new spirit will triumphantly rise.'

Books burned included works by socialists such as Bertolt Brecht, communists such as Karl Marx and supporters of the Weimar Republic such as Thomas Mann. American authors such as Ernest Hemingway and Jack London were targeted for their pacifism or calling for improved conditions for workers, and Jewish writers, such as Franz Werfel and Max Brod, were also included on a list of some 75 German and foreign authors. It was, of course, a deeply symbolic act. Hitler, a self-educated high-school drop-out, was fiercely anti-intellectual. His vision of a return to traditional German and Nordic values of loyalty, struggle, self-sacrifice, family, race and *Volk*, free from Jewish 'foreign' and 'degenerate' influences, was far more important than formal education.

## Rise and rise of the *Hitlerjugend*

Following the success of the book burning, Baldur von Schirach was riding high. In June, Hitler promoted him to Youth Leader of Germany, answerable directly to Hitler himself. In *Mein Kampf*, Hitler had written, 'He alone who owns the youth gains the future.' For him, it was essential to ensure the loyalty of youth to the Nazi cause in order to guarantee the thousand-year Third Reich. As historian Michael Kater said, 'He had to have recruits, people who would take over as grown-ups and continue the ideology of the Third Reich.'[42] Schirach's task was a big one.

Following his promotion, he acted quickly against some of the 400 other existing youth groups in Germany. His first move was to take over the Berlin offices and staff of the Reich Committee of German Youth Associations, who represented some 6 million youngsters. He ordered raids on Jewish, socialist and communist youth groups' headquarters, seizing assets, disbanding the organizations and encouraging their members to join the Hitler Youth ranks. Some refused and others joined because they were scared not to, but many, particularly Protestant groups, complied immediately. Only the Catholic Youth League held out, helped by a concordat between the Nazis and the Vatican. However, this offered little protection for Catholics, who continued to suffer persecution. The Jehovah's Witnesses held out too, even refusing to salute the Nazi flag. Many of those who refused to comply were trucked off to the ever-expanding concentration camps, where many were killed.

As a result of such pressure, within six months, the majority of Germany's youth organizations had been absorbed into the *Hitlerjugend*, either voluntarily or by force. Membership numbers swelled exponentially: in 1932, combined membership of various Hitler Youth groups, including the BDM, was 107,956; a year later it stood at 2,292,041. With such huge numbers joining, Schirach organized a restructure. For boys, informal membership was available from the age of six, with the youngsters informally known as *Pimpfen*, they joined the *Jungvolk* from the age of 10 to 14 and then the HJ itself from 14 to 18. Each boy was given a performance booklet recording his progress in athletics and Nazi indoctrination throughout all of his years in the HJ. Girls aged 10 to 14 joined the *Jungmädelbund* (JM or Young Girls' League) before joining the BDM proper from ages 14 to 18. The girls wore a schoolgirl-style uniform with skirts and blouses along with hiking boots. In 1938, a further, voluntary group was added. *Glaube und Schönheit* (Faith and Beauty Society) was intended to prepare girls for marriage, domestic duties and motherhood, though education and job training was also given.

## Indoctrination begins

In the early days of the *Hitlerjugend*, activities for its members included culture, education and propaganda, as well as encouraging outdoor activities, such as sports, camping, marching and music. Many of these ideas were inherited from groups such as the *Wandervögel*, though the militaristic organization and uniforms had been added and developed by Gustav Lenk and Kurt Gruber. Those entering the fold under Schirach's watch were not pampered in any way. New recruits were required to swear an oath, written by Schirach and designed to impress on them the responsibilities they were undertaking:

> *In the presence of this blood banner which represents our Führer,*
> *I swear to devote all my energies and my strength to the saviour of*
> *our country, Adolf Hitler. I am willing and ready to give up my life*
> *for him, so help me God!*

The *Blutfahne* (blood banner), in the presence of which the oath had to be taken, was said to have been soaked in the blood of the martyrs who died during the failed putsch in 1923.

Hitler Youth meetings would be held regularly, after school during the week and all day at weekends. The weekday meetings, called 'Home Evenings', would be held in local halls, cellars, barns and other places. There would be no adults present, only leaders not much older than the other members. Instructions on how to run the meetings would be sent by letter from the Hitler Youth headquarters. The children, some of them for the first time, would have access to leisure activities, such as arts and crafts, model planes, singing and learning to play musical instruments, though all, of course, with instructions intended to teach them how to be good Nazis. They might, for example, listen to approved readings or be asked to read propaganda leaflets and even listen to special radio broadcasts explaining the ideas of National Socialism and Nazi ideology.

On weekends, they might have access to a sports field or a swimming pool, or they went on long hikes, eating outside round a campfire and sleeping in tents. In the summer, there might be sports competitions or holiday trips away from home. Both boys and girls were introduced to serious fitness regimes, and required to achieve certain minimum requirements in, for example, running, swimming and long jump. They practised gymnastics, sailing and diving. They also practised marching and singing and took part in Winter Aid charity collections. War games were a big part of weekend meetings. The boys would divide up into

Hitlerjugend *summer camps provided opportunities to take part in a range of activities and sports including boxing.*

platoons with different-coloured armbands. The aim was to 'hunt down the enemy' and take off their armbands. These games often ended in real fights, which were encouraged by the older boys, keen to toughen up their charges. All these activities had a strong element of competition, between individuals or teams, which was intended to drive them to excellence. For many, these events were exciting, a chance to get away from their home environment. The children made friends, learned to look after themselves and developed a feeling of belonging – to the group, to Nazi ideals and to the *Volksgemeinschaft*.

## Developing 'soldiers of an idea'

Although the *Hitlerjugend* was in itself separate from the other NSDAP organizations, its members were intended to pass up through the age groups and straight into some form of Nazi service, which at first was the SA. Certain preparations for this were compulsory for HJ members. For example, all members had to greet each other with the *Deutscher Gruss* (German salute), standing to attention with the left hand on the belt buckle and a rigid right arm raised a little higher than the right shoulder, saying 'Heil Hitler' while clicking heels. It was also common to refer to colleagues as *Kamerad* (comrade) and to greet and say goodbye to others by saying 'Sieg Heil!' (Hail Victory).

Discipline was severe, with punishments a regular part of life in the HJ.[43] As the organization grew, so discipline became more important. Many of the new members came from the now-disbanded non-Nazi organizations, some without Nazi sentiments and many unable to deal with the more militaristic style of discipline required by the HJ. Added to that was a shortage of trained, politically reliable local youth leaders. To deal with this issue, Schirach announced that 1934 was to be 'The Year of Training' and set up a number of *Reichsführer* (leadership) schools across Germany teaching three-week courses on Nazi racial principles and ideology, and German history. Those attending also learned practical leadership skills, PE and rifle shooting. By August, more than 30,000 youngsters had completed the courses. Although the HJ had always been a work in progress, it was fast becoming an army, complete with iron discipline, uniforms, a strict hierarchy, regiments and weapons. Schirach made his intentions clear in a speech at the beginning of the year. He said, 'Whoever marches in the Hitler Youth is not a number among millions but the soldier of an idea. The individual member's value to the whole is determined by the degree to which he is permeated by the idea. The best Hitler Youth, irrespective of rank and office, is he who completely surrenders himself to the National Socialist worldview.' In other words, through its drills and marches, the Hitler Youth were learning to obey their leader, to think and act as one. Known as the *Führerprinzip* (leadership principle), this required 'absolute obedience to superiors.'[44]

## Limitless power

In the early months of 1934, Hitler appeared to be in complete control in Germany. However, like most dictators, he was always looking out for potential rivals from inside and outside the party. His 'divide and rule' tactic meant that party leaders, such as Göring, Goebbels, Himmler, Heydrich and Ernst Röhm, leader of the SA, developed a dislike for each other as they jostled for the Führer's favour. Though Hitler liked Röhm and was grateful for the SA's help in defeating the opposition in 1932 and 1933, he also feared him. In 1934, the SA had more than 3 million men, easily outnumbering the regular *Reichswehr*, and completely capable of removing him from office. Tensions between the Nazi hierarchy and the SA were already high. With plans for the future of the army already under discussion, the fear was that Röhm could take advantage of a reorganization and take over as leader of Germany's *Wehrmacht*, as the army was soon to be renamed. Others voiced their criticism of Röhm, for his socialist views on the economy, his claims that the real revolution was still to come and the fact that he was a homosexual.

When rumours of a coup led by Röhm but including Gregor Strasser, whom Hitler hated, were put about, notably by Göring and Himmler, Hitler decided to act. On 29 June, SA leaders and others deemed enemies of the Nazis were summoned to a meeting in Bad Wiessee. During the next 24 hours, some 200 senior SA officers were murdered, including Röhm and Strasser. Other killings, from a list of 'Unwanted Persons' compiled by Göring and Himmler, were rolled into what was called Operation Hummingbird, included Ferdinand von Bredow, head of Germany's military intelligence, former chancellor Kurt von Schleicher, Gustav von Kahr, for his part in the suppression of the Beer Hall Putsch in 1923, and the leaders of various youth groups who were rivals to the Hitler Youth.

Details of the operation were kept secret since the Nazis planned media coverage to portray the event as a preventative measure against a violent revolutionary force, rather than a series of politically motivated murders. Details were revealed in a speech on 13 July, when Hitler reported the purge, naming it 'Night of the Long Knives', a phrase from a popular Nazi song. Claiming that 74 people had been shot resisting arrest, he justified the move by saying: 'In this hour I was responsible for the fate of the German people, and thereby I become the supreme judge of the German people. I gave the order to shoot the ringleaders in this treason.'

There is some debate as to the number of victims that night – others claim as many as a thousand people were killed – but there was no doubt that as Germany's 'supreme judge', Hitler was placing himself above the law. There were other consequences, too. Deprived of its leadership, the SA lost its power immediately and Hitler announced the independent status of both the SS and the Hitler Youth. The army, pleased at the removal of Röhm and the subsequent collapse of the once-powerful SA, decided their allegiance was with Hitler. When President Hindenburg died on 2 August, the army announced its support for Hitler's request to merge the offices of chancellor and president and occupy the position himself. The approval of the people was achieved with a massive majority in a vote on 19 August, thus removing any limits to Hitler's power.

At last freed of the yoke of the SA, Schirach made plans for the Reich Party rally in Nuremberg. On 8 September 1934, 60,000 Hitler Youths marched into the Städtisches Stadion to salute their leader. The event was staged beautifully by Albert Speer and filmed by Leni Riefenstahl. The subsequent film, *Triumph of the Will*, shows Hitler, Schirach and the Hitler Youth in all their glory. Hitler arrives at the stadium amid a thunderous cacophony of drums, trumpets and pipes, the crowd roars its approval, the shouts of '*Heil*' seem endless. The boys seem gripped

*Hitler salutes the massed ranks of the Hitler Youth as he arrives at the Städtisches Stadion in Nuremberg for the Nazis' annual party rally. After 1933, the rallies took played a big part in the Nazi propaganda campaign, conveying the image of a unified and strong Germany under Nazi control.*

by adulation, greeting their leader with almost religious fervour. After fanfares, the band plays 'We Boys' as the entourage makes its way to the podium. Hitler's speech presses all the right buttons. 'Regardless of what we create and do, we shall pass away, but in Germany you will live on. And I know it cannot be otherwise for you are the flesh of our flesh, blood of our blood, and your young minds are filled with the same will that dominates us ... And when the great columns of our movement march through Germany today, I know that you will join these columns. And we know that Germany is before us, within us and behind us.' Filled with confidence in the ranks of devoted youth he was addressing, he expressed his wish and belief in a 'Thousand-Year Reich'. As he finished, a storm of applause filled the stadium, and then the 60,000 boys belted out their signature song, 'Our Flag Showing Us the Way'.[45]

## 'Blood and soil'

'The Year of Training' had been a busy one for the Hitler Youth. Along with Nazi labour leader Robert Ley, Schirach had introduced a National Vocation competition for those learning trades to show their new skills. In October, the new Landdienst (Land Service) was introduced, aimed at removing urban youths from towns and cities so they could get 'back to the land'. Some 200,000 youths worked on farms from springtime to harvest time, giving them the chance to experience life on the farm and learn the value of hard work. In the winter, they would travel around the villages, many of which were cut off from any Nazi influence, and spread the word of the scheme's slogan, 'Blut und Boden' ('Blood and Soil').

The following year was even busier. In 1935, 60 per cent of Germany's young people were members of the Hitler Youth, which now boasted more than 3 million members. Declared 'The Year of Physical Training', the summer months witnessed a huge and prestigious sports competition. School timetables were altered to allow for a least one hour of physical training in the morning and another in the evening, to raise standards. In his speech at the Nuremberg rally, Hitler said, 'We must bring up a new type of human being, men and girls who are disciplined and healthy to the core. We have undertaken to give the German people an education that begins already in youth and will never come to an end.'

For the Nazi propaganda machine, images of healthy, smiling, bronzed youths working on the land, playing on the sports fields and marching in regimented order were ideal in portraying Nazi Germany as united in discipline and excellence. With mass communication still in its infancy, it was relatively easy to impress the outside world. On returning from a trip to meet Hitler, former British Prime Minister Lloyd George said, 'Whatever one may think of his methods ... there

*Posters were an integral part of the Nazi propaganda machine. They were designed carefully to appeal to a specific audience depending on the message they intended to convey, such as these recruitment posters for the Hitlerjugend. Using photos, artwork, clear lettering and pictorial language, they were intended to set the Nazis apart from the Weimar Republic, representing a Germany 'that is modern, that is new and that is different'.*

can be no doubt that he has achieved a marvellous transformation in the spirit of the people, in their attitude towards each other, and in their social and economic outlook … There is for the first time since the war a general sense of security. The people are more cheerful. There is a greater sense of general gaiety of spirit throughout the land.'[46]

The reality was somewhat different.

# Chapter 6

# The Nazification of Education

Despite his initial disinterest in Gustav Lenk's suggestion to organize a youth section of the DAP in 1921, it is clear from the thoughts and ideas Adolf Hitler laid down in *Mein Kampf* that he had much to say on the subject of education. He himself had been a poor student, had few schoolfriends and disliked many of his teachers. In his first year at the high school for science in Linz, in Austria, he was marked down as 'unsatisfactory' and had to repeat the year. His class teacher, Dr Eduard Huemer, described him as 'stubborn, high-handed, dogmatic and hot-tempered.'[47] In his final year, 1904–05, he failed to reach even a mediocre level and left school without being awarded the *Abitur* (secondary school diploma).

In Hitler's memory, only one teacher stood out, Dr Leopold Pötsch, who taught history, his favourite subject alongside geography. Like many people living in German-speaking Upper Austria, Pötsch was a German nationalist, and he filled the heads of his pupils with stories of its military victories over France in 1870 and 1871 and was critical of the Habsburgs for not becoming involved in these triumphs. Hitler wrote that Pötsch, 'used our budding nationalistic fanaticism as a means of educating us, frequently appealing to our sense of national honour. By this alone he was able to discipline us little ruffians more easily than would have been possible by any other means ... And indeed, though he had no such intention, it was then that I became a little revolutionary. For who could have studied German history under such a teacher without becoming an enemy of the state which, through its ruling house, exerted so disastrous an influence on the destinies of the nation? And who could retain his loyalty to a dynasty which in past and present betrayed the needs of the German people again and again for shameless private advantage?'[48]

## Years of failure

As well as history and geography, Hitler had enjoyed art, and in the first years after leaving school he began to dream of a future career as an artist. In 1907, he applied to join the prestigious Academy of Art in Vienna. Although his work showed some talent, particularly in his depiction of architecture and landscapes, his drawings of humans and especially human faces did not meet the standards required. He is said to have drawn iconic and Biblical scenes that impressed the examiners, but they rejected the work in his previously prepared portfolio in which they said he had painted 'too few heads' – the drawing of people was particularly important to the Academy judges. He applied again the following year, but was rejected for a second time and advised to try for a place at the Academy's school of architecture instead. However, admission for that required the *Abitur*, which he had not passed, so he did not apply at all.

It seems very likely that Hitler's concept of education that was imposed on children in Nazi Germany had its roots in those years of failure. He blamed his lack of success on his teachers, criticizing their 'excessive emphasis on purely mental training', suggesting instead that a German boy, 'After his day's other work … must strengthen his young body like steel so that when life puts him to the test, it will not find him too delicate. It is the responsibility of those educating youth to prepare their bodies and not just pour knowledge or so-called wisdom in their heads.' In Hitler's thinking, with physical fitness would come mental alertness strong enough to understand that the 'racial idea' of purity and unadulterated blood would ensure the cultural progress of the German people.

As for the teaching of his favourite subject, he said, 'We must reduce the amount of material students are required to learn, especially in history classes. The main reason anyone learns history is to grasp the big picture and understand historical development and how it affects current events. The more we focus what is taught, the more hope there is that the individual's knowledge will later create a return that will benefit the entire community. We do not learn history in order to know what has happened in the past, but we learn history so that it may be our guide for the future.'[49]

## Educational changes

When Hitler took power in March 1933, the reorganization of education became one of the major concerns of the Nazi regime, as the 'most important instrument for the promotion of Nazi stability.'[50] Hitler was clear in his opinion that, 'Universal education is the most corroding and disintegrating poison that liberalism has ever invented for its own destruction.' However, through education, taught with discipline, training and order, the Nazis planned to get rid of the cancer of Marxism, liberalism and democracy. Freedom of thought, intellectual independence and judgement were to be eradicated, as they benefitted the individual rather than society as a whole. Therefore, went their thinking, rather than developing the intellect, formal education should be aimed at strengthening the emotions, which will result in loyalty, self-sacrifice, strength of will and the joyful acceptance of responsibility. Henceforward, the starting point in education was not to be the child but *das Volk* (the people) and their needs. Like life, education was to be rooted in blood and soil.

The first educational decrees were issued by Hitler and Minister of the Interior Wilhelm Frick. On 1 May, former secondary schoolteacher Dr Bernhard Rust was appointed Federal Minister of Science, Education and Public Culture. In the next few months there were several policy announcements. The authority of the teacher was reinforced, and corporal punishment was re-established, religious instruction was made compulsory, sex education classes (said to be a Marxist invention) were banned and the teaching of heredity and race knowledge was introduced as a strand of biology. The teaching of history and nationalism was promoted with special emphasis on the superiority of the Nordic race in culture and civilization, on militarism and the Heroic ideal. The previous two decades were to be covered in detail with the idea of further discrediting the republic and glorifying the National Socialist Revolution. Geography, too, had a new emphasis, that of geopolitics and the advancement of the Nazi *Weltanschauung* (worldview).

Every classroom was to be overlooked by a portrait of the Führer, which was to be saluted with a '*Heil Hitler*' at the beginning and the end of every lesson. Alongside this, a programme of physical regeneration had been developed. Combining pre-military training with sport, it was intended to lay the foundations of the national army of the future. Another innovation was the *Landschuljahr*, the rural school year, which stated that on leaving urban elementary schools at the age of 14, all boys and girls were required to spend a year in the country. There were many advantages to this idea: it got impressionable children away from the temptations of the city, gave them an understanding of peasant life and presented them with another opportunity for physical training. In the longer term, it was hoped that some of them would take up life in the country and, in the event of another war, be able to assist in food production. A less successful idea, for girls of the same age, was a voluntary year-long apprenticeship in housekeeping. For 18-year-olds, the *Arbeitsdienst* (labour service) was run along the same lines.

This emphasis on sports training was the main characteristic of the new Nazi education system but was only one example of a shift away from the intellectual traditions of the past. Though it can be argued that the Nazis 'inherited a very conservative educational system,'[51] its reputation among civilized nations, for its 'broad curriculum, the quality of its teachers ... and its tradition of academic freedom' was second to none.[52] In his book, *The Rise and Fall of the Third Reich*, William Shirer declared, 'The result of so much Nazification was catastrophic for German education and for German learning.'[53] Louis Snyder, a German-American Exchange Fellow in Frankfurt from 1928 to 1931, had a more nuanced explanation: 'There were to be two basic educational ideas in his [Hitler's] ideal state. First, there must be burnt into the heart and brains of youth the sense of race. Second, German youth must be made ready for war, educated for victory or death. The ultimate purpose of education was to fashion citizens conscious of the glory of country and filled with fanatical devotion to the national cause.'[54] Nazi Minister of Education Bernhard Rust was even more direct, explaining that, 'The whole function of education is to create a Nazi.'

## The Jewish purge

Before the Nazification of the school system could begin, those most opposed to Hitler's plans had to be removed. Obvious candidates were Jewish teachers, along with Social Democrats and liberals working in the education system. In April 1933, the Law against Overcrowding in German Schools and Universities was enacted. Although it did not mention Jews, the law was specifically aimed at Jewish students and teachers. Bernhard Rust later explained the reasons for this decision: 'As a consequence of the demand thus clearly formulated ... Jewish teachers and Jewish pupils have had to quit German schools, and schools of their own have been provided by and for them as far as possible. In this way, the natural race instincts of German boys and girls are preserved; and the young people are made aware of their duty to maintain their racial purity and to bequeath it to succeeding generations.' The purge began immediately. Within six months, 15 per cent of German schoolteachers and some 1,200 university lecturers had lost their jobs. In Prussia, so many teachers lost their jobs that the start of the new school year in 1934 was delayed.

Other teachers too came under suspicion if they did not show overt support for the new regime and its teaching. Many of the older teachers, particularly those who had fought in the First World War or been members of the *Freikorps*, were inherently nationalistic. Many of the younger ones had grown up through the ranks of the Hitler Youth. As such, they welcomed the Nazi reforms. In fact, at least 25 per cent of teachers were Nazi Party members in the early 1930s and saw the opportunity to reverse Weimar policies that had led to unemployment and poor school funding. The situation for those who were not so inclined became more difficult. Should a teacher's views come under suspicion, they might receive a visit from the Gestapo. They would be questioned, often in front of the class. If their answers were not good enough, then they would be arrested and taken away. One 16-year-old girl later wrote, 'Teachers had to pretend to be Nazis in order to remain in their posts, and most of the men teachers had families which depended on them. If somebody wanted to be promoted, he had to show what a fine Nazi he was, whether he really believed what he was saying or not. In the last two years, it was very difficult for me to accept any teaching at all, because I never knew how much the teacher believed in or not.'[55] The consequences of not toeing the line were serious. A

38-year-old teacher in Düsseldorf told a joke to her class of 12-year-olds that was slightly critical of Adolf Hitler. She realized her mistake and pleaded with the children not to tell anybody about it. One of the children told his parents, who informed the Gestapo. She immediately lost her job and was sent to prison for three weeks.[56]

In a speech he gave in November 1933, Hitler said, 'When an opponent declares, "I will not come over to your side," I calmly say, "Your child belongs to us already... What are you? You will pass on. Your descendants, however, now stand in the new camp. In a short time they will know nothing else but this new community."' A change in the balance of power was now underway.

In many ways, the fate of Jewish schoolchildren was even worse. Although it was slowly introduced, the teaching of *Rassenkunde*, anti-semitic racial theory, was compulsory for all pupils for half an hour every morning.[57] As a result, Jewish children were gradually ostracized by their classmates and teachers for reasons that many of them did not understand; they were bullied, insulted, beaten and subjected to regular hostility. Jews were painted as 'inferior' beings, parasitical, a threat to Germany and world peace; they were also held to be responsible for Germany's defeat in 1918. Alfons Heck, a schoolboy in the Rhineland in the 1930s, admitted bullying Jewish pupils in his class and recalled his teacher doing the same. 'Herr Becker made the Jewish children sit in a corner, which he sneeringly designated "Israel". He never called on them, which I perceived as a blessing, but we quickly realized that he wanted us to despise the Jews.' As a result, many Jewish children joined special Jewish schools; others left the education system altogether.

By the end of 1933, as well as teaching, German Jews were excluded from a whole range of jobs, ranging from public office, journalism and radio to theatre and farming. In September 1935, the Nuremberg race laws essentially stripped Jews of their citizenship and isolated them from political, professional and social life. The laws stated that only racially pure so-called Aryan Germans, people 'of German or related blood', could hold German citizenship. For the Nazis, Jews were not Aryan, so they could not therefore be citizens and so had no political rights. Sexual relations and intermarriage between members of these groups were forbidden.

A supplementary law followed in November the same year that defined three categories of Jew. First, those individuals with three or more Jewish grandparents were classified as full Jews. Second, those with two Jewish grandparents were said to be 'first degree Mischlings' or half-Jews. Third, those with one Jewish grandparent were considered 'second degree Mischlings' or quarter-Jews. The laws eventually excluded Jewish children from German schools altogether.

## Radical syllabus revision

In the two years following Hitler's rise to power, education in Germany was subject to complete overhaul. By November 1935, almost all Jews – teachers and pupils – had been expelled. All teaching bodies, assorted associations and trade unions had been disbanded and replaced by a new association, the *Nationalsozialistische-Lehrerbund* (National Socialist Teachers' Alliance). Teachers rushed to join. Some – generally younger ones – because they believed in the Nazi cause, others because they felt it was 'necessary and unavoidable' to continue their careers. Whatever the applicant's beliefs, they had to provide an ancestry table and official documents proving their German bloodline. It has been estimated that by 1936 more than 32 per cent of teachers were also members of the Nazi Party, a much higher figure than that in other professions.

Although there were no major changes in the structure of education in Germany, there was a radical revision of the syllabus. Censorship of school textbooks was immediately employed by Goebbels, who ordered the removal of any 'alien' or 'decadent' literature. Many of the textbooks were withdrawn and 'edited' by the Party Censorship Office, while

*Classroom charts, like this one entitled 'German Youth, Jewish Youth', were used in classrooms to point out the superior physical – and therefore racial – characteristics of the Aryans over the Jews, a key aspect of National Socialist racial ideology.*

others were replaced with newly published books that reflected Nazi ideology. Every new textbook included a frontispiece with an illustration of Hitler along with one of his sayings, for example, 'Learn to sacrifice for your Fatherland', 'In your race is your strength', or 'You must be true, you must be daring and courageous, and with each other form a great and wonderful comradeship.'

The repetition of National Socialist messages was relentless. School noticeboards and classroom walls were covered in Nazi propaganda posters and teachers were often required to read out anti-Semitic articles that portrayed Jews as ugly, greedy swindlers who lived off the sweat of others. One slogan taught in the classroom was: 'Judas the Jew betrayed Jesus the German to the Jews.' One textbook, *The Jewish Question in Classroom Instruction*, was written by noted anti-Semitist Fritz Fink with an introduction by Julius Streicher, the powerful Gauleiter of Franconia. Streicher wrote, 'The National Socialist state requires its teachers to teach German children racial theory. For the German people, racial theory means the Jewish problem.' The book itself included detailed instructions and photos on the 'identification of Jews', and included passages such as 'Jews have different noses, ears, lips, chins and different faces than Germans' and 'they walk differently, have flat feet … their arms are longer and they speak differently.'

There were other such propaganda books whose purpose was to teach anti-Semitism to children as young as six. Many of these, such as *Trau keinem Fuchs auf grüner Heid und keinem Jud bei seinem Eid* (*Trust No Fox on His Green Heath and No Jew on His Oath*), *Der Giftpilz* (*The Poisonous Mushroom*) and *Der Pudelmopsdachelpinscher* (*The Poodle-Pug-Dachshund-Pinscher*) were published by the *Der Stürmer* publishing house. Although these were not official Nazi publications, they were based around a very successful, virulently anti-Semitic weekly tabloid newspaper of the same name, owned and run by Julius Streicher. *Trust No Fox…* was written and illustrated by an 18-year-old art student,

Elvira Bauer. Both the fox and the Jew in the title are depicted with the traditional European prejudices of anti-semitism: the fox is clever and deceitful, eager to kill its prey, while the Jew is shown as small and bulky with black hair, ready to 'swear a false oath under the star of David'. Rather than a linear story, the book simply reinforces the differences between the German and Jews. On one page a tall, blond, shirtless German worker leans on his spade and looks across at the shifty, cigar-smoking Jew. Small, stout, with sloping shoulders and dark hair, the Jew carries an attaché case and has a financial newspaper in his pocket. The page has text as follows:

*This illustration from Elvira Bauer's book* Trust No Fox ..., *published in 1936, depicts the expulsion of Jewish teachers and students from German schools. The accompanying text reads: 'It's going to be fine in the schools at last, For all the Jews must leave'.*

*But the Germans – they stand foursquare.*
*Look, children, and the two compare,*
*The German and the Jew.*
*Take a good look at the two*
*In the picture drawn for you.*
*A joke – you think it is only that?*
*Easy to guess which is which, I say:*
*The German stands up, the Jew gives way.*
*The German is a proud young man,*
*Able to work and able to fight.*
*Because he is a fine big chap,*
*For danger does not care a rap,*
*The Jew has always hated him!*
*Here is the Jew, as all can see,*
*Biggest ruffian in our country;*
*He thinks himself the greatest beau*
*And yet is the ugliest, you know!*

The book's final picture suggests the Nazis' solution to the Jewish Question: the expulsion of all Jews from Germany. Published in 1936, there are estimated to have been some 70,000 copies in circulation.

In a similar vein, neither *The Poisonous Mushroom*, published in 1938, nor *The Poodle-Pug…*, which followed two years later, leave the reader in any doubt about the Nazis' solution to the so-called 'Jewish problem'. The former is based around a popular German pastime of picking wild mushrooms in the forest. A mother explains how difficult it is to tell the difference between edible and poisonous varieties. She equates the edible ones to good people and the poisonous ones to bad people and the most dangerous, of course, to Jews. She goes on to explain that as with mushrooms, it is difficult to tell Jews from non-Jews because Jews are the Devil's work and can appear in any form. There follows some helpful advice on the 'physical characteristics' of Jews to help in identifying them. The book also deliberately misinterprets the Talmud, the central text of Rabbinic Judaism, suggesting it is filled with images of the morally decadent Jew taking advantage of the morally upstanding German. The images in the book show repugnant Jews and defenceless young blonde-haired women and children and contain suggestions of pornographic character. Another picture storybook, *The Poodle-Pug...* centres on the animal world. It contains stories based around the unattractive traits of certain animals. For example, the cuckoo that throws other birds out of their nests, hyenas that prey on wounded animals, the bedbug that sucks blood, the poisonous snake and the tapeworm, and finishes with the (Jewish) Poodle-Pug, an inferior race created by cross-breeding. Both books close with the clear message that the only way to rid the world of poisonous mushrooms and Poodle-Pugs is to eliminate them – thinly veiled suggestions of *Endlöesung* (Final Solution), the Nazi plan for the genocide of the Jews to come in 1942.

## Other school subjects

Maths was regarded as a naturally Aryan subject, but the Nazis still attempted to impose their ideology though its teaching. A mathematical problem could be given racial connotations, for example, 'How many children must a family produce in order to secure the quantitative continuance of the German *Volk*?' Alternatively, a problem might touch on eugenics or 'racial hygiene', such as, 'A mentally handicapped person costs the republic 4 Reichsmarks per day, a cripple 5.5 Reichsmarks and a convicted criminal 3.5 Reichsmarks. Estimates state that within the boundaries of the German Reich 300,000 persons are being cared for in public mental institutions. How many marriage loans at 1,000 Reichsmarks per couple could annually be financed from the funds allocated to these institutions?'[58] Of course, questions about the Jews were also popular. 'The Jews are aliens in Germany – in 1933 there were 66,060,000 inhabitants in the German Reich, of whom 499,682 were Jews. What percentage of the population is made up of aliens?' There were more practical questions, too, particularly based around warfare. 'An aeroplane flies at the rate of 240 kilometres per hour to a place at a distance of 210 kilometres in order to drop bombs. When may it be expected to return if the dropping of bombs takes seven and a half minutes?'

Nazi physics concentrated on the principles of ballistics, aviation and bridge building. For Hitler, Jewish involvement in physics, such as the work of Albert Einstein, had no place in Nazi Germany and was discredited. The Theory of Relativity, for example, was held up as a plot by world Jewry bent on world domination. Ironically, some historians see this rejection of what Hitler called 'Jewish science' as the reason Germany failed to create the atomic bomb. In chemistry, teachers emphasized the importance of chemical warfare and explosives – it was a disastrous policy and led to a serious decline in the standard of German scientific advances.

Biology was one of the Nazis' core subjects. Teaching centred around 'raciology' – the superiority of the German race. Children were constantly reminded of their racial duties to the 'national community'. They learned about worthy and unworthy races, about breeding and hereditary diseases. 'They measured their heads with tape measures, checked the colour of their eyes and compared the texture of their hair against charts of Aryan or Nordic types, and constructed their own family trees to establish their biological, not historical, ancestry ... They also expanded on the racial inferiority of the Jews.'[59] In addition, Hitler himself had decreed that 'no boy or girl should leave school without complete knowledge of the necessity and meaning of blood purity.'

In Nazi thinking, the purpose of geography was to 'teach the destructive consequences of the Treaty of Versailles and point out the need for space for the German people to live.' Even before the Nazis had begun their invasions, new globes and atlases appeared in classrooms featuring 'Greater Germany', which included Austria, Czechoslovakia and Lithuania. The only language teaching available, apart from German, was English, for which translation exercises were taken from Hitler's *Mein Kampf*. Art, too, was an important but soft subject. It was favoured because, as one art teacher reminded a promising pupil, 'The Führer needs artists – he himself is one'. However, under *Gleichschaltung*, the government had taken complete control of the art world and was very hostile to modern art, which was deemed 'degenerate'.

At the top of the tree, of course, was history. Wilhelm Frick, Minister of the Interior, outlined the Nazi approach, pointing out that the idea that history teaching should be objective was a fallacy of liberalism.[60] For him, 'The purpose of history was to teach people that life was always dominated by struggle, that race and blood were central to everything that happened in the past, present and future, and that leadership determined the fate of peoples. Central themes in the new teaching including courage in battle, sacrifice for a greater cause, boundless admiration for the Führer and hatred of Germany's enemies, the Jews'. History was seen as an exciting way to develop children's sense of national pride through the nation's heroic past and the possibility of future glories that would come from the Nazis''national renewal'. Many Nazi history textbooks only covered German history, with great rulers of the past, such as Frederick the Great, held up as examples of 'heroic leadership, ceaseless service to the state, military successes and, inevitably, parallels to Hitler'.[61] Recent history, of course, was given prominence in new textbooks, such as *Nation and Leader: German History for Schools*, particularly the 'glorious' Munich Putsch in 1923, the heroic Horst Wessel and Hitler himself. Pupils were asked to write essays with titles such as, 'Adolf Hitler, the Saviour of the Fatherland' or 'What Enables Adolf Hitler to be the German Führer and Reichschancellor?' Additionally, the Weimar Republic was painted as a national disgrace, both for signing the shameful Treaty of Versailles and for the extreme permissiveness of urban society caused by the economic hardships of the Weimar years that shocked many conservative-thinking Germans.

## Special schools

In 1933, Bernhard Rust founded the first of a series of elite schools, called *Nationalpolitische Erziehungsanstalten* (Napolas for short). Run by the SS, their main task was the 'education of national socialists, efficient in body and soul for service to the people and the state.' That same year saw the establishment of three special *Adolf Hitler Schulen* (Adolf Hitler Schools) to train the Nazi elite and a series of *Ordensburgen* (Order Castles), which were seen as finishing schools for budding party leaders. Pupils attending these establishments were intended to be the future leaders of Germany in political, administrative and military spheres. They were modelled on English public schools. Selection for entry included pure racial origins, physical fitness and a clean report card from the Hitler Youth. Although they were administered separately from other German secondary schools, they followed a similar syllabus but with much more emphasis on sports, such as boxing, rowing, sailing, gliding and shooting. Over the next few years, 39 of these schools were established, of which only two catered for girls. By 1939, however, these schools specialized in preparing pupils for entry into the Wehrmacht and the Waffen-SS.

## Declining academic standards

Between 1933 and 1936, the Nazi assault on Germany's educational system began to take its toll. With the enforced removal of Jewish and other teachers deemed politically 'unsuitable' by the new regime and their replacement by new, often younger, teachers who were likely to be selected for their posts not for their teaching skills but rather for the strength of their National Socialist beliefs, the usual high academic standards began to plummet. In 1936, an article in a Nazi magazine aimed at women titled 'The Educational Principles of the New Germany' explained that there was no longer any place for high academic standards in schools. It explained that 'The four iron pillars of the national school and educational system are: race, military training, leadership and religion'. For teachers, pupils and their parents, the situation quickly became intolerable.

For teachers, continual changes in the curriculum were bewildering, and they were under pressure to support the Nazi Party and teach its ideology, whether they supported it or not. By 1938, two-thirds of elementary schoolteachers were indoctrinated in Nazi ideology at special camps. Attendance at the month-long courses was compulsory and attendees were expected to pass on what they learned to their students. Some teachers were already members of the party and wore their uniforms in the classroom, some pretended to agree with National Socialist thinking, while others were quietly anti-Nazi. A Dr Shuster, a geography teacher at the time, said, 'I am trying through the teaching of geography to do everything in my power to give the boys knowledge and I hope later on, judgement, so that when, as they grow older, the Nazi fever dies down and it again becomes possible to offer some opposition, they may be prepared.'

Pressure on teachers came from another pernicious source too – that of the Hitler Youth, whose influence was greatly extended by the Law Concerning the Hitler Youth passed on 1 December 1936. The law banned all other youth organizations and declared that membership of the Hitler Youth was mandatory for children from the age of ten onwards. Membership of the movement soared to almost 6 million.

As early as 1934, a report on the effects of the Hitler Youth and the Nazi government on the education system was damning, 'Everything that has been built up over a century of work by the teaching profession is no longer there in essence ... They have been wilfully destroyed from above. No thought any more of proper working methods in school, or of the freedom of teaching. In their place we have cramming and beating schools, prescribed methods of learning and... learning materials. Instead of freedom of learning, we have the most narrow-minded school supervision and spying on teachers and pupils. No free speech is permitted for teachers and pupils, no inner, personal empathy. The whole thing has been taken over by the military spirit.'[62]

By 1938, problems for teachers increased further. With the growing influence of Hitler Youth leaders who were still at school came a gradual decline in morale and discipline in the classroom. One teacher, who did not support Hitler, wrote the following in a letter to a friend, 'In the schools it is not the teacher, but the pupils, who exercise authority. Party functionaries train their children to be spies and agent provocateurs. The youth organizations, particularly the Hitler Youth, have been accorded powers of control which enable every boy and girl to exercise authority backed up by threats. Children have been deliberately taken away from parents who refused to acknowledge their belief in National Socialism. The refusal of parents to "allow their children to join the youth organization" is regarded as an adequate reason for taking the children away.'[63]

There was also an alarming drop in attendances at school, particularly since school authorities were instructed to grant leave of absence for pupils attending Hitler Youth events. One school in Westphalia reported 23,000 days lost because of extramural activities in one academic year. There was also a growing problem with the recruitment of teachers, not just because of the growing political pressure, but also because of a fall in teachers' pay. Starting salaries of 2,000 marks per year were offered. After deductions, this meant about 140 marks per month, little more than the average for a low-paid worker. In the summer of 1938, it was said that one teaching post in 12 was unfilled and that there were 17,000 fewer teachers than there had been in 1933.

## Chapter 7

# Time is Running Out

On 5 September 1934, the first day of the 6th Nazi Party Congress held in Nuremberg, Adolph Wagner, the Gauleiter in Munich and the so-called 'Speaker of the Party', read a proclamation written by Hitler in which he declared the arrival of the Nazi millennium, predicting that the Third Reich would last a thousand years. There was much work to do.

During his time in Landsberg prison and the writing of *Mein Kampf*, Hitler had been quick to realize the importance of youth in a National Socialist state. He outlined his ideas and hinted at the path he would take on his release, explaining that, 'By educating the young generation along the right lines, the People's State will have to see to it that a generation of mankind is formed which will be adequate to this supreme combat that will decide the destinies of the world.'[64] By 1933, his vision was beginning to take on a concrete form: 'I am beginning with the young,' he said, 'we older ones are used up. Yes, we are old already. We are rotten to the marrow. We have no unrestrained instincts left. We are cowardly and sentimental. We are bearing the burden of a humiliating past, and have in our blood the dull recollection of serfdom and servility. But my magnificent youngsters! Are there finer ones anywhere in the world? Look at these young men and boys! What material! With them, I can make a new world.'[65]

## Social forces

As a result of this thinking, following his rise to power, education had been 'seized upon' because of the possibilities it offered for the promotion of Nazi values, ideology and stability'. But in addition to changes in the classroom, the Nazis were able to alter the structure of youths' extra-curricular activities through the ever-expanding *Hitlerjugend* and the *Bund Deutscher Mädel* in order to further their ideological agenda. Dr Ernest Kreick, a Nazi professor who wrote extensively on the merits of National Socialism in education, believed: 'An efficient and logical education can be established not by a reform of methods but by the interplay of all social forces (family, religion, vocation and State) in the formation of an all-round citizen, integrated harmoniously with his right and duties for life has meaning only in a great organic whole.'

Despite his 'boyish looks, plump physique and effeminate manners',[66] aristocratic upbringing in Weimar and youthful interest in literature, painting and poetry, none of which had any place in Nazi thinking, Baldur von Schirach's strong will, organizational flair and ability to inspire his youthful charges was highly regarded by Hitler. In return, Schirach's devotion to the Führer, his vision for the HJ and the energy with which he undertook his role as *Reichsjugendführer* had been highly effective. Following his custom of naming each calendar year, Schirach called 1936 'Der Jahre das Jungvolk' ('The Year of the *Jungvolk*'). As a present for Hitler's birthday, he intended to enroll the entire population of ten-year-olds in Germany into the Hitler Youth. A huge recruitment drive was launched, and pressure was put on children across the country – in schools by Nazi-affiliated teachers, at home with local meetings for parents, and at play, when they were accosted by uniformed members and asked to join neighbourhood marches and special sing-alongs. On 20 April 1936, the Führer's 47th birthday, the new recruits were presented at their oath-taking ceremony at Marienburg Castle, home of the Teutonic Order of knights who had participated in the Crusades in the 12th century.

One by one, the ten-year-olds stepped into the glow of torch lights, amid solemn drum beats and a fanfare of trumpets, to swear the blood banner oath (page 96):

*In April 1939, with space at a premium because of the numbers joining, the solemn swearing-in ceremony for the HJ and the BDM, which included pledging fealty to Hitler, rather than to the German state, was held in the refectory at Marienburg.*

This was followed by the singing of the Hitler Youth anthem, the *'Fahnenlied'* ('Banner Song'), which had been written by Schirach:

> *Our banner flutters before us*
> *Our banner represents a new era*
> *And our banner leads to eternity!*
> *Yes, our banner means more to us than death!*

For the first few months, new recruits were on probation, while undergoing training from older, more experienced HJ members. They were required to learn the words of the *'Horst Wessel Lied'*, which had been adopted as the Nazi marching song. They also had to learn the answers to questions on Nazi racial and political ideology, on the history of the National Socialist Party, Germany's rightful place in the world and on the life of the Führer. They were required to meet physical challenges, too, including running 60 m (66 yards) in 12 seconds, accomplishing a long jump of 3.5 m (11.5 ft), completing a 15 km (9.3 miles) cross-country hike in one day and hitting the bull's eye on a target at a distance of 8 m (26.2 ft) with an air gun. The recruits' final test was called a *Mutprobe* (courage test), which might involve leaping over a burning campfire or jumping from the window of a one- or two-storey building on to a sheet of canvas held taut by other members of the group. On the successful completion of all these tasks, the recruit was issued with the hallowed uniform, including a brown shirt with the insignia of the *Jungvolk*, black toggle tie, black shorts and brown socks. Of particular significance, each recruit was given a leather belt complete with a silver buckle decorated with the Sieg rune, symbolic of victory, and a leather shoulder strap with a scabbard for holding the Hitler Youth dagger, which bore the inscription *'Blut und Ehre'* ('Blood and Honour').

## Exponential expansion

Following Schirach's reorganization of the HJ, which had begun in 1933, the movement had expanded exponentially, particularly after the passing of the law concerning the Hitler Youth in December 1936, which stated, 'The future of the German nation depends upon its youth and German youth will have to be prepared for its duties. The Reich Government has therefore decided that ... the whole of German youth within the frontiers of the Reich is organized in the Hitler Youth. The German youth, besides being reared in the parental home and school, shall be educated physically, intellectually and morally in the spirit of National Socialism to serve the people and community, through the Hitler Youth.'

As well as expanding membership, of both boys and girls, the law was intended to ensure, through academic and physical education, that the future of Nazism was secure in the hands of an ideologically and racially aware youth. It also set out who had to join, and who was prohibited from joining (including Jews, Gypsies and other undesirables, such as the disabled). As well as racial prohibitions, children who were struggling in school and deemed unable to progress without exclusion were not required to take part in the otherwise mandatory activities. Parents who did not enroll their children into the Hitler Youth were penalized in conjunction with the law. A fine of 150 marks, or confinement, was the penalty for not registering children by a 15 March deadline each year. Preventing children from attending Hitler Youth meetings could have led to imprisonment.

There were other, more ominous, developments within the HJ. One was the appearance in 1934 of the *HJ-Streifendienst* (Patrol Force), who were likened to a junior Gestapo, under whose command they operated. The roles of these specially selected 16 to 18-year-olds were to keep order at HJ meetings, doling out beatings when necessary; to police wayward members of the HJ; and to keep a lookout for anyone who was disloyal or who criticized Hitler or Nazism and report them to the authorities. They received special training, under the auspices of Heinrich Himmler, at the time *Reichsführer* of the SS, who was keen to organize a conveyer belt of Nazi talent directly from the HJ to the SS.

## Keen to join

With a membership of almost six million, the Hitler Youth became bloated with bureaucracy and its offices in Berlin began to resemble a giant governmental institution. Despite this, life in the Hitler Youth was, almost, as the Nazi authorities intended – a combination of 'energetic activity, excitement, discipline, compulsion and indoctrination.'[67] Shot through with military values, it placed maximum value on 'the idea of physical perfection dedicated to the greater glory of the Fatherland.'[68] Hitler himself had set the bar high in a speech at the 1934 Nuremberg rally when he said, 'We do not want this nation to become soft. Instead, it should be hard and you will have to harden yourselves while you are young. You must learn to accept deprivations without ever giving in. Regardless of whatever we create and do, we shall pass away, but in you, Germany will live on. And when nothing is left of us you will have to hold up the banner which some time ago we raised from nothing.'

For the youngsters themselves, reasons for joining were numerous. For example, Erwin Hammel, born in Cologne in 1924, explained: 'As children, we didn't have the opportunity to travel, so we didn't get to know Germany from another point of view. We didn't have that at all. This made the propaganda that we were exposed to seem very plausible. We heard and saw nothing else.'[69] Another, Rolf Heberer, born in 1927, joined the Hitler Youth in Freital as soon as he was old enough. His father was a member of the Nazi Party and brought him up to support the government. 'Until 1933 there was the period of unemployment. And then Adolf basically got the unemployed off the streets with the measures he took, like building the Autobahn. The people were content. They had a job ... the Hitler Youth were always making trips somewhere.

One felt like part of a community. Mostly it was the case that those you went to school with or who were in your class were all involved … the Nazis understood well how to fill people with enthusiasm for certain things.'[70] Bert Trautmann, who would later find international fame as a professional footballer, joined at the age of ten, having seen newsreel images: 'The newspapers and cinemas were soon full of idealized images of blond young athletes in white vests and flannels, shot-putting, hurdling, running, javelin throwing, swinging on the parallel bars; whole fields of them putting on a display of gymnastics at some Nazi rally, row upon row of perfect Aryan specimens, muscles taut, eyes blank, all facing the Führer standing on a distant podium festooned with laurel leaves and swastikas.'[71]

## Beasts of prey

Of course, underlying the obsessive pursuit of exercise and sports in terms of health was the Nazi plan to prove the 'truth' of the superiority of the 'Aryan Master Race' and, ultimately, to prepare for the establishment of the Thousand-Year Reich. Hitler had set out his plans for German youth in 1934, saying, 'I will have the youth fully trained in all physical exercises. I want to have an athletic youth, that is the first and chief thing. In this way I can eradicate the thousands of years of human domestication. Then I shall have in front of me the pure and noble natural material. With that, I can create the new order … Education in a national state must be targeted on the creation of extremely fit bodies which are healthy to the core … I will have no intellectual training. Knowledge is ruin to my young men. A violently active, dominating, brutal youth – that is what I am after. Youth must be indifferent to pain. There must be no weakness or tenderness to it. I want to see once more in its eyes the gleam and pride and independence of the beast of prey.'[72]

Life for those in the Hitler Youth developed quickly after the Nazis took power because members, particularly boys, were always intended to be the soldiers of the future. Despite the ban on military preparations imposed by the Treaty of Versailles, new activities and 'sports' were regularly introduced. Countryside hikes and singing songs round the campfire were replaced with weekend camps and military-style marches, complete with music and an early morning roll call, weapons handling, target sports, semaphore, bicycle repairs, cable laying and the use of air guns – all skills useful to the military.

In 1935, Hitler announced that Germany was rearming and would no longer abide by the rules of the Treaty of Versailles, but the HJ's military preparations, which by then included flying gliders, riding motorbikes, sailing, kayaking, map-reading, camouflage skills, radio communications and Morse code, were still kept hush-hush.

## The power of music

One thing that united the boys' and girls' Hitler Youth movements was music. From the earliest days of both groups, music was regarded as a fundamental part of its existence and purpose. Music, in particular the martial variety, and song featured predominantly in the HJ's educational curriculum. Schirach and his music chief Wolfgang Stumme, an educator, editor and advocate of National Socialist ideas, realized how powerful music could be in forging political unity both inside and outside the organization. Over the years, some 900 musical groups were established, including, 'orchestras, instrumental groups, marching bands, groups of wind-playing comrades, music teams, sport and fanfare teams, song-playing, puppet shows and radio groups'[73] with children given regular classes in formal vocal and instrumental musical training. Those with particular musical talent were sent to special music schools. In 1937, these schools turned out some 60,000 musicians. With the HJ's activities including military exercises, Nazi festivals, educational programmes, marches, camping and community services, there were plenty of opportunities to play and sing to build group cohesion, obedience, state indoctrination and public morale. One former HJ member recalled, '… in the songs that we sang, in the poems that we recited, everything was bright, shiny and clear, the sun and earth were ours, and tomorrow so, too, would be the whole world.'

Group singing was considered particularly important as a means of building group cohesion and obedience, and numerous songbooks were published for this purpose. Many of the songs they learned were old German folk songs, music of the *Volk*, regarded by the Führer as 'our nation's most valuable cultural heritage', though many of the songs had the lyrics changed to promote the Nazi worldview. In terms of instruments, the boys tended to favour trumpets and drums while the girls were more likely to specialize in playing recorders and singing.

Germany has long had a special connection with music, whether via Bach, Beethoven, Schubert or Hitler's personal favourite, Richard Wagner. The Nazis were keen to use this legacy to justify the defence and expansion of German culture against the so-called 'cultural bolshevism' of 'degenerate' music, like that composed by Jews such as Mahler and Mendelssohn, or swing or jazz.

Perhaps the most effective use of music in the Nazi annual calendar came during the first week of September when the week-long Party rally, held in Nuremberg between 1927 and 1938, took place. The rallies, attended by thousands of spectators and participants, were full of ecstasy, delirium and nationalist exultation, set off by jubilant colours, lights and triumphal music in an orgy of self-glorification. Mass performances and mass demonstrations were held in support of what seemed like the Führer's messianic mission. It is no surprise that Leni Riefenstahl chose to highlight the group musical activities of the Hitler Youth in her famous propaganda film of the 1934 rally, *Triumph of the Will*.

## The *Bund Deutscher Mädel*

As in the *Hitlerjugend*, there were two separate sections of the *Bund Deutscher Mädel* according to age: the *Jungmädelbund* for girls aged

10–14 and the *Bund Deutscher Mädel* (the BDM proper) for girls aged 14–18, although activities were somewhat different from those of the HJ. Sports and tough physical exercise were paramount from the start of the organization in 1932, but Hitler's belief was that young girls had to undergo this training to make them fit and strong enough to be good mothers in order to ensure the survival of the Reich. 'They should glow from fresh air and exercise, Hitler thought, or better yet, from pregnancy.'[74] In 1933, responsibility for the BDM was given to former postal service worker Trude Mohr, although she was a direct report to Schirach. Mohr was married in 1937, became pregnant and had to give up her position. She was replaced by Dr Jutta Rüdiger, who led the organization until it ended in 1945. Run, like the HJ, by young leaders who were taught in special sessions at provincial schools, the purpose of the movement was to 'give girls and young women a sense of pride and self-worth, and produce political and racial conformity in the young so that they would go on as adults to have unquestionable loyalty and faith to the Führer.'[75] Like the HJ, the BDM adhered to the Nazi principle that 'youth should be led by youth'.

Although playing a full part in maintaining Nazi rule in Germany, their duties were in keeping with the role of females from the Nazi viewpoint. As a result of Hitler's firm belief that men were superior to women, the girls' organizations were subservient to those of the boys at all levels of seniority. The girls' and women's primary role was to give birth to healthy, racially pure Aryan baby boys. A key part of its instruction, therefore, centred on them avoiding *Rassenschande* (the racial defilement or 'blood disgrace' that resulted from sexual relations between Aryans and non-Aryans). 'German schoolgirls were not taught subjects such as Latin, since knowledge of this kind was not necessary for future mothers. Instead, girls were given pamphlets with advice on how to pick a husband: the first question to ask a prospective mate was, "What is your racial background?"'[76] Additional domestic and home-making tasks to help the family were taught along the lines of the so-called three 'Ks' – *Kinder, Kirche, Küche* (children, church, kitchen), for example, sewing, nursing, cooking and household chores.

Conformity was the key in all aspects of the organization. The girls wore uniforms: dark blue skirts, brown jackets, white blouses with a black neckerchief, and heavy marching shoes. Make-up was not permitted as 'Nazi girls were intended to be natural beauties that did not rely on cosmetics.'[77]

Activities of the JM and the BDM were similar to those of the boys. Although the BDM's regular weekly 'home evenings' concentrated on domestic training, Saturday mornings involved outdoor exercise and physical training. In sports, there was great focus on swimming, athletics and gymnastics. These were often collective and synchronized, rather than competitive and individual, intended to demonstrate the value of working together. In order to be granted membership, girls had to pass certain physical tests. They had to run 60 m (66 yards) in 12 seconds, jump more than 2.5 m (8.2 ft), throw a ball over 20 m (65.6 ft), swim 100 m (109 yards) and complete a two-hour route march. Those who passed the test were entitled to wear a special neckerchief ring. Other sports, such as fencing and tightrope walking, were not considered to be appropriate for women at the time and complaints about this from parents were common. Summer camps involved more sports and plenty of campfire chats comprising folk tales, German traditions, stories of Nazi martyrs, and all aspects of the Nazi 'worldview' education, including anti-Semitism. All these events were designed to present a highly organized and comprehensive indoctrination into the Nazi belief system.

## Freedom ... of a sort

Once again, girls who joined the movement were happy to explain their reasons. For example, Hedwig Ertl, born in 1923, joined at the age

*Synchronized group exercises, particularly focused on athletics and gymnastics, played a major part in BDM physical training. Collective exercises were intended to demonstrate the value of working together and to ensure the creation of strong girls who were fit for child-bearing.*

of ten. She said: 'There were no class differences. You went on trips together without paying for it, and you were given exactly the same amount of pocket money as those who had lots of money and now you could go riding and skating and so on, when before you couldn't afford it. You could go to the cinema for 30 pfennigs. We could never go to the cinema before, and suddenly things that had been impossible were there for us. That was incredible, those beautiful Nazi movies.'[78] Others joined in for different reasons. Marianne Gärtner joined the local branch in Potsdam. This involved taking the oath: 'I promise always to do my duty in the Hitler Youth, in love and loyalty to the Führer.' Other mottos she was taught included: 'Führer, let's have your orders, we are following you!', 'Remember that you are a German!' and 'One Reich, one people, one Führer!' As she later admitted: 'I was, however, not thinking of the Führer, nor of serving the German people when

I raised my right hand, but of the attractive prospect of participating in games, sports, hiking, singing, camping and other exciting activities away from school and home...'[79]

In early 1938, a new voluntary section for women aged 18–21 was added to the BDM, called *Glaube und Schönheit*, to bridge the gap between the BDM and the *NS-Frauenschaft*, the official National Socialist Women's association. It was a sort of finishing school and aimed to turn out perfect Nazi women. Those selected for membership had to have a staunch devotion to Nazi ideology and tended to be blonde and blue-eyed and blessed with 'superior intellectual gifts and grace of mind and body.'[80] As well as the standard BDM curriculum, members also indulged in riding, driving cars, pistol shooting, dancing, playing tennis and sunbathing. Fees were high and costs had to be met by parents. The best dancers performed at Nazi Party rallies and many of them ended up marrying members of the leadership corps of the NSDAP and the SS.

As war approached, in 1939, there were 4.5 million members of the BDM. In preparation for the war effort, BDM girls were ordered to help out in hospitals, kindergartens and homes with large families. They were also tasked with helping to raise funds and collect clothes and other useful goods for Nazi charitable organizations, knit socks, grow vegetables and send care packages to the soldiers on their way to the front line.

## Seizure of power

Of course, the development of both the HJ and the BDM was not without problems. Immediately after the Nazis came to power, the struggle between schools and the Hitler Youth for the attention of German children became something of a see-saw. It was hardly a fair fight, as Minister of Education Bernhard Rust was an old man with a love of the bottle, and Schirach was a young and energetic operator.

Schirach had the advantage immediately, because while schools were administered by the state, the HJ was an institution of both party and state. Following the passing of the Civil Service Law in 1933, all teachers were subject to screening routines to weed out not only Jews, Social Democrats and Communists but also those clearly opposed to the growing demands of the Hitler Youth, whose spreading influence among the pupils made their job as educators even harder. In addition, though some of the teachers were conservatives and happy with the idea of totalitarian education, the majority were not Nazis and simply wanted to get on with their jobs teaching German children without interference.

Gradually, however, the HJ carried out their own 'seizure of power', particularly in urban schools. Many of the teachers and pupils turned up in the mornings in their uniforms and teaching took place in classrooms

*After the Nazi takeover of power in 1933, school classrooms became a battleground between educators and Nazi ideologists. The Hitler Youth played a huge part in ensuring that the National Socialists prevailed in the struggle.*

adorned with Nazi banners and pictures. Disobedience became commonplace, teachers' meetings were disrupted and, in one case, in Munich, 'uniformed Hitler Youths smashed the windows of the flat of a Latin mistress notorious for giving low marks.'[81] Rust responded to the incident, saying, 'The authority of the school in the racial state must not be violated.' Measures to reassure concerned parents were taken by the Ministry of Education.

Schirach responded by insisting that every school should have a *Vertrauenslehrer* (liaison teacher), who would represent the interests of the HJ, ensuring high standards of Nazi indoctrination were maintained and acting as a recruitment officer. As the influence of the HJ grew, so educational standards dropped further. In 1938, with war on the horizon and fewer and fewer people applying for teaching jobs, Rust was forced to cut secondary education by a year. Soon afterwards, as one schoolboy – a member of the Hitler Youth and a soldier – not without cynicism later recorded in his memoirs, 'Learning was postponed to the period after the Final Victory.'[82]

The BDM had its own set of problems. The Nazi government encouraged the mixing of the sexes, which was seen as a method of encouraging children to get away from the family. One newspaper claimed that mixed social dances 'had a more beneficial effect on the relationship between boys and girls than any number of exhortations and lectures.'[83] However, sometimes it went too far. For example, in 1936 when an estimated 100,000 members of the HJ and the BDM attended the Nuremberg Rally, some 900 girls aged between 15 and 18 returned home pregnant.[84]

The organization grew slowly between 1933 and 1939, when membership became compulsory. The huge influx of numbers that followed meant that leadership became a real problem. There were simply not enough women of the right age and with the right experience to fulfil the roles. As a result, although the organization still ran its programmes, many members had become disillusioned, and the BDM began to lose its momentum.

## Time is running out

In April 1935, Hitler's real intentions on the world stage were gradually revealing themselves. For those at the top of the Nazi hierarchy, time for preparation was running out. Having announced that Germany was rearming, general conscription was introduced. Minister of the Armed Forces Werner von Blomberg noted that, 'Service in the Wehrmacht is the last and highest step in the general educational process of any young German, from the home to the school, to the HJ and Labour Service.'[85] Enthusiasm was infectious. One group of *Jungvolk* members were reported to be heard marching to the chant of, 'What are we now? *Pimpfen*. What do we want to be? Soldiers!'

The following year, 1936, with Hitler's invasion plans still officially under wraps but hiding in plain sight, troops reoccupied the Rhineland, and a new regime was established in the *Hitlerjugend* with even greater emphasis on paramilitary training, often in direct association with the Wehrmacht, the Luftwaffe and the Kriegsmarine (navy). For members of the Hitler Youth, the years of playing soldiers were gone. Instead of potential warriors, they were preparing for real battle. A Reich shooting school was set up in Obermassfeld in Thuringia where almost 2 million boys were trained in rifle shooting and other military field skills from instructors provided by Himmler's SS. Some 50,000 of them were awarded a medal for near perfect shooting at a distance of 50 m (54.7 yards).[86] Erwin Rommel, a legendary war hero, was appointed first liaison officer to the Hitler Youth in charge of military training. Tasked with trying to persuade the Hitler Youth to become part of the army rather than the SS or the NSDAP, he clashed with Schirach. Although Rommel's plan was dismissed, the leadership connection between the HJ and the Wehrmacht had become explicit.[87]

*With the possibility of war increasing, weapons training for boys in the HJ was stepped up. This image shows a Wehrmacht officer giving his young charges small-calibre rifle target practice during a Hitler Youth summer camp on the Baltic Sea.*

With the Wehrmacht and the Waffen-SS almost in competition for the potential talent coming through from the HJ, help was available from both for Schirach in terms of land, building materials, labour and skilled instructors and soon hundreds of shooting ranges had been set up, along with secure areas for use in terrain manoeuvres. Demands on all members of the HJ increased in terms of hours, and physical and mental energy. Soon, paramilitary training had become paramount with school time, work time and holidays taking a back seat, as the Ministry of the Interior began to set quotas for boys to be battle-ready. Recruits in the Flieger-HJ (Hitler Youth Flyers) learned both the theory and practice of flying. They built and flew gliders, visited Luftwaffe facilities and flew in fighters and bombers. The best and the brightest students were earmarked for future transfer to the Luftwaffe while others had to be content manning FLAK guns and searchlights. The Marine-HJ had two sections: one trained boys for the high seas fleet and the other for river and lake activity. According to an Allied report, 'The Marine-HJ is generally composed of boys living in coastal regions and furnishes replacements for the Navy and Merchant Navy. Training is under the supervision of naval personnel, and includes practically all phases of naval activities.'[88] The Motor-HJ was to train future recruits for the motorized and armoured divisions of the army. Training included practical and mechanical knowledge of all motor vehicles, including on-the-spot repairs. Other units gave training in signalling, field medicine, anti-aircraft operations and the duties of air-raid wardens.

## Ready for war

Two events in late 1938 proved that the Hitler Youth were prepared for their duties. The first was the biggest and best-ever Nuremberg rally, dedicated to the theme of 'Greater Germany' in celebration of the annexation of Austria earlier in the year, and held in Berlin's Olympic Stadium in early September. Festivities lasted for a week and some 700,000 members of the different Nazi organizations attended. Day Five, a Saturday, was the Day of the Hitler Youth. Some 80,000 members of the HJ marched into the stadium to perform military manoeuvres they had been practising for a year. To finish, the massed ranks moved into position to spell out the name of their beloved Führer, Adolf Hitler, to thunderous applause from the huge crowd. Hitler responded in his speech, saying, 'You, my youth, are our nation's most precious guarantee for a great future, and you are destined to be the leaders of a glorious new order under the supremacy of National Socialism. Never forget that one day you will rule the world!'[89]

On 7 November, a 17-year-old Polish Jew, Herschel Grynszpan, shot and killed Ernst vom Rath, a German embassy official stationed in Paris. Grynszpan had just heard the news that his parents, resident in Germany since 1911, had been expelled from the Reich along with thousands of other Jews of Polish citizenship. At a meeting of Nazi leaders that evening, Goebbels suggested that as a consequence there should be 'spontaneous' anti-Jewish riots across the country. To provoke this 'response', Reinhard Heydrich issued orders to all police headquarters for the destruction of all Jewish places of worship in Nazi Germany and suggestions as to how to start these disturbances. Heinrich Mueller, head of the Secret Political Police, sent out an order to regional and local police: 'Operations against Jews, in particular against their synagogues, will commence very soon throughout Germany. There must be no interference.'

With the police, the SA and the SS nominally responsible, anti-Semitic violence began to erupt in the late evening and early morning of 9 and 10 November. Although not officially required to attend, many HJ members, juiced up by their training and preparation for war, joined in the organized destruction of Jewish-owned homes, businesses, schools, hospitals, cemeteries and synagogues. The actions occurred in cities, towns and villages throughout Germany, annexed Austria and the Sudetenland, that had been recently occupied by German soldiers. Many of the units involved wore plain clothes to support the idea that these actions were 'spontaneous'. Mobs of brown-shirted SA and HJ roamed the streets, armed with torches and bricks. To Schirach's apparent despair, there were reports of members of the Hitler Youth beating Jews with lead piping while women looked on, some holding up their children to get a better look. Large numbers of ordinary people joined in too, looting and plundering. Jews were turfed out of their homes and shops and humiliated or beaten up in the street. Some bystanders were egged on by peer pressure, but many now believed that 'Jews are our misfortune' and that it was 'time to put them in their place.'

Paul Briscoe, a young English boy living in a small town in Germany at the time, recalled looking out of the window and seeing the shop across the street with a mob outside: '[you] could hear the crowd chanting "Jews out! Jews out!" … I didn't understand it. The shop was owned by Mira. Everybody in Miltenberg knew her. Mira wasn't a Jew; she was a person. She was Jewish, yes, but not like the Jews. They were dirty, subhuman, money-grabbing parasites – every schoolboy knew that – but Mira was – well, Mira: a little old woman who was polite and friendly if you spoke to her, but generally kept herself to herself. But the crowd didn't seem to know this: they must be outsiders. Nobody in Miltenberg could possibly have made such a mistake. I was frightened for her … A crash rang out. Someone had put a brick through her shop window. The top half of the pane hung for a moment, like a jagged guillotine, then fell to the pavement below. The crowd roared its approval.'[90]

For Alfons Heck, just ten at the time and ready to sign up for the HJ, it was an exhilarating experience: 'After my return from Nuremberg, life in the town seemed quite boring. But all of a sudden, on 9 November 1938, excitement broke loose. It was the *Kristallnacht*, the night of the broken glass. It seemed like a frenzy of hatred, all of a sudden, as we were crossing the marketplace, a van stopped, and there were perhaps 18, at the most 20 people on it. One of them was shouting, "let's get to the synagogue and take it apart." Literally seconds later, the stained-glass window came crashing into the road, and a few minutes later, one of the stormtroopers was up on the roof. And he released the rolls of the Torah, and he was shouting, "wipe your asses with it."

'Even to me, as a ten-year-old, the events of the *Kristallnacht*, my witnessing the brutality committed on townspeople that I had known all of my life, signified the end of German innocence. From now on, not one of us could ever maintain that we did not know what was in store for the Jews.'[91]

The pogrom was particularly destructive in Berlin and Vienna, home to the two largest Jewish communities in the Reich. Some 1,400 synagogues were destroyed, many burned along with their Torah scrolls, prayer books and benches, while local firefighters stood and watched. An estimated 7,500 shops and businesses had their windows smashed and premises vandalized and looted. Hundreds of Jews were injured in the violence and though the official statistics say that 91 were killed, it seems most likely that the figure was much higher. In the days following the pogrom, orders were issued to arrest as many Jews as local prisons could hold, preferably young, healthy men to perform hard labour. By 16 November, SS units and Gestapo had rounded up some 30,000 Jewish males and most of them were sent on to camps at Dachau, Buchenwald and Sachsenhausen. Hundreds died in the camps as a result of the brutal treatment they received but others were released on the condition that they made plans to leave Germany as soon as possible. This led to a huge increase in the emigration of Jews from Germany.

The Nazis euphemistically called this pogrom *Kristallnacht* ('Night of Broken Glass'); the harmless sound of the name intentionally disguised the terror and devastation of the events and the demoralization faced by Jews across Europe. Today, it is more commonly called what it was: the November Pogroms.

# Chapter 8

# Families in Nazi Germany

Although the characters in Taika Waititi's 2019 film *Jojo Rabbit* – in which Jojo, a ten-year-old member of the *Jungvolk* who has Hitler as an imaginary friend, finds out that his mother is hiding a Jewish girl, Elsa, in their house – are fictional, in reality the youth group of which Jojo was a member had a huge effect on families in Nazi Germany. As the film shows, while many youngsters had a deep and almost religious belief in their Führer, others, like Jojo, were 'ten-year-old kids who like dressing up in a funny uniform and want to be part of a club.'

## Women in the Weimar Republic

For German families, the 1920s had been difficult: the political situation was polarized and volatile, creating a climate of fear and violence on many city streets, the effects of the Treaty of Versailles began to bite, the Ruhr was occupied by French and Belgian troops, the economy crashed, which led to a period of hyperinflation, and then the Depression came along to destabilize the Weimar Republic and create fear and anger among the struggling population. But the troubles for German families went back further than that.

With more than 2 million soldiers killed in the First World War, many families had lost the head of the house. Many of the 'lucky ones' who had returned from the war were disabled, 'approximately, 2.7 million ... had lost more than just the use of their bodies ... [they] were robbed of the security of culturally transmitted bodily certainties by the war. This security was part of their masculine identity.'[92] Rather than returning as heroes, they came home damaged in body and spirit. Many of the men struggled to regain their sense of masculinity.

Deprived of their breadwinner, the burden for women with families grew heavier. Not only did they have to bring up the children, but they also had to find the money, the food and the spirit to do so. Many children, particularly the older ones, left home in the hope of finding work and reducing the number of mouths to feed. However, with so many men gone, new job opportunities were created, for example, in transport, shops and factories. Some women even became lawyers and doctors. In 1918, 11 million women were in work. The following year, Article 109 of the Weimar Constitution stated that men and women had the same rights, including the right to vote and hold office. As a result, during the years of the Weimar Republic, the majority of the electorate was female. Even as men returning from the war began to get back to work, women continued to take posts as teachers, social workers and secretaries. For some of these 'new women', this was a period of liberation, but they tended to be found in the big cities. Elsewhere, expectations for women remained as they were, as traditional and conservative wives and mothers.

## Men productive, women reproductive

For those in the so-called 'Hitler Youth generation' – people born between 1925 and 1933 – life was to prove increasingly conflicted under the new regime. The Nazis intended to make the family unit the central building block of their new society – the 'primordial cell of the *Volk*', as Reich Minister of the Interior Wilhelm Frick called it. As with many Nazi policies, their ideas on the family were not particularly new or original, but were a mixture of existing opinions that the party manipulated for its own ambitions. For the new Nazi *Volksgemeinschaft* (national community), it was necessary to raise the birth rate, which had been in decline in the latter years of the Weimar Republic.

The National Socialists believed the two sexes had distinct roles in the family: 'In the Nazi view, the chief difference was that man was essentially productive and woman fundamentally reproductive.'[93] The Mother and Child Welfare Office was set up with specific responsibility for mothers and babies. In June 1933, a marriage loan was introduced to help out newly married couples. The loan was for 600 Reichsmarks, which was the average income over four months. A quarter of the loan was cancelled for every child a couple had, so four children would mean no repayments. The only condition was that the wife had to give up work if she was employed when she got married. To pay for these loans, single men and childless couples were taxed more heavily.

But the Nazis were not just interested in more babies; they were interested in more healthy 'Aryan' babies. Female members of the 'inferior' races, such as Jews, Gypsies and other 'asocial' families, were forced, by law, to undergo compulsory sterilization. To underline the point, abortion was prohibited for healthy pure-blooded German women; those who had one were accused of 'racial suicide'. Worse still, couples from inferior races, which also included those with hereditary illness and mental disorders, who had babies were accused of 'racial degeneration'.

## 'But Who Are You?'

At the heart of these racial policies was the Nazi obsession with 'racial purity'. After identifying and eventually legislating against the regime's racial enemies, principally the Jews, laws were also drawn up for ordinary German citizens to determine their 'racial value'. Nazi ideology heralded the idea of eugenics – the idea that human society could be improved through selective breeding. Through this, the Nazis wanted to create a pure-blood 'Aryan' population. Soon after they took power, the authorities decided that anyone wanting to join the Nazi Party, perform military service or practise law or medicine had to provide evidence of 'ancestral proof of "Aryan descent"'. In 1935, the Nuremberg Laws (*see* page 110) extended this to couples who wanted to get married in case they had Jewish ancestors, so-called 'hereditary illnesses'.

To help with this process, the authorities produced brochures, such as 'But Who Are You?', and a book titled *My Book of Ancestors* in which people could collate all the necessary documents and data. Birth, marriage and death certificates, and baptism records of both the individual and the individual's ancestors were all required. In the pamphlet's introduction, Reich minister Dr Frick wrote, 'We want every fellow German, in days to come, to take an interest in his ancestry and to realize what value his ancestors hold for him personally, for his family, and thus for his people, his race. This is essential, if we are to know, in the new Germany, who is a member of the German people and who is not.'[94] The pamphlet also contained detailed information of how to go about the huge task of researching your 'parents, Grandparents, Great-grandparents and Great-great grandparents etc' using civil registry and pastoral offices, church registers, libraries, kinship research offices and so on. Those who successfully proved their racial heritage were rewarded with a stamped and signed *Ahnenpass*. It was a tall order but an important tool for the Nazi concept of the superiority of the German *Volk* and the inferiority of those who could not prove their 'Aryan' bloodline.

## Meat and drink for the Nazis

Whatever was to happen later, there is no doubt that Hitler and the Nazis were popular when they were 'elected', albeit illegally, as Germany's governing party. The Weimar Republic had proved unable to deal with the effects of the Depression and had no answers to the rise of unemployment and poverty that followed. German historian Hans-Ulrich Wehler argues that there was a 'broad consensus' of support for the regime at the outset. This support was maintained by Hitler's promises to everyone: bread for the hungry, work for the unemployed, profits to industry, bringing order to chaos and making Germany strong again. As a result of this, there existed an 'unreserved agreement between the rule of the Führer and the opinion of the people.'[95]

The dire economic situation in early 1930s' Germany affected middle-class families in many ways. As well as losing jobs, incomes and often their savings, many parents could no longer offer their children protection and security. Social tensions rose, since many parents had lost their status through poverty and unemployment, which led to conflict between the haves and the have-nots as well as between generations. These tensions, which caused such a crisis in German families, were meat and drink to the new regime.

As Nazi hopes of power began to grow, they sought to appeal to both men and women, aware that they needed as many votes as possible and both sexes to create their racially pure state. Conditions were ripe for the kind of stability that Hitler and the National Socialists were offering. For the men of the household – for example, office workers, civil servants and teachers in the nation's towns and cities – Hitler offered a return to the old ways, with work and income, a chance to put food on the table, a rekindling of the patriarchy of the 'good old days'. For wealthy businessmen and the middle classes, he offered strong government. In rural areas, farmers, shopkeepers, artisans and agricultural labourers gave him their votes. All of them were seemingly attracted by the idea of the 'national community' and further swayed by 'nationalist, super-patriotic and German romantic notions'[96] and the strength of Hitler's leadership.

His appeal among women was different but just as ardent. As it was for the men, Hitler's promise to end unemployment and restore order was effective for those women desperate to see an end to street fighting between rival political gangs. Ideology was less important to them, but his solutions to unemployment and poverty, which had brought discord to German families who saw their standards of living deteriorating, moved them greatly. For women, the 'Hitler cult' was powerful. Helene Radtke, the wife of a German soldier in her thirties, said that it was her 'divine duty to forget about all my household chores and to perform my service to my homeland.' Another, Agnes Molster-Surm, called Hitler her 'God-given Führer and saviour, Adolf Hitler, for Germany's honour, Germany's fortune and Germany's freedom.'

In the elections in 1933, the Nazis offered simple solutions and the people accepted them. Voting records show that the NSDAP received a larger share of the female than of the male vote.

## Family – germ cell of the *Volk*

In his first speech as chancellor, in February 1933, Hitler outlined the focus of his new regime. He said, 'Peasants, workers and bourgeoisie must all join together to provide the building blocks for the new Reich. The government will therefore regard it as its first and foremost duty to re-establish the *Volksgemeinschaft* – the unity of spirit and will of our *Volk*. It will preserve and defend the foundations upon which the power of our nation rests. It will extend its strong, protecting hand over Christianity as the basis of our entire morality, and the family as the germ cell of the body of our *Volk* and State ... It will establish reverence for our great past and pride in our old traditions as the basis for the education of our German Youth.'

At that point, more than 11 million women were employed, of whom almost 5 million were either married or widowed. Although the Nazis understood that many women worked to earn extra money, they were most concerned with those who had to work because of poverty. Dr Frick claimed that because so many women were in the workplace instead of the home, family life was being destroyed. The Nazi priority was to get women to leave the workplace, both to have more babies and to create more jobs for the huge numbers of unemployed men.

In March that year, Joseph Goebbels gave a speech ostensibly addressing growing complaints about the Nazis' reactionary attitudes to women. He said, 'We do not see the woman as inferior, but as having a different mission ... we believe the German woman, who more than any other in the world is a woman in the best sense of the word, should use her strength and abilities in other areas than the man.

'The first, best, and most suitable place for the women is in the family, and her most glorious duty is to give children to her people and nation, children who can continue the line of generations and who guarantee the immortality of the nation ... If the family is the nation's source of strength, the woman is its core and centre. The best place for the woman to serve her people is in her marriage, in the family, in motherhood.'[97]

Hitler himself spoke on the same subject the following year, claiming that the 'emancipation of women' was a Jewish conceit associated with Marxism. A propaganda campaign was launched that elevated women and glorified motherhood. 'The breastfeeding mother appeared on sometimes graphically deplorable posters and was sculptured for placing in public spaces. Painters depicted mothers surrounded by their families in warm, soft-toned agricultural settings, intended to invoke the peasant rural idyll within which the Nazi fantasy of ideal family life was framed.'[98] In reality, of course, the Nazis had their own agenda.

*In 1935 the Nazis founded the Lebensborn Programme in an effort to reduce the 600,000 abortions annually undertaken in Germany at the time. It provided space, medical care and a safe space to raise children with Aryan features, such as those pictured here.*

## Stunning brutality

Although the Nazis used 'terror tactics' against their enemies as soon as they took the reins of power, in the early days of the regime some historians claim that those enemies were small groups of social outcasts, such as communists, vagrants, homosexuals and criminals, who did not affect the lives of ordinary Germans – though the communists were hardly social outcasts, having polled almost 6 million votes in the election of November 1932. Many Germans were aware of the concentration camps but thought of them with approval rather than fear. As Canadian historian Robert Gellately said, 'The Nazi revolution did not begin with a sweeping onslaught on German society, but moved forward in tune with what the great majority of people wanted or would tolerate.'[99] In the first few weeks of their regime, the Nazis appeared to be restoring law and order after the chaos of the previous few years. In fact, a phrase commonly used by German historians recently to describe this era of

Nazism is a 'dictatorship by consent'. But things soon changed, as serious and sometimes deadly violence was unleashed, particularly against Social Democrat politicians, councillors and supporters. Victims of this behaviour, normally meted out by gangs of SA stormtroopers, soon included trade unionists and other organizations that represented the working classes – the Nazis' enemies were no longer 'small groups of social outcasts'.

Some people were genuinely convinced by the Nazi messages. Alfons Heck, for example, was born in Wittlich, a small town in the Rhineland, in 1928. Upon joining school aged six, Alfons was bombarded with Nazi ideology and propaganda. He joined the Hitler Youth aged ten, and was invited to hear Hitler speak at the Party rally in Nuremberg. He recalled, 'Hitler said, "We will be one people, one nation, and you, my youths, you are going to be that people and that nation." After he had uttered this sentence, I belonged to Hitler, body and soul. He went on, "Before us lies Germany. In us, Germany marches, and after us comes Germany." It was mesmerizing to hear the Führer speak. That's the feeling that I had at the end of Hitler's speech. Suddenly, you had become invincible.' Soon after his return from Nuremberg, Alfons witnessed the brutal events of *Kristallnacht* and stood among the watching crowd as uniformed stormtroopers brutally beat up innocent Jews and smashed up their property and belongings. 'The brutality of it was stunning,' he said, 'but I also experienced an unmistakable feeling of excitement.'[100]

Henry Metelmann was born near Hamburg in 1922. His father, a committed socialist, disapproved of the Hitler Youth, the 'Brown Pest' as he called it. He tried to get Henry to understand that in war there was no heroism, 'only desperation, fright and unbelievable brutality'. In the end, he relented for fear of the consequences. Henry recalled, 'even though Father hated everything connected with the Nazis, I liked it in the Hitler Youth. I thought the uniform was smashing … The songs we sung were beautifully melodic, all about our great race, our *Lebensraum* in the East, and the glory of fighting and dying for the Fatherland. I liked the comradeship, the marching and the war games. We were brought up to love our Führer, who was to me like a second God, and when we were told about his great love for us, the German nation, I was often close to tears.'[101]

## Rebellion in the family

Despite Hitler's claims that he placed the family at the heart of the new *Volksgemeinschaft*, the goals of Nazi policies on family were in reality a means to an end. As a direct result of these policies, which were intended to redefine family dynamics, there was a breakdown of traditional family roles and relationships. Conflicts between German children and their parents became more common. The impact on families was immense, with pressure from within the household, from school and from the Hitler Youth. Melita Maschmann, born in Berlin in 1918, came from a wealthy family, and her parents were members of the German National Party and disliked Hitler. However, Melita was bored at home with her conventional and conservative parents, and joining the Nazis was a way for her to rebel against them. Having been taken by her parents to watch the torchlight parade in celebration of Hitler's appointment as chancellor on 30 January 1933, she recalled, 'I longed to hurl myself into this current, to be submerged and borne along by it … The crashing tread of the feet, the sombre pomp of the red and black flags, the flickering light from the torches on the faces and the songs with melodies that were at once aggressive and sentimental … I was overcome with a burning desire to belong to these people for whom it was a matter of life and death.'[102] Her parents refused to let her join the BDM, but she did so anyway, sneaking out to their weekly meetings in secret.

Arguments like these upset many parents, who felt that the Nazi Party was taking control over their children. There were already conflicts at school, with a new curriculum, new textbooks, new teachers, new rules, crucifixes replaced by portraits of Hitler, a new sense of race and incessant indoctrination, all intended to educate their children 'in the spirit of National Socialism'. By 1936, the demands on children's time increased further. Five days a week at school, one evening and sports on Saturday morning with the HJ had been replaced; the school day was shortened and required physical training was increased to three hours every weekday and the whole of Saturday and sometimes Sunday if a weekend campout was organized. This often resulted in exhausted children and an alarming drop in attendances at school.

However, the appeal of the Hitler Youth was strong. Hedwig Ertl noted the extra power she had over her parents since joining the BDM: 'As a young person, you were taken seriously. You did things which were important ... Your dependence on your parents was reduced, because all the time it was your work for the Hitler Youth that came first, and your parents came second ... All the time you were kept busy and interested, and you really believed you had to change the world.'[103]

Splits were appearing in the traditional family unit, not only financially and politically, but also generationally. Hildegard Koch, born in Steglitz, Berlin in 1918, joined the BDM aged 15 and argued constantly with her mother about her membership. 'After all,' she said, 'we were the new youth; the old people just had to learn to think in a new way and it was our job to make them see the ideals of the new nationalised Germany.'[104]

## Claustrophobia!

With the Nazis in control, normal family life became impossible, as one by one, basic everyday civil liberties were lost. It was illegal to join any political organization apart from the Nazi Party, or any non-Nazi organization of any kind, apart from the churches and the army. Censorship was rife as *Gleichschaltung* began to take effect both on those who supported the Nazis and those who were less sure but were swept up into the huge tidal wave of nationalist emotion they created. Many of those who clearly disapproved of the Nazis came under severe pressure, exerted by the party and the HJ, on parents, teachers and employers. Some parents were fearful for their jobs and livelihoods, others for their children's future prospects. Economic decline was a reality; Hitler seemed like the only alternative.

Amid all this pressure, people were bombarded with pro-Nazi propaganda and, at the same time, denied access to any alternative thinking. The atmosphere was claustrophobic, as the ideology of the NSDAP seeped into every aspect of German society under the auspices of Joseph Goebbels, minister of the Reich Ministry of Popular Enlightenment and Propaganda. He explained his thinking, '... the secret of propaganda [is to] permeate the person it aims to grasp, without his even knowing that he is being permeated. Of course, propaganda has a purpose, but the purpose must be concealed with such cleverness and virtuosity that the person on whom this purpose is to be carried out doesn't notice it at all.'[105] All newspapers were censored, as were radio broadcasts; a new Radio Law was passed that forbade Germans from listening to foreign stations. Films were censored, books were burned; the work of artists and musicians who practised so-called 'cultural Bolshevism' was removed from galleries, concert halls and clubs. Sermons from the pulpits of Protestant and Catholic churches were monitored for dissent. Public meetings, other ceremonies and foreign press relations all came under scrutiny. Even conversation was censored; anyone daring to speak out against Hitler or the Nazi Party could face imprisonment or execution, and even telling an anti-Nazi joke was a crime and could lead to a fine or even imprisonment. Telephones were tapped, a task made easier by telephone operators who would listen in on private conversations and report suspicious talk to the Gestapo, and even personal letters were not safe. Within 20 months of taking power, Germany had become a police state in which 'violence was used deliberately and openly to intimidate opposition and potential opposition. It was used to create a public sphere permeated by violence and it provided a ready reminder for anyone who stepped out of line, who failed to show loyalty to the new order.'[106]

## Families replaced by the state

Although supposedly at the heart of the Nazis' *Volksgemeinschaft*, in reality their policies were driving families apart. For a population forced to participate in the new Reich, whether they liked it or not, the family had been replaced by the state. It had been sacrificed at the altar of the *Volk*, or as its slogan had it, 'You are nothing – your *Volk* is everything.' Individuality, free will and choice were now regarded as a revolt against the natural order.[107] New social policies emptied the family home, with each member involved in different party activities and organizations. The head of the house was replaced by the Führer, who became the figure of authority in the family home. Members of the HJ and the BDM spent longer and longer attending meetings and events, sharing experiences with leaders not much older than themselves. They grew closer to their friends, weakening the ties with parents and siblings. Moreover, youth leaders actively encouraged children to rebel against their parents, giving them new norms and values. Parents began to worry about speaking honestly in front of their children in case their remarks were relayed to the youth leaders. 'Many parents got picked up by the Gestapo because their children turned them in. It reached the point where children could not trust their parents and parents could not trust their children,' remembers Karl Schnibbe, born in Hamburg in 1924.[108] Dorothy Fleming, born in Vienna in 1928, had just started high school in 1938 when the Nazis invaded Austria. As a Jew, she was immediately ostracized in the classroom. She recalls her teacher speaking seriously to the class: 'At home I want you to keep your eyes and ears open and listen carefully to what your parents, their friends and your brothers and sisters are saying. If you hear them saying anything nasty or critical about our new system, you are to report it to me.'[109]

Perhaps the ultimate examples of the effectiveness of this form of coercion come from the stories of Walter Hess and Elisabeth Fetter. In the mid-1930s, Walter Hess was an active and enthusiastic member of the HJ, though at school he was unpopular and considered to be a bully. Rumours circulated that he hated his father. At home one day, Walter's father, a former Communist, called Hitler a 'blood-crazed maniac'. Caught up in his beliefs in Hitler's political ideas and in an attempt to curry favour, Walter reported his father to his youth leader. He was arrested the same day and sent to Dachau, where he died, aged 40, of sudden 'heart failure'. In return, Walter received a promotion. Elsewhere, one evening, eight-year-old Elisabeth Vetter returned from a BDM meeting and told her parents that she no longer belonged to them, she now belonged to Hitler. Her parents were shocked. 'They opened the door and said, "If you belong to Hitler, then go to him now." They pointed her outside and closed the door behind her.' Her youth leader happened to pass by the house and see Elisabeth crying on the steps outside and asked her what was wrong. Elisabeth told her what had happened. The youth leader reported the parents to the authorities, and they were arrested and taken away. Elisabeth did not see them for three or four weeks. The incident was never mentioned in the family again.[110]

## Intimidation, fear and coercion

Judging by the brutality of violence they unleased, usually at the hands of the SA, the Nazis clearly knew that there would be opposition when they took power in 1933. As well as the laws they passed, the new legal system they controlled and the huge propaganda campaign they launched in their early days and weeks in power, the Nazis sought to control the German people using intimidation, fear and coercion, which stretched its roots deep into all areas of society.

The key tools at their disposal were the Gestapo, the SS, the SA and the SD, concentration camps and block wardens. The Gestapo was set up in 1933 as a small unit of Nazi secret police with 1,000 employees. Between then and 1945, it established a reputation of terror among the German population. Through violence, blackmail, entrapment, denunciation, intimidation and extortion, it carried out Nazi policies, crushing its opponents and keeping society in line. This was no small task given that at its peak in 1944, it had 16,000 active officers to police a population of 66 million.

Once armed with its fearful reputation, it expanded by absorbing members of the SA and the SS and was given extraordinary powers to act 'as the instrument of the Führer's authority.'[111] Early actions against Communists and ordinary members of other left-wing groups in which individuals were rounded up and sent to the concentration camps served an additional purpose, making members of the public think twice about criticizing the regime at all. Secret arrests, often at night, created uncertainty in the community, a feeling increased as rumours about the treatment of those arrested began to spread. Added to this was the growing fear of being sent to the concentration camps. Ideally for a force with limited manpower, these actions gave birth to the idea that 'only total compliance with the regime was acceptable.'[112] Because of the effectiveness of this tactic, the Gestapo began to rely on the population as their main source of information.

At every level, the Gestapo began to use coercion and denunciation to further control the population. As the pressure to conform grew, so did the fear for personal safety as it became clear that not co-operating with the regime could threaten anyone. This fear led to thousands of instances of denunciation, as one individual would accuse another of 'sedition' to deflect suspicion from their own actions. Letters and other forms of communication arrived at Gestapo offices every day reporting on family, friends and neighbours. Some of these may have been genuine, but many involved personal gain, such as getting rights to an occupied apartment, or personal revenge for a domestic dispute. Jewish people were particularly at risk of denunciation, especially following the passing of the Nuremberg Laws in 1935.

Of course, coercion did not need to involve arrest or a spell in one of the camps; politicians were threatened with the loss of their jobs if they did not join the Nazi Party, as were others employed by the state, such as schoolteachers, university professors, civil servants, and post office and public transport workers.

## Creeping paranoia

But the roots of Nazi power went even deeper. The Nazis had organized a pyramid of officials to enforce surveillance and control of all German citizens. The Gestapo sat at the top, but lower-level officials were just as important. Recently, historians have focused on the effectiveness of the cell block warden or *Blockleiter*, a sort of glorified janitor for a block of apartments or a group of houses in towns and cities across the country. Official duties included making sure that flags were put up on Hitler's birthday, that proper air-raid precautions were taken, and that rubble was cleared afterwards. But, as active Nazis, their primary duty was to form a link between the authorities and the general population, enforce Nazi doctrine and keep an eye out for the regime's enemies, particularly former socialist and communist activists. One Nazi propagandist magazine article explained, 'Their primary task is to anchor the party members of their cell or block ever more firmly to the party, and to win those who live in their cell or block more and more to National Socialist thinking.' They had power, too, and were able to stop offenders' welfare payments and report them to local party officials. They were not popular, but they were effective in monitoring political and social deviance.

There were similar low-ranking but effective officials in the workplace. Officials in the Labour Front dealt with troublesome workers, for example those who might have complained about working conditions or poor wages, who could be threatened with reassignment to dirty and difficult jobs miles away from home if they did not toe the line. Coercion was also used as a weapon in German schools, where Hitler Youth leaders used the threat of refusing pupils their school leaving certificates against those unwilling to join the HJ. Without that document, prospects of finding an apprenticeship or job were slim.

Under such coercion, life for ordinary German families was stifling; there was no room to breathe, no opportunity to speak out and say what you really thought. A sort of creeping paranoia developed; individuals felt themselves under constant surveillance, you could never be quite sure when talking to someone that they were not a police agent or even a cell block warden. Ordinary Germans were living in a climate of fear and many, not surprisingly, retreated into private life. However, the household had lost its dominant role in the upbringing of children. Education was earmarked to serve as an ideological function and the Hitler Youth took up most of the time that had been spent working at home. For the young men and women conscripted into the Labour Service and the armed forces, state duties now superseded those of the household.

# Chapter 9

# The Fighting Starts

For those members of the Hitler Youth who were dedicated to the cause, the years building up to the by-now inevitable war were disappointing. Apart from the 'excitement' of *Kristallnacht*, life had settled into one of repetitive routine of physical exercise, 'achievement sports', marksmanship, orienteering and other 'terrain manoeuvres'. In the early 1930s, there had been a sense of movement, as they worked towards preparedness for war; now they seemed to be going through the motions.

## Rising anticipation

However, levels of anticipation went up on 13 March 1938, when German troops marched into Austria. Crossing the frontier at 5 am that Sunday morning, they were met with cheers and flowers. The *Anschluss* (Union), as it became known, expressly forbidden by the Treaty of Versailles, had long been a Germanic dream, particularly among those living in German-speaking territory of the former Habsburg empire over which Austria had claimed sovereignty at the end of the First World War. In fact, Austrian Nazis, with help from their German colleagues, had attempted a coup in 1934 but it had been unsuccessful. Tensions simmered between the two neighbours with Hitler insisting that ethnic Germans in Austria should have the right to self-determination. Writing in *Mein Kampf* in 1925, he said '... the unification [of Germany and Austria] is a life task to be carried out by all means. Germany-Austria must be restored to the great German Motherland ... People of the same blood should be in the same REICH.'[113] Within days of the troops' arrival, the country's Jews were dispossessed and stripped of their citizenship and their leaders were sent to Dachau, along with Austria's former chancellor, Kurt von Schuschnigg. In addition, thousands of political opponents and 'antisocial persons' were arrested and incarcerated. Austria was used as a 'laboratory' for the Nazis' anti-Jewish policies.

At the final peacetime Party rally at Nuremberg in September 1938, dedicated to the theme of Greater Germany, both Hitler and Göring hinted at their plans for a further annexation, that of the Sudetenland in northern Czechoslovakia. The country had only been founded as a result of the Treaty of Versailles. During the 1920s, it had become one of the most industrially advanced and politically progressive states in Europe. Hitler wanted this industrial might for himself. On the pretext of supposed poor treatment of the majority German-speaking population of the Sudetenland, he instigated a massive propaganda campaign to promote German nationalistic sentiment in the region and demanded that the Czech government cede it to Germany or face war. The Führer's speech on the matter on 12 September sparked a wave of violence by the Sudeten Germans, targeting Czechs and Jews, and riots and general unrest continued until the German invasion. The watching world took note of the warning and, fearing a repeat of the conflict of 1914–18, the British and French agreed to appease Hitler's demands and hand over the territory in exchange for a promise of peace. The intended invasion began on 1 October when thousands of German troops flooded over the border into Bohemia and Moravia. Although it was a bloodless victory, in a matter of months Czechoslovakia had ceased to exist.

## Reopening the 'Polish Corridor'

Poland had been the subject of German interest since it had been given the German provinces of West Prussia, Poznan and Upper Silesia under the Treaty of Versailles. These areas were home to many ethnic Germans, particularly the Polish Corridor, which included the city of Danzig on the Baltic Sea coast. On taking power in 1933, one of Hitler's first moves was to offer Poland a non-aggression pact in order to avoid the possibility of a military alliance between the Poles and the French. He then began suggesting that Danzig, the population of which had expressed their wish for annexation by Germany at the ballot box, be reincorporated into Germany. He also hinted at other plans for the region, admitting in private that Danzig was not the issue. For him, *Lebensraum* was the priority. The Polish government remained suspicious of his motives and fearful for their independence. Hitler had announced before the war that he intended to clear the Poles out of Poland and bring in German settlers instead. In effect, Poland was to serve the same function for Germany as Australia had for Britain, or the American West for the USA: it was to be a colony of settlement, in which the supposedly racially inferior indigenous inhabitants would be removed by one means or another to make room for the invading Aryan Master Race.

Hitler had not hidden his feelings about the Poles. 'The Führer's judgement on the Poles is annihilatory', reported Goebbels. 'More animals than men, totally dull and formless ... The filth of the Poles is unimaginable.'[114] 'The Poles,' Hitler told the Nazi Party ideologue Alfred Rosenberg, consisted of 'a thin Germanic layer: underneath frightful material. The towns thick with dirt ... If Poland had gone on ruling the old German parts for a few more decades everything would have become lice-ridden and decayed. What was needed now was a determined and masterful hand to rule.'[115]

Plans for the invasion of Poland were in place by early summer. In August, the Nazi propaganda machine went into overdrive in its attempts to justify aggression against its near neighbours. As it had done in Czechoslovakia, it published reports of atrocities against *Volksdeutsche* (ethnic Germans) in Poland – stories of rape, dismemberment and mass slaughter. Like all effective propaganda, there was some truth in this. They also spread rumours that Poland, Britain and France were planning to surround and attack Germany. On 31 August, the SS carried out a false flag attack on a radio station in Upper Silesia using German soldiers in Polish uniforms. The following day, under the pretext of annexing the mostly German free city of Danzig and reopening the so-called 'Polish Corridor' to the Baltic, Germany invaded Poland. Danzig was a symbolic target for the guns of the battleship *Schleswig-Holstein*, which shelled the city's munitions depot and marked the first action of the Second World War. It was an action approved by ordinary Germans to help heal the wounds of the humiliation of the Treaty of Versailles.

## The HJ moves on

Schirach had not ordered HJ involvement in the anti-Semitic pogrom of 9 November 1938, and was furious on hearing reports of it (*see* page 140). Summoning a meeting of local leaders, many of whom had been involved in its organization, he condemned what he described as these 'criminal actions' and ordered that it never happen again. This action, clearly out of step with the Nazi hierarchy, indicated that his tenure was coming to an end. He resigned his post in 1940 and was rewarded with an appointment as Gauleiter of Vienna.

Schirach was replaced by Artur Axmann, a Hitler Youth leader of considerable talent since 1928. Axmann's appointment was not without controversy. In his role as *Reichsführer* of the SS, Heinrich Himmler was interested in establishing a smooth flow of talent from the HJ to his own organization, and favoured Schirach's deputy Hartmann Lauterbacher for the post. Unfortunately for Himmler, his colleagues preferred Axmann. The new man's first job, however, was to fight on the Russian front. In 1941, he was seriously injured and lost an arm. He returned as a war hero, and rose considerably in Himmler's estimation, sealing the relationship between the HJ and the SS that Himmler was after. Both these actions brought a new wave of membership into the Hitler Youth.

Following the declaration of war on Germany by Britain and France on 3 September, in response to the invasion of Poland, a new sense of urgency was introduced to Hitler Youth training. The original purpose of the HJ had been to bring Hitler to power; its new mission was victory in war. Although militarism had always been a major theme in the education of the HJ – membership of which, by the end of 1938, stood at 8.8 million aged from 10 to 18, of which almost half were girls – new rules were drawn up. Across the board, in all four HJ organizations, the hours were increased. Copious amounts of school time were sacrificed for paramilitary training. 'Terrain Games' took on a more aggressive edge, with boys involved in realistic wartime activities involving outwitting, ambushing and assaulting rival groups.

Much of this training took place during three-week summer infantry camps intended to prepare youths for military life. On arrival, the boys would walk under a sign on the gate that read, 'We are born to die for Germany'. The programme was tough: cleanliness, tidiness, obedience and teamwork were expected. Each day's activities were highly regimented: reveille at six, breakfast at seven then games of football, athletics and gymnastic exercises. Afternoons would be spent in the field, digging trenches or foxholes, learning how to stalk and ambush enemies and how to handle weapons. On other days, the boys would take part in long marches carrying heavy backpacks. Talking was not permitted

*German youths born between 1926 and 1929 are commonly known in German culture as the 'Flakhelfer-Generation' (Flakhelper). School life of these youths, of both sexes, was interrupted by ideological indoctrination and strict military training in preparation for dangerous and often deadly work.*

because instructors would shout commands at random that required the boys to dive for cover in ditches or bushes to avoid imagined 'enemy' activity. In the evenings there would be newsreels to watch or lectures on the importance of obeying orders, their commitment to fight, kill and, if necessary, die for Germany.

As well as target practice, training now included the use of explosives, grenades, rocket launchers and anti-aircraft weapons. Increasing importance was given to HJ specialist groups, the Flieger-HJ, the Motor-HJ and the Marine-HJ as well as smaller formations who specialized in anti-aircraft operations, air-raid precautions, Morse code, practical field medicine and cavalry units specially designed to attract rural youths. Girls also received training as auxiliary nurses and in air-raid duties.

## Invasion of Poland

As the war began in earnest, over a million Hitler Youth boys of draft age – 18 and over – were called up to the Wehrmacht and the Waffen-SS. They had been schooled for war. They were ready – to fight, to kill and to die if necessary. Filled with optimism for a quick victory, with belief that what they were doing was justified and with the certainty of their membership of the Aryan Master Race, they crossed the border into Poland.

The German invasion was unprovoked and unannounced. Starting at dawn, some 2,000 tanks, 900 bombers and more than 400 fighter planes began the attack, supported by more than a million soldiers. They crossed the border from the north, the south and the west via the Polish Corridor, advancing on Warsaw and aiming to encircle the city. Germany's new and immediately successful war tactic, *blitzkrieg* (lightning war), saw surprise attacks by bombers from the air, supported by tanks on the ground. The infantry would then move in to occupy the territory. Optimism and enthusiasm among Germany's young soldiers was high. Images created by years of Nazi ideology held good: killing Polish soldiers was righteous revenge for their pre-war killing of ethnic Germans; shooting civilians and looting shops were justified, as was the killing of sub-human Jews. Unhindered progress and easy victories engendered a sense of immortality among the German troops, unshaken by the death of a comrade or a personal injury.

In a speech to military commanders ten days before the attack on Poland, Hitler had set the tenor of the conflict to come, saying, 'Our strength lies in our speed and our brutality. Genghis Khan hunted millions of women and children to their deaths, consciously and with a joyous heart. History sees in him only the great founder of a state ... I have issued a command – and I will have everyone who utters even a single word of criticism shot – that the aim of the war lies not in reaching particular lines but in the physical annihilation of the enemy. Thus, so far only in the east, I have put my Death's Head formations [SS units] at the ready with the command to send every man, woman and child of Polish descent and language to their deaths, pitilessly and remorselessly ... Poland will be depopulated and settled with Germans.'[116]

## Dividing the spoils

In the event, the German invasion of Poland was intended to create *Lebensraum* and so the Wehrmacht were ordered to fight the Polish people as well as the army. The disparity in resources and equipment was huge: thin lines of Polish troops were unable to defend on three frontiers. On 16 September, 328,000 kg (723,116 lb) of bombs were dropped on defenceless Polish positions. Within a week, Polish forces were in disarray, and the government had gone into exile. On 17 September, it was announced that the Red Army had crossed into Poland's eastern border and the end was inevitable. On 28 September, Warsaw was bombed by 1,200 German aircraft, killing 20,000 civilians and destroying over 10 per cent of the city's buildings. The city's garrison surrendered. By 6 October, Poland had been defeated with 250,000 soldiers killed and wounded and over a million taken prisoner. In addition, some 16,000 civilians had been executed.

The Germans and the Russians carved Poland up between them. These measures extended the borders of the Third Reich up to 200 km (124 miles) eastwards, which contained around 10 million people, mostly Polish. The eastern side of the country was given to Russia in accordance with a secret protocol in the Molotov-Ribbentrop non-aggression pact agreed by Hitler and Soviet leader Joseph Stalin a week before the German invasion. In June 1940, the Russians also moved into the Baltic states of Lithuania, Latvia and Estonia. The German portion – referred to as Greater Germany – was divided in two: the Reichsgau Wartheland or 'Warthegau', which bordered Germany; and, for logistical purposes, the General Government, a German colony of some 11 million people, which formed a sort of 'buffer zone' between Germany and Russia.

In the summer of 1939, with plans for the invasion in place, the SS leadership, which included Heinrich Himmler and Reinhard Heydrich, drew up occupation plans for the various services under their control: the Security Service, the Gestapo, the police and a number of other specialized offices. Plans put in place included the politicization of the police, many of whom were not fanatical Nazis, and the creation of five new *Einsatzgruppen* (mobile killing units) – task forces to follow the army into Poland and carry out Nazi ideological policies. The SS were instructed to instigate a 'clear-out: Jews, intelligentsia, priesthood, aristocracy'. The 'rabble' were to be eradicated from German territory.

## Widespread and indiscriminate cruelty

Now in total control of western and central Poland, the Nazis unleashed the full force of their racial ideology – a model that Hitler intended to impose throughout Eastern Europe, the area intended as living space for the Aryan Master Race. The invasion had been brutal, but what followed was even worse. The SS began a massive campaign of arrests, deportations and murders. Cruelty was widespread and indiscriminate. When one soldier was stabbed in a brawl with locals, as a punishment, 122 people from the village were rounded up and shot dead. Not content with that, a local train was stopped and several passengers were taken off and executed immediately. In another incident, a window in the local police station in Obluze, near Gdynia, was smashed by a schoolboy. Fifty boys were rounded up and asked who had done it. No one owned up. The boys' parents were told to beat them. They refused. So the SS men beat them with rifle butts and shot ten of them dead. One stormtrooper had 55 Polish prisoners taken out of their cells and killed in a drunken fit of rage. Incidents like these, involving task forces, police and the regular army, were daily occurrences during the autumn and winter of 1939–40.

More organized reprisals were also dealt with harshly. On 10 September, German Colonel-General von Bock issued an order: 'If there is a shooting from a village behind the front and it proves impossible to identify the house from which the shots came, then the whole village is to be burned to the ground.'[117] One unnamed stormtrooper recalled his unit being fired on in another Polish village, 'Soon burning houses were lining our route, and out of the flames there sounded the screams of the people who had hidden in them and were unable any more to rescue themselves. The animals were bellowing in fear of death, a dog howled until it was burned up, but worst of all was the screaming of the people. It was dreadful. It's still ringing in my ears even today. But they shot at us and so they deserved death.'[118] By 26 October 1939, 531 towns and villages had been burned to the ground and 16,376 Poles had been executed.

## *Einsatzgruppen* – mobile 'death squads'

German barbarism knew no bounds. In fact, many of the operations undertaken by the *Einsatzgruppen* were done out of sight of the regular army, whose job, once the fighting was over on 6 October, was to restore order, a task made harder by the cruelty of these 'death squads'. In early September, *Einsatzgruppen z.b.V.* was formed, headed up by Lieutenant General Udo von Woyrsch of the SS. Ostensibly required to mop up behind the front-line troops, this particular group had special instructions issued by Himmler for the 'ruthless suppression' of the Polish uprising in East Upper Silesia and, in particular, the indiscriminate killing of Jews. Upper Silesia was formerly part of Prussia and had been taken from Germany by the Treaty of Versailles and furthermore was rich with mineral resources, mines, iron and steel mills on which the Nazis had their beady eyes. In addition, Operation Tannenberg, as it was known, involved the killing, if possible, of prominent Poles – Catholic clergy, nobility and those who had participated in the uprising, as well as prominent Jews – who were all listed in the *Sonderfahndungsbuch* (Special Prosecution Book), a ledger compiled by the Gestapo, of which each group had a copy. The preliminary list contained the names of 61,000 people.

Hitler's orders were to 'spread fear and terror in the population' – orders these mobile units followed to the letter. In Bedzin, patrols moved through the area searching Jewish homes and businesses for weapons; some businesses were wrecked, and three men were executed when weapons were found in their possession. Other orthodox Jews were humiliated, having their beards and ear-locks cut off. The city rang with the sound of gunshots as 29 'hostages' were executed. They used flamethrowers to set fire to the synagogue and then shot the people fleeing from the building. The synagogue in Katowice was also torched and other Jews were shot in Krzeszowice, Dulowa and Trzebina. In Wieliczka, near Kraków, they smashed up Jewish homes, arresting 32 males aged 14 and over. They loaded them into trucks, took them to the forest and shot them. In Dynów, a small town near Przemyśl, they came across a synagogue with a dozen or so Jews inside. They locked them in and burned it down. They then rounded up a further 60 or so Jewish men from the locality and drove them into the forest, where they were forced to dig their own mass grave. They were then shot.

But for this particular unit, the worst was reserved for Przemyśl. They combed the city looting and destroying Jewish homes and businesses while searching for any prominent Jewish citizens listed in the *Sonderfahndungsbuch*. A hundred or so Jewish men were assembled in the market place. Once again, they were transported to the forest and executed.[119]

While it is perfectly rational to think that these actions were borne simply of Nazi racial hatred for the Slavs and the Jews, it also had a practical purpose: Hitler wanted Poland cleared of Poles and Jews in order to make space for the Aryan Master Race and assist in the Germanization of the occupied territories. After the war, Bruno Streckenbach, commander of another *Einsatzgruppe*, confirmed that Von Woyrsch's orders from Himmler to use extreme terror were genuine but that the intention was to 'force the flight of the Jewish population.' According to the transcript of a court martial inquiry in September 1939, investigators found evidence that Von Woyrsch was given the 'special task' of forcing the Jewish population to flee east. In addition, of course, it was also a blueprint for German military tactics and genocide to come.[120]

While it is impossible to say for certain whether any of the Hitler Youths recently called up took part in any of these atrocities, some must have witnessed them or even been ordered to participate. What price their youthful optimism afterwards?

## *Generalplan Ost*

As well as creating 'room for living' for Germans in the east, Hitler's plan was to exploit the labour force of conquered territories. The Nazis had previous experience of slave labour, which began in earnest in 1937 when rearmament caused a labour shortage. Forced labour camps were set up throughout Germany to house workers, at first comprising 'unreliable elements' such as petty criminals, communists, Jews, the homeless and homosexuals. When the war started, they were replaced by workers arriving from newly conquered territories in the east. In Poland, a campaign was launched by the Reich Propaganda Unit to try to attract youngsters to help with farm work in Germany – an appealing prospect at the time in comparison to life under the Nazis in occupied Poland. Some 15 per cent of Polish workers volunteered. The remainder – Polish Jews and Poles over the age of 12, in the end numbering some 1.4 million – were deported to Germany as slave workers. They were set to work in the war industry, construction, repairing bombed railways and bridges, or working on farms.

Conditions of life in the camps were appalling and no attention was paid to the health of the 'prisoners'. There was little food, equipment, medicine or clothing. The work was hard, with long hours and little time to rest. As a result, death rates were extremely high.

As the deportations began, they were accompanied by a huge campaign of looting and requisitioning by the German occupation forces. They requisitioned properties – stealing jewellery and money when they found it – and farms to secure food for the troops, and emptied shops of their wares. They confiscated scientific equipment from university laboratories, and searched widely for metals, such as copper, lead and zinc, all of which were transported back to Germany, along with saucepans, garden gates and railings. When winter came, they took sheepskin coats from anyone they saw wearing one. To add insult to injury, they began raiding villages and confiscated all bank notes they found there, legally or illegally if necessary.

If anything, life was worse for those living in the General Government. Hitler had appointed Hans Frank, the Nazi Party's legal expert and a cruel anti-Semite, as the new colony's governor-general. Frank was a civilian and a great admirer of Hitler. His job was to oversee an area intended to serve as a racial dumping ground, providing an endless supply of slave labour, and later, sites for the mass extermination of European Jews. Life inside this pseudo-state was appalling, a constant struggle against hunger – because food had to be turned over to the Germans and rations were pitiful – random street round-ups, public executions, deportations and pacifications. Jews had all rights taken away and were forced into ghettos. Eventually, they were deported to concentration camps set up in the colony, such as Belzéc, Sobibór and Treblinka.

## The HJ back home

With the 18-year-old HJ away on the front lines, youth leaders who remained at home were therefore 16- or 17-year-olds, although they were helped by students, teachers and party members who had experience of youth activities. Organized into groups of 500 or 600 and allocated certain districts, roads and blocks, their charges were tasked with collecting materials in support of the war effort: brass, copper, scrap metal, razor blades, paper and bottles. Others delivered draft notices in their neighbourhoods, as well as the new ration cards, which went out once a month to every household. Members of the BDM stood on railway station platforms offering encouragement and refreshments to soldiers departing for the front and helped to care for wounded soldiers in hospitals. They also helped out in kindergartens and rendered assistance to households with large families.

Other important functions for the HJ included involvement in the *Kinderlandverschickung* (KLV) programme of evacuation of children to the countryside. Announced in September 1939, at first evacuations were limited to school-age children from Berlin and Hamburg, which were deemed the cities most likely to be bombed. As the Allied bombing campaign was stepped up, so more children were moved. By 1942, over 850,000 had left their homes and moved to rural East Prussia, the Warthegau section of Poland, Upper Silesia and even Slovakia. They were housed in private homes, camps, youth hostels, farms and holiday camps, where they were looked after, by and large, by girls from the BDM. The camps, run by Nazi-approved leaders and Hitler Youth leaders, ostensibly served as de facto grammar schools, which had all been closed by the bombing. As such, the children continued to receive indoctrination and militarization. Between 1940 and 1945 more than 2.8 million children spent time in KLV camps.

Inevitably, as the war began to take its toll on Germany, members of the HJ became more involved in military activities. By the end of 1940, boys aged ten and older started terrain manoeuvres and target practice; soon Axmann was boasting that a million boys were practising with live rounds and that they had produced 31,000 first-class marksmen. In the cities and towns, a shortage of men saw boys used as an auxiliary military force, firefighting, fulfilling air-raid duties, manning rescue squads and technical emergency services, manning anti-aircraft batteries, operating searchlights, and transporting ammunition supplies and dispatches. Trained by members of the SS, they also patrolled the streets, ensuring that curfews and blackouts were observed, and formed search parties hunting prison or camp escapees and Allied airmen who had been shot down.

## Lebensraum

With Hitler's actions in Austria, Czechoslovakia and Poland, he had taken the first steps in acquiring his much-lauded *Lebensraum* in the east. While he had not anticipated the declaration of war by Britain and France, the early success of his *blitzkrieg* tactics in Poland and his other conquests in Northern Europe occupied his thoughts.

In 1936, in their search for a cure to unemployment, the Nazis had introduced the *Reichsarbeitsdienst* (Reich Labour Service), in which all high school graduates in the HJ were required to serve for six months. As part of their 'duty to serve' they were required to perform socially useful tasks which, in turn, would create more new jobs. It was an invaluable source of cheap labour. Their duties included clearing forests and draining swamps to create more land for farming, and also road building, including the much-vaunted Autobahns. Members of the BDM were also required to 'volunteer' on graduation. The girls would be transported all over Germany to help with farm work and food production. Conditions were spartan, the hours were long – at harvest time, sometimes up to 15 hours per day – and the work was hard. For Melita Maschmann, however, who did her service in East Prussia, it was an uplifting experience. 'Amongst us there were peasant girls, students, factory girls, hairdressers, schoolgirls, office workers and so on ... The knowledge that this model of a National Community had affected me such intense happiness gave birth to an optimism to which I clung obstinately until 1945.'[121]

Due to the success of this scheme, a new law, the Youth Service Law, was decreed in 1939 requiring 18-year-old HJ to perform year-long public service called *Landdienst*. For the Nazis, this represented the completion of the required smooth progression of Hitler Youth to labour service and then the Wehrmacht, which would process every German youth from the age of ten. Robert Ley, the Nazi labour chief, set out the achievement in stark terms: 'We begin with the child when he is three years old. As soon as he begins to think, he gets a little flag put into his hand. Then he follows the school, the Hitler Youth, the SA and military training. We don't let him go. And then when adolescence is passed, then comes the *Arbeitsfront*, which takes him again and does not let him go until he dies, whether he likes it or not.'[122]

Under the new system, at the end of eighth grade, groups of boys and girls were sent to the country to help plant and tend crops and then bring in the harvests. Girls were also expected to help out in the fields along with housework and babysitting for the farmers' families. Camps were built to house the youngsters, and were run along military lines. Girls and boys were housed separately, and strict discipline was enforced by supervising army officers. This service was well supported by the Nazi leadership; the optics were good, and it played well with their promise of 'work and bread for all'. Former Hitler Youth member Hörst Krüger said, 'The Labour Service was a good thing. Those spades slanting over shoulders made sense to the people. A surge of greatness seemed to course through the country.'[123] They believed that the camps instilled discipline, obedience and respect for hard work. The groups also included youngsters from all walks of life, encouraging

*Heinrich Himmler and Artur Axmann inspect a cohort of HJ recruits in 1941. Himmler was keen to establish a smooth flow of talent from the HJ to the SS. By agreeing to this, new HJ leader Axmann was able to access funds from the SS to finance his Landdienst project.*

camaraderie between Germans of all classes. In practical terms, the scheme was also hugely successful in producing large quantities of fresh vegetables and fruit.

The return from the front of the injured war hero and new leader of the Hitler Youth Artur Axmann in 1941 marked a turning point in the progress of the *Landdienst*. Using his connections to Himmler and the SS in securing finance, more than 16,000 HJ were sent to camps in the German countryside, with a further 3,000 despatched to recently conquered regions. By 1942, this figure had increased to 30,000, mostly in Poland and western Ukraine. Ambitious plans were drawn up for the colonizers, youths to till the soil and older settlers drawn there because of a huge Nazi propaganda campaign, involving generous payments and the prospect of land ownership. But the numbers did not stack up. More Hitler Youths arrived, but many did not come because of strong objections from parents concerned for the safety of their children so near the war zone. Some 400,000 German civilians did arrive but almost all as administrators or merchants, contributing very little to the hoped-for agricultural colonization. Numbers were bolstered by German-speakers from Poland and surrounding countries who were promised land, but the space available was too big to fill. Then, almost all this activity was stopped on 22 June 1941 when Adolf Hitler launched Operation Barbarossa, Germany's invasion of the Soviet Union.

# Chapter 10

# Boy Soldiers

By 1941, the 18-year-old *Hitlerjugend* who had joined up at the start of the war had become seasoned veterans. But each year the ranks of the Wehrmacht, the Waffen-SS and the SS were refreshed with a delivery of new young recruits whose zeal for the Nazi cause was as great if not even greater than theirs. Their training had been better and longer, following the setting up of *Wehrertüchtigungslager*, special schools where, in addition to their existing paramilitary training, HJ members aged 15 and over took mandatory three-week courses in war training, under the supervision of the Wehrmacht. Weapons training included handling the standard weapons of the infantry: pistols, machine guns, hand grenades and *Panzerfausts* (a type of anti-tank bazooka).

## The failure of Operation Barbarossa

Germany's initial military successes in Europe benefitted from their non-aggression treaty with the Soviet Union, allowing Hitler to expand his plans in Europe. In May 1939 and 1940, the German war machine pushed on into Scandinavia, Belgium, the Netherlands and France, which was conquered in six weeks. But on 22 June 1940, they launched a surprise attack on their so-called 'allies'. Operation Barbarossa, named 'Red Beard' in honour of Holy Roman Emperor Frederick I, was a colossal undertaking and regarded by Hitler as the ultimate goal of his quest for *Lebensraum*. Hitler's aim was to destroy Stalin's 'Jewish Bolshevist' regime, enslave the Soviet Union's Slavic populations and establish German hegemony in Europe.

Three army groups were involved, comprising 3.5 million German and Axis troops (including Italian, Finnish and Slovakian soldiers among others), 3,400 tanks and 2,700 aircraft – it was one of the largest ever invasion forces in history. Army Group North headed towards the Baltic and ultimately Leningrad. Army Group South attacked the Ukraine and the Donbas industrial region, while Army Group Centre were to take Minsk, Smolensk and Moscow. The invasion was expected to last ten weeks.

The initial thrust of the Axis forces was hugely successful because Stalin was not expecting it and the Red Army was therefore not prepared.

German forces advanced quickly, taking millions of Soviet soldiers as prisoners of war (POWs). It is estimated that more than 3 million Red Army troops were deliberately starved to death or otherwise killed as part of the Nazis' 'Hunger Plan' to exterminate the Slavic population and ease German food shortages. The *Einsatzgruppen* followed in the army's wake, seeking out and killing civilians, especially Soviet Jews. Hitler's directives for the invasion included the Commissar Order, which authorized the immediate execution of all captured enemy officers.

While they made territorial gains, German forces also sustained heavy casualties, since the Soviets' numerical advantage and the strength of their resistance proved greater than expected. At the end of August, Hitler ordered – over the protests of his generals – that the drive against Moscow be delayed in favour of focusing on resource-rich Ukraine to the south, which Hitler regarded as more important. By the end of

September, Kiev had fallen. In the north, the Germans managed (with the aid of their Finnish allies) to cut Leningrad off from the rest of Russia, but they weren't strong enough to take the city itself. Instead, Hitler ordered his forces to starve the city into submission, beginning a siege that lasted 872 days.

In early October, Hitler returned his attention to Operation Typhoon, the offensive against Moscow. The month's delay had given the Soviets time to strengthen the defence of their capital with some million troops and a thousand new T-34 tanks. After a successful initial assault, the muddy roads of autumn – known as *Rasputitsa* (quagmire season) – literally stalled the German offensive outside the city, where they had run into the improved Russian defences. In mid-November, Panzer divisions attempted to encircle Moscow, but reinforcements from Siberia helped the Red Army halt the German offensive, just as the brutal winter weather arrived. Soviet forces mounted a surprise counter-attack in early December, forcing the Germans to retreat.

Despite the territorial gains and damage inflicted on the Red Army, Operation Barbarossa was a failure, because it did not force the Russians to capitulate. Though Hitler blamed the winter weather for the failure of the Moscow offensive, the entire operation had suffered from a lack of long-term strategic planning. Counting on a quick victory, the Germans had failed to set up adequate supply lines to deal with the vast distances involved, icy weather and harsh terrain. They had also underestimated the strength of the Soviet resistance, which Stalin skilfully encouraged with his calls to defend Mother Russia. Hitler's Commissar Order and other ruthless behaviour on the part of the Germans also served to harden the Red Army's resolve to fight until the end. Similar mistakes were made the following year, when the Germans launched another offensive that came to grief on the steppe at Stalingrad – a defeat that ultimately changed the course of the war.

## The Waffen-SS

As war approached, most HJ who transitioned into the military joined the Wehrmacht, although there was a smooth flow of recruits going directly into the SS because of the relationship between Himmler and Axmann. However, in 1939, Himmler established the Waffen-SS, the military arm of the *Schutzstaffel*. Recruits were chosen based on a policy of strict racial selection with an emphasis on political indoctrination, particularly involving anti-Semitism. They had to prove Aryan ancestry, be between the ages of 17 and 23, over a certain height, have 20/20 vision and no fillings. With increasing casualty rates from the Eastern Front, the SS and the Wehrmacht suddenly had a rival for the annual delivery of battle-ready HJ. Although the SS normally had the edge in this contest, the Waffen-SS positioned itself as the elite. Both groups earned the resentment of the regular army. Recruitment drives by all three organizations led to a power struggle, which was also common in the Nazi leadership due to Hitler's favoured 'divide and rule' policy.

Following intense combat training, the Waffen-SS fought alongside the regular soldiers in Austria, Czechoslovakia and Poland. As membership increased, they were divided into brigades and then divisions, which included the SS-*Totenkopfverbände* (Death's Head formations) that would eventually get involved in most of the major campaigns of the war as well as in mass shootings, anti-partisan warfare, notably in the Soviet Union, and in supplying guards for the concentration camps. Being elite, soldiers in these divisions were expected to fight to the bitter end. Recruits were left in no doubt that they would be involved in war crimes and that therefore their treatment in captivity or after Germany's defeat would not be like that of the normal soldier. This did not stop almost 20,000 members of the Hitler Youth from signing up in 1940.

Chapter 10

# The home front

As the war progressed, pressure on the German war machine on the home front increased. With soldiers now away fighting on the Eastern and Western fronts, reliance on the HJ intensified. There was little time for training and little point in worrying about whether the youths were affiliated to the *Jungvolk* or the HJ before deciding on their duties. Night-time bombing raids had become a regular feature in Germany's industrial centres, such as Berlin, Hamburg, Dortmund, Leipzig and Essen, and the *Luftwaffenhelfer*, commonly known as *Flakhelfer* (anti-aircraft helpers), were in big demand. In early 1943, it was decided that anti-aircraft batteries were to be manned by HJ aged 15 and upwards. In reality, 13- and 14-year-olds were regularly pressed into service. Although they were still expected to carry on their education while in their flak positions, this was impossible.

The older boys would read the radar signals and man the guns, while the younger ones would operate the searchlights and keep communications open. When enemy aircraft were spotted, sirens would go off. Members of the HJ would then head for the air-raid shelters, open the steel doors and operate the machinery that pumped fresh air into the bunkers. People would rush to black out their windows and head for safety. Once inside the shelters, the HJ and the BDM would offer assistance in the form of food, milk and toys for those who required it. Others would brave the bombs, patrolling the streets to make sure that blackout precautions had been taken, since any light could draw the attention of the bombers above. When enemy planes came within 10 km (6.2 miles), the guns – often 88 mm anti-aircraft cannons – would start firing in an effort to bring them down. It was dangerous work: razor-sharp shrapnel flew through the air as bombs exploded and the batteries were, of course, preferred targets of the Allied aircraft.

Following the all-clear signal there was much work to do. Though most commonly at night and on military targets, Allied bombers also targeted residential areas, civilians, schools, transport infrastructure, even in daylight – anything to undermine the morale of German citizens. It is estimated that 600,000 German civilians were killed in air raids. Almost one-third of all houses were destroyed or damaged beyond repair. Following an air raid, clouds of smoke and ashes filled the air of bombed city streets and fires burned. Margarete Zettel recalled the aftermath of the air raid on Hamburg in June 1943: 'When we came out of the shelter it was just a pure inferno, chaos, an unbelievable storm, it's something you can't really imagine ... The first thing we noticed was this horrible smell, a smell I still have in my nose even today. The neighbouring house was just a pile of rubble. People were buried in it. There was the smell of blood and cement and burning all mixed together – it was horrible, revolting. It took me a long, long time to get over that.'[124]

While the BDM assisted the injured with first aid, handed out food and did their best to find shelter for families whose homes had been destroyed, the HJ had the task of putting out the fires and collecting the bodies of the dead, which were often buried in mass graves. They then got to work clearing the tons of rubble left behind. Looting became a major problem during air raids and was a crime punishable by long prison sentences, and even immediate execution – it is estimated that more than 16,000 Germans were executed for looting between 1938 and 1945.

German youths, both boys and later, girls, born between 1926 and 1929 became known as the 'Flakhelfer generation'. They served for a year or even 18 months before transferring to the Reichsarbeitsdienst and then on to the Wehrmacht. Some 200,000 youngsters from Germany and Eastern Europe served as Flakhelfer, and the death toll was very high, particularly in Berlin.

The success of the KLV programme (see page 173) meant that at any one time some 500,000 youngsters were evacuated to camps in the east. The failure of the German campaign on the Eastern Front and the possibility of a Russian invasion caused rumblings of discontent among the parents of those camped in the border regions. The evacuees, in turn, wondered about the safety of their parents living in cities that sat under the hail of Allied bombing raids. In the summer of 1944, the psychological burden on German adults and children was considerable. In response to the threat of invasion in East Prussia, Hitler Youths were ordered to join local citizens in a massive operation to dig anti-tank barriers. These were, in effect, ditches 5.5 m (18 ft) wide and 4.6 m (15 ft) deep that stretched for miles along Germany's eastern border and were intended to prevent tanks from entering German territory. They toiled ten hours a day, seven days a week in the burning sunshine. At night, they fell asleep in the flickering red light of fire-flashes, which were accompanied by the constant rumbling of the as yet still distant conflict.

## The Final Solution takes shape

Although the Nazis began their official persecution of Jews as soon as Hitler took power in 1933, the process took a while to gain traction. Nazi policies – on education, on the civil service, on medicine, on Jewish-non-Jewish relationships – were gradually formalized by the Nuremberg Laws in 1935. The turning point came in November 1938, when 30,000 Jews were arrested, and their homes and businesses were destroyed on *Kristallnacht*. From then on, Nazi racial policies were revealed in their full horror. A purge of all non-Aryans – Jews, Gypsies, Jehovah's Witnesses, homosexuals, prostitutes, criminals, alcoholics, vagrants, the work-shy, the disabled and the mentally ill, anyone who could dilute the blood of the so-called Aryan Master Race – began. Many were sterilized, many were executed, many were 'euthanized' and many were sent to concentration camps.

In a speech to the Reichstag on 30 January 1939, Hitler said: 'Today I will be once more a prophet: if the international Jewish financiers in and outside Europe should succeed in plunging the nations once more into a world war, then the result will not be the Bolshevizing of the earth, and thus the victory of Jewry, but the annihilation of the Jewish race in Europe!'[125] When the invasion of Poland took place later that year, his prophesy began to come into effect. In each territory conquered, the Jews were isolated, herded and brutally driven into ghettos, where there was little food, infectious diseases and regular executions. As the German army moved east, extermination had become part of the solution, with the SS *Einsatzgruppen* death squads murdering 750,000 Russian and Lithuanian Jews in the first year of the war.

Concentration camps had first been set up in 1933, under the control of the SS, to house political enemies of the new regime. Hitler was particularly impressed with Himmler's work in setting up Dachau, which became the model for the camps that followed. By 1937, only four camps had been built; by 1944, this number had increased to 30 main camps and hundreds of sub-camps. As Greater Germany took shape after 1938, the population of the camps increased exponentially as the Nazis realized the potential of the prisoners as forced labourers to help in the production of construction materials and the building of new German settlements in Poland and the Soviet Union. Camps at Sachsenhausen, Buchenwald and Mauthausen were deliberately constructed near areas with soil suitable for brickmaking, close to brickmaking factories or to stone quarries. Similar reasons saw the construction of the Auschwitz-Birkenau and Lublin-Majdanek camps, made ready to house thousands of Soviet POWs.

## 'Death camps'

At some point in 1941, Hitler had authorized his plan to eliminate all Jews living in German-occupied Europe, some 11 million people. The so-called Final Solution to the Jewish Question was communicated to Nazi officials and the German government by SS General Reinhard

Heydrich at the Wannsee Conference in January 1942. Soon afterwards, Jews from all over Europe were being transported to the camps, particularly those in Poland, some of which were now designated as 'death camps'.

Having witnessed a mass shooting, Heinrich Himmler decided that using guns and bullets in this way was wasting time and money. New ideas were needed. The first was trialled at Chełmno, near Lodz in Poland, in December 1941. After handing over their valuables and clothes, the prisoners were led down a ramp and into the back of a large, panelled truck with room for 50–70 people. The doors were closed and sealed. A tube was attached to the van's exhaust pipe and the engine started, pumping carbon monoxide into the van, so the prisoners were asphyxiated. The van was then driven to the forest and the bodies were dumped in pre-dug graves. Any survivors were shot. Further experiments with static gas chambers took place at Belzec, Sobibór and Treblinka in 1942.

However, the bulk of the killing took place at Auschwitz-Birkenau, 64 km (40 miles) west of Krakow in southern Poland after it was linked into the main railway network. Comprising a labour camp, a concentration camp, large gas chambers and crematoria, and covering some 40 sq km (15.4 sq miles), the Auschwitz complex was the most notorious of the six Nazi extermination camps. Between 1942 and 1944, well over a million Jewish men and women along with Poles, Hungarians, Russians, Gypsies and others were transported in overcrowded cattle trucks with no food or water. Those who survived the journey had their valuables, money, jewellery, clothes, shoes, spectacles and hair taken from them. Many were killed immediately on arrival at the camp, using Zyklon B gas pumped into what the prisoners were told were 'showers'. After death, they had their gold teeth extracted and their bodies were burned in ovens. When the crematoria were at capacity, groups of 500 or fewer were shot in the back of the head and thrown on to a burning pyre, whether they were dead or not. Others were worked in appalling conditions for long hours with little food or water in the war industry. Death was almost certain. Being sent to Auschwitz meant being exploited, beaten, starved, tortured and killed because of their so-called racial origins. It remains the greatest symbol of humanity's cruelty to its fellow human beings in the 20th century.

In 1933, Himmler had appointed Theodor Eicke commandant of Dachau. He was responsible for creating the model for other camps, including a disciplinary code for the treatment of prisoners and a system of camp functionaries, for administration, including roles for prisoners and soldiers. Following the dissolution of the SA in 1934, the SS took control of all the concentration camps. The camp guards, whose duties were to guard the camps and work details, were provided by the SS-*Totenkopfverbände* units, part of the Waffen-SS. They were known for their brutal treatment of prisoners, who were subjected to controlled, disciplined brutality, instilled into members of the unit as a doctrine of 'no pity' by Eicke. The same units were also the main providers (some 34 per cent) of troops for the *Einsatzgruppen* death squads. It seems highly likely that these units were full of former Hitler Youth now old enough to join the SS elite formations. By this time, the Hitler Youth had become an integral part of the Nazi machinery of murder.

## Trying to hide the truth

The Germans had taken steps to keep news of the mass killings and death camps to a minimum. Deceiving victims and the outside world, they used code words to describe mass executions, such as 'special actions', 'resettlements', 'cleansings', 'selections', 'Final Solution' and the sign bearing the words *Arbeit Macht Frei* ('Freedom through work') that greeted those arriving at Auschwitz, to hide their malevolence. The camp administrators used collaborators to do the real dirty work, like the *Sonderkommandos* – Jews who cleared out the gas chamber victims and the crematoria. Some were forced to do so, others chose to in return for extra rations, alcohol and three or four months of extra life, before being executed so they could not tell tales. They also used the *Judenrats*, Jewish councils who administered the ghettos, in an effort to equate the oppressed with the oppressors, jointly involving both sides in evil endeavour.

The mass killings, which reached a peak in 1941 when 1.5 million people were executed – including 33,000 Jews from Kiev shot at the ravine in Babi Yar in the Ukraine – and the estimated 2.7 million, mostly Jews, killed in the extermination camps were not without consequences. Many of the Nazi leaders had little or no moral compunction with these actions, believing them to be the Final Solution of the Jewish Question. For example, SS-*Oberscharführer* Muhsfeldt shot 80 sick prisoners in the head one evening at Auschwitz before ordering that their bodies be burned. Later that night he reported to the camp doctor complaining of an erratic heartbeat and a headache. The doctor, who had witnessed the killings from his window, could find nothing wrong apart from a slightly raised pulse, suggested that his actions earlier might have been the reason for his symptoms. 'Your diagnosis is wrong,' shouted Muhsfeldt, 'It is of no concern to me if I shoot eighty or a thousand people. It doesn't upset me in the slightest. Do you know why I am so nervous? It is because I drink too much!'[126] Of course, many of the worse jobs were forced on collaborators, but there were huge psychological problems for the soldiers who carried out the executions: some became openly sadistic, others were unable to stop crying; some suffered breakdowns and others became deranged and shot at their own comrades.

Of course, the Nazis could not hide the truth. News travelled, often via civilians who lived near one of the camps or via soldiers' gossip. There was much talk in Germany, too, though, as the writer Primo Levi, a Holocaust survivor, suggested, many Germans were suffering from 'intentional ignorance' at the time. Not for much longer. In the last months of the war, as the Nazi empire began to collapse, Allied troops arrived in Poland and then Germany. The liberations of the camps began when the Red Army reached Auschwitz in January 1945. The first camp liberated on the Western Front, in April, was a sub-camp at Buchenwald, where General Eisenhower ordered that a film record be taken of what they found to prove to those in the future that those things had really happened. When American troops arrived at Dachau, they were so horrified by what they found that they dispensed summary justice by shooting almost all of the 500 SS guards still in the camp. Allied soldiers made a practice of forcing local townspeople and members of Hitler Youth groups to view the carnage and help in burying the corpses. In towns and cities all over Germany, people were forced to watch documentary footage of what the Allied soldiers had encountered.

## The ordinary actions of ordinary people

Though the first Nuremberg Trials began in November 1945, they only dispensed justice on the Nazi leadership. The crimes of the estimated 8 million 'ordinary' rank-and-file Nazis, such as camp guards, took much longer. Indeed, many escaped justice altogether. Within a few years of the end of the war, at least 36,000 cases against Nazi underlings, including 300 Auschwitz staff, were dropped, as the Americans turned their attention to the new communist threat. In 1949, responsibility for these prosecutions was taken over by the newly partitioned Germany. In both East and West Germany, lawyers struggled. In 1954, West Germany decided to pursue these crimes under the German penal code, thus treating deaths in the Holocaust like any other murder. There were further trials in the 1960s but only 17 Auschwitz personnel of the estimated 6,000 or 7,000 who survived the war were found guilty and only six were given life sentences.

In 2011, a new legal strategy was adopted arguing that anyone who served in one of the death camps could be held responsible as part of a killing machine. This resulted in the successful prosecution of the Ukrainian camp guard John Demjanjuk as an accessory to 28,060 murders at Sobibór. In 2015, former SS officer Oskar Gröning, who had served in the Hitler Youth and the Waffen-SS before his posting to Auschwitz in September 1942, was accused of being an accessory to the murders of 300,000 Jews. His job at the camp was to itemize money and valuables taken from new arrivals at the death camp. Recently released figures have calculated that by February 1943, the value of these items, including at least 5.5 tonnes (6 tons) of gold teeth, were in the region of 326 million Reichsmarks, the equivalent of $2 billion in US currency of the early 2020s. Denying any personal involvement in the genocide, but admitting he had seen mass killings, he asked for forgiveness and accepted his share of moral guilt. He was sentenced to four years' imprisonment but died, aged 96, before his sentence began.

There was much debate in Germany about the point of this and other recent trials of Nazis in their 90s. Perhaps their real value lies in the way they show that the Holocaust was the product not of a conspiracy of extraordinarily cruel individuals, but rather the ordinary actions of ordinary people. 'They remind us that this genocide would never have taken place without these lowly foot soldiers,' said Amherst historian Lawrence Douglas. 'Things can go wrong in a hurry in countries, and when they do, it is shocking how willing people are to go along with it.'

## Formation of the 12th SS Panzer Division

In a speech at the Berlin Sportpalast a few days after Germany's catastrophic war-changing defeat at Stalingrad in early 1943, Joseph Goebbels called for 'total war'. In May that year, German strongholds in North Africa fell to the Allies, in July they were defeated by the Red Army at the Battle of Kursk, and in September the Allies invaded Italy. Whether he genuinely believed that this all-out sacrifice of both military and civilian lives and resources would turn Germany's fortunes around or that it was a last desperate attempt to prop up the ailing Third Reich is debatable. But the German campaign was in desperate need of a new impetus. Stalingrad had cost a total of some half-million German soldiers, including 91,000 taken prisoner. In order to mitigate this huge loss of manpower, the SS mounted another recruitment drive, aimed at members of the HJ born in 1926, with the specific purpose of creating a special division within the Waffen-SS – an idea first suggested to Himmler by Artur Axmann. German youth, galvanized by Goebbels' call, responded in their thousands. The recruiters were helped by the lowering of the age of military service from 18 to 17, though boys of 16 and under were also signed up. The Führer's wish was for the new division to 'exemplify the brand of sacrifice and fighting spirit that "total war" would require.'[127]

The formal order to set up the new division was issued in June and was to be under the command of 34-year-old Franz Witt and 33-year-old Kurt Meyer, both SS *Brigadeführer* in the Waffen-SS. In July and August some 10,000 recruits travelled from the divisional base in Kaiserslautern to Beverloo in Belgium for basic training from officers and NCOs recruited from the Eastern Front. There was little need for square bashing and endless drills; the qualities of the recruits were impressive despite their youth. In fact, it was often the officers who needed training, particularly in explaining the reasons behind their orders, which would help the young recruits understand why these orders should be obeyed. The parade ground was forgotten as exercises took place on a realistic war footing with live ammunition. Time was short. The only bone of contention seemed to be that boys under the age of 18 received a sweet ration rather than the usual cigarettes!

In October, the division was officially named the 12th SS Panzer Division *Hitlerjugend*, by far the youngest unit in the German armed forces. It was reorganized into one Panzer, one artillery and two infantry regiments and an engineer battalion, each with its own recon detachment

*A Panzer tank and combat-ready crew belonging to the 12th SS Panzer Division en route for Caen in early June 1944.*

*Despite establishing a reputation for fierce fighting as a result of their bravery in action in Caen and the Falaise Pocket, within 11 months the division had lost 10,000 men killed and taken prisoner when they surrendered to US forces.*

and anti-tank, anti-aircraft and signalling sections. Training, which continued day and night in all terrains and all weathers for six months, included long marches with heavy packs, digging foxholes, crawling, running with fixed bayonets, clearing mines and attacking infantry positions and armoured vehicles. Individual training turned into unit training, then company-, battalion- and regimental-level training to foster team spirit. 'Each Waffen SS soldier was trained to take over from his superior if that person was wounded or killed, to assume his mantle and carry on with fulfilling the mission.'[128] In spite of organizational difficulties and a shortage of materials and weaponry, the 20,540 boy soldiers were ordered to move from Flanders to Normandy in France in April in advance of the expected Allied landings. Juiced up from years of indoctrination, from brutal training, from fear of what was happening to their families back home under the constant Allied bombing and in anticipation of what was to come, the youngsters' first action was to execute local civilians in reprisal after the railway line their train was travelling on was blown up at Ascq in northern France. Altogether 70 men who lived in the houses on both sides of the track were summarily executed, and another 16 men from the village were also shot. Further investigations by the Gestapo led to six more executions by firing squad.

## Kill or be killed

The division was deemed to be combat-ready by 1 June 1944 and it was in the forefront of German defensive operations at Caen on 7 June, the day after D-Day. The young troops did not disappoint. A British tank commander recalled that they fought 'like wolves' with a tenacity and ferocity not seen in battles with the Wehrmacht troops. They pushed the Allied troops back to the Sword and Juno beaches. But their own advance was severely hampered, by Allied air attacks, from which they had little defence, and by faulty intelligence, which meant that they were spread out more widely than necessary. That evening, 11 Canadian

POWs were executed in the gardens of the Ardennes Abbey. At the end of the war, it was discovered that these scattered killings, by then known as the Normandy Massacres, were just a part of 156 killings of POWs carried out by the Germans during this battle.

Despite setbacks and casualties, the 12th SS Panzer Division counter-attacked the following day near the abbey. The 'Baby Division', as they were by now nicknamed by the Canadian troops they faced, fought ferociously and again forced the enemy to retreat despite facing more bomber attacks, big guns and tank shells. The fighting continued, with the Germans holding Caen but the Allies in control of Bayeux and aiming to capture Rots, where tank battles continued night and day. It was here that the Hitler Youth battalion cemented its reputation for battle madness despite being outnumbered and at the mercy of anti-tank guns and long-range fire from Royal Navy warships in the English Channel.

On 16 June, the commander, Franz Witt, was killed by flying shrapnel and replaced by Kurt Meyer, whose combat style had already earned him several medals for bravery and the nickname 'Panzermeyer'. Whether the young soldiers were brave or foolhardy is summed up by the story of SS-*Unterscharführer* Emil Dürr. On 26 June, holding a position outside the village of St-Manvieu-Norrey, the division was attacked by Sherman tanks, including a Crocodile flamethrower tank that positioned itself in front of the German command post. Responding to the order, 'That tank has to go,' Dürr grabbed a *Panzerfaust* and slipped over a wall before running towards the tank. He fired but did not pierce the armour. Shot in the chest, he ran back over the wall, grabbed another *Panzerfaust* and ran back towards the tank. Too far away to damage the tank shell, he aimed for the wheel track. A hit immobilized the vehicle, but it was not destroyed. Again he was hit by machine-gun fire but managed to crawl back to his position. This time he grabbed a *Panzerknacker*, a magnetic anti-tank grenade, before heading over the wall for a third time, still bleeding from his wounds. He attached the grenade to the tank, but it fell off as he turned to run. He turned back, picked up the explosive and held it in place until it exploded and destroyed the vehicle. By now seriously wounded, he made it back to the command post, where he died four hours later. Emil Dürr was later awarded the Knight's Cross, the highest grade of the Iron Cross.[129]

Despite heroics like these, Caen fell to the Allies in early July. The exhausted troops were removed from the field and rested for a few days. There were no new tanks or weapons, but the repair and supply units restored tanks and other vehicles and were able to provide ammunition and petrol. During August, the division saw action in the Falaise Pocket, an area south of Caen in which the retreating German army were trapped. An estimated 100,000 soldiers were surrounded by the Canadian, British, US and Polish armies. The 12th SS Panzers were tasked to punch their way through the Polish troops to the south-west and open up an escape route. The young troops fought like madmen. According to a Canadian unit's war diary, 'few prisoners were taken; the enemy preferred to die rather than give in.'[130]

Losses on both sides were huge in the bitter seven-day battle, which ended when the Allies sealed the pocket on 21 August with 50,000 German troops inside. However, the actions of the division had allowed some 40,000 soldiers to escape.

Now severely reduced in terms of numbers, the remaining *Hitlerjugend* troops continued their retreat. After 12 weeks in the field, the division had lost almost all of its tanks, 70 per cent of its armoured vehicles, 60 per cent of its artillery, 50 per cent of its motor vehicles and half the division's men – lost, killed, wounded or missing – including Kurt Meyer, who had been arrested by a Belgian policeman and handed over to the Americans. They reached Germany on 8 September for a major programme of rearming, refitting and the replacement of personnel.

# Chapter 11

# Reality and Resistance

In his memoir, *If This is a Man*, Primo Levi describes his arrival at Auschwitz in February 1944. After having the number 174517 tattooed on his left forearm, he and his fellow Italian deportees were locked up in an empty barrack. 'Driven by thirst, I eyed a fine icicle outside the window, within reach of my hand,' Levi writes. 'I opened the window and broke off the icicle, but at once a large, heavy guard prowling outside brutally snatched it away. "*Warum?*" [Why?] I asked in my poor German. "*Hier ist kein warum*" [Here there is no why], he replied, shoving me back inside.'[131]

## Warum?

It is easy to believe that Hitler and the Nazi regime had it all its own way, particularly during the early years – the era dubbed *Gleichschaltung* in which they set out to reform all aspects of German society – when early histories implied that they functioned as a 'well-organized, highly efficient, top down government.'[132] Traditional histories of the Third Reich point out that there was little in the way of resistance from the German people following Hitler's election victory in 1933.

And whatever opposition there was had little practical effect on the totalitarian National Socialist regime. However, more recent histories take a different view. Although many Germans did support the Nazi programme, many tolerated it, many hated it and some resisted it and even posed the same question: 'Why?'; 'Why do German people behave so apathetically in the face of all these abominable crimes, crimes so unworthy of the human race?', '… why do you not bestir yourselves, why do you allow these men who are in power to rob you step by step, openly and in secret, of one domain of your rights after another, until one day nothing, nothing at all will be left but a mechanized state system presided over by criminals and drunks?'[133] Interestingly, these histories also suggest that by looking at the youth – in this case the Hitler Youth – one can gain a greater understanding of how the Nazis succeeded in obtaining power. In fact, the same can be said about the resisters, particularly those youngsters who did not conform to draconian rules, who proved that the 100 per cent control over German life the Nazis craved could never be achieved. Because of their brave actions, which often ended in torture and death, it seems high time to add another category to the traditional division of German people during the war years as perpetrators, victims, bystanders and now resisters.

## The illusion of democracy

As we have already seen (*see* chapter 4), in terms of elections and plebiscites, the popularity of the Nazis had been artificially boosted. In March 1933, for example, they failed to get the majority vote that Hitler had expected and the passage of the Enabling Act was neither free nor fair and only possible because of the arrest of Communist and Social Democrat MPs who were imprisoned until after the vote had been held. The votes on Hitler's appointment as head of state in 1934 and on the union with Austria four years later took place in an atmosphere of violence and intimidation. Stormtroopers roamed the streets on polling day rounding up the voters and making it absolutely clear which way they should vote. In some places, voting took place in the open air in full view of the intimidating brownshirts, while in others, booths were labelled 'only traitors enter here'. There were also reports of people collecting their voting slips with the 'yes' vote already filled in, 'no' votes thrown away and replaced by 'yes' votes, and spoiled papers going into the 'yes' boxes for counting. The 1938 vote on Austria was even coupled with a vote of confidence in Hitler. A 'no' note therefore would mean committing treason under newly passed Treason Laws.

There is other evidence, too, from the ballot box. Between 1928 and 1932, the German economy imploded as a consequence of the Great Depression, and more than a quarter of gross national product was lost. Unemployment began to rise, and thousands of businesses faced bankruptcy. In these circumstances, the voters of any country would want to get rid of the ruling parties. To improve their popularity, the Nazis focused on job creation in industry and agriculture, land reclamation, and road and house building. Their tactics worked but were not as effective as they'd hoped even in these parlous circumstances. Their vote peaked at 43.9 per cent (17.2 million votes) in March 1933.

A survey of elderly Germans, conducted in the 1990s, is equally revealing.[134] Of those asked three questions – whether they believed in National Socialism, whether they admired Hitler and whether they shared Nazi ideals – only 18 per cent answered yes to all three and 31 per cent said yes to two of the questions. Although the survey was conducted so long after the events, the questions were put to people born between 1910 and 1928. As such, they were members of the so-called Nazi Youth generation – those most influenced by the Nazi propaganda campaigns – and the results were hardly reflective of a political regime supposedly swept in on a tidal wave of popularity. However, the popularity of the Nazis was bolstered by other factors, enabling them to maintain the illusion of democracy.

## Propaganda and fear of violence

In reality, government in Germany during the Third Reich was chaotic and confusing. Hitler showed little interest in actual government; one of his personal staff said that, 'He disliked the study of documents [and] … took the view that many things sorted themselves out on their own if one did not interfere.'[135] Nonetheless, he was in charge. According to his biographer, Ian Kershaw, '… he set the tone for the regime, made his wishes known, and then allowed those below him in the hierarchy to create policy and make decisions in line with what they interpreted to be Hitler's wishes.'[136] If this is the case, then clearly Hitler was cautious during the early months of his leadership, perhaps because his party had not secured the desired majority. Goebbels too addressed the issue in his speech to the press after the announcement of the new Reich Ministry for Popular Enlightenment and Propaganda on 15 March 1933. Famous for painting things in a favourable light, he said: 'If this government is determined never and under no circumstances to give way, then it has no need of the lifeless power of the bayonet, and in the long run will not be content with 52 per cent behind it [only achieved because of a coalition with the German National People's Party (DNVP)] and with terrorizing the remaining 48 per cent, but will see its most immediate task as being to win over that remaining 48 per cent.'[137]

Of course, politics then was similar to politics today: some people were interested, and others were not. Politics had been high on the agenda in Germany following the First World War but had settled down during the more stable era of the Weimar government. However, the catalyst for change came with the Great Depression. Once in power, they used propaganda to push the policies they knew would meet with approval through slogans such as 'Bread and Work' and posters depicting 'Mother and Child' perfection. They also offered protection from communism, protection for businesses from the trade unions, and strong authoritarian leadership. Perhaps most importantly, Hitler pointed his finger at those who were to blame for Germany's parlous state: the Weimar government who had agreed to the ruinous terms of the Treaty of Versailles, the Communists who were trying to take over the country, and the Jews.

A campaign of violence and intimidation began in the big cities soon after the election 'victory' of March 1933, but the Nazis chose their targets carefully – a combination of factors aimed at creating a climate of fear while gaining favour among those who had not voted for them, such as the middle classes. Serious violence was used by SA thugs on communists, Social Democrats, trade unionists, the working classes and Jews who were stripped, beaten, horsewhipped, tortured, publicly humiliated and murdered. At least 100,000 Germans were arrested and detained without trial at specially built camps at Dachau, Moringen and elsewhere. Actions against those less opposed to the new regime, such as Catholics, nationalists and conservatives, were taken when necessary but were less severe. Nevertheless, their actions were effective. 'Violence ... during the early months of 1933, was used deliberately and openly to intimidate opposition and potential opposition. It was used to create a public sphere permeated by violence and it provided a ready reminder of what might be in store for *anyone* who stepped out of line, who failed to show loyalty to the new order.'[138] The following year, it became clear to the Nazi leadership that the SA, which had grown in membership to 3 million, was out of control. There were complaints too from conservatives and members of the public. Aware that the Nazis needed to appear moderate and democratic in order to maintain the illusion of democracy, they acted quickly. On 30 June 1944, most of the leadership of the SA, including its leader Ernst Röhm, were murdered and the organization decimated. The 'Night of the Long Knives', as it became known, was hugely popular and welcomed by the middle-class citizens, who had so far been afraid of the violence, but saw this as a move towards law and order.

## Painting a picture

As well as being a useful tool in pushing forward the parts of the Nazis' radical programme that required the acquiescence of the German population, this move was also essential in manipulating and deceiving the people and the outside world over their true ideological goals of genocide, invasion, war and eventual world domination. Having crushed any political dissent, they painted a picture of a new, united German nation. They played on the public's hopes, fears and prejudices. They rearmed the military, carefully portraying Germany as a victim of the Treaty of Versailles, thereby portraying it as an act of self defence against communism rather than revealing their real aims of territorial expansion and racial warfare.

They exerted control over all areas of mass communication – newspapers, radio, film, newsreels, theatres and music. They published more newspapers than any other nation in Europe, banning most of those that opposed them. In January 1933, radio ownership in Germany was on the increase. Realizing the potential this offered, Goebbels declared in March that year: 'We make no secret of it: broadcasting belongs to us, no one else! And we will place broadcasting in the service of our ideas, and no other idea will be given a chance to speak.' The Nazis then helped in the design and production of the *Volksempfänger* (people's receiver), which only broadcast German programmes, thus preventing German citizens from hearing news from elsewhere. Propaganda and most importantly Hitler's speeches were therefore heard in homes, factories and even in the streets of German towns and cities.

Films too were used as a tool for Nazi propaganda, with Germany becoming Europe's largest film producer in the 1930s. Many were films with a political message, such as Leni Riefenstahl's *The Triumph of the Will* and the hugely successful *Olympia*, a two-film package covering the 1936 Summer Olympics in Berlin. But Goebbels was aware that other, less political films, were also needed to get audiences into the cinemas.

Once there, they would watch the main feature but also get the news from newsreels. The output of Germany's four independent newsreel companies was heavily censored, and the news was presented with loud triumphant military music and biased reporting. Nazi successes were reported widely, portraying the new regime as one of action and change that was restoring national self-confidence and traditional German moral values and forging a true national community, *die Volksgemeinschaft*.

## Much said, much unsaid

But whatever was said, much was unsaid. Although anti-Semitism was a central part of Nazi ideology, there had been a long history of it among Catholic and Protestant Europe, for example, in Germany, Poland, Russia and elsewhere. When Hitler came to power in 1933, there were more Jews in Germany that in any other country in Western Europe, albeit comprising less than 1 per cent of the population. Severe economic hardship and the fact that Jews had been big supporters of the Weimar Republic meant they were easy pickings for the new regime. Added to this, there were advantages to be gained from Jewish misfortune. For example, medical students were pleased at the diminished competition for future employment when Jewish students were banned from studying in 1933. As Jews began to be deported to purpose-built ghettos, tens of thousands of properties were made available to German families, often at discount prices.

Action against those not included in the *Volksgemeinschaft* began immediately, some of it conducted in public but much of it out of the public eye. Political opponents of the regime were dealt with in the full glare of publicity, as were those regarded as 'anti-social elements', such as tramps, Gypsies, Jehovah's Witnesses, homosexuals and career criminals, all of whom were rounded up and sent to the newly opened concentration camps. Few people cared about them, and many were pleased to hear of their treatment. The Nazis were more sensitive about their treatment of the Jews. Although they had made their anti-Semitic position clear, they were right to be cautious; a Nazi-organized boycott of Jewish businesses arranged for 1 April 1933 was a disaster, lasting only a day and ignored by the German public. However, the deportations that followed marked the beginning of a concerted nationwide campaign against Jews that would culminate in the Holocaust.

In time, Nazi policies grew more radical. Gradually, Germany was transformed into a police state, administered by coercion, by the newly formed *Geheime Staatspolizei* (the Secret State Police or Gestapo), by the *Kriminalpolizei* (the Criminal Police or Kripo) and backed up by an ever-increasing series of new laws designed to punish the regime's opponents and do away with opposition and dissent. Laws against Jews grew increasingly repressive as Nazi propaganda began to make anti-Semitism acceptable. First, Jews were not allowed to hold public office, anti-Semitic 'race science' began to be taught in schools and then, with the passage of the Nuremberg Laws starting in 1935, which effectively stripped Jews of their rights as Germans, they were no longer allowed to work, marry, have children and – ultimately – live.

## Unspoken truths

Other laws attacked civil liberties and treason laws were expanded. Transgressors was liable to serious punishment, including imprisonment without trial and the death penalty. Malicious gossip was made illegal, membership of all non-Nazi organizations, apart from the Catholic and Protestant churches, were illegal, and it was even illegal to make jokes about Hitler. The authorities were given sweeping powers, to open personal letters and tap telephones, to have political opponents sacked, to throw people out of their homes. On the streets, the block wardens poked their noses into everyone's business and kept a close watch for illegal or subversive activities, as did the Hitler Youth leaders. The presence of these 'representatives' of the authorities and the possibilities of denunciation to agencies of state like the Gestapo led to a serious reduction in social intercourse.

The Nazis took great care to keep policies and actions they knew would be unpopular as confidential as possible. They introduced one such action in July 1933, passing the Law for the Prevention of Progeny with Hereditary Diseases, which called for the sterilization of everyone who suffered from what were considered hereditary diseases: including learning disabilities, physical deformity, mental illness, blindness, deafness, epilepsy and severe alcoholism. It was the first step in their quest towards the creation of the Aryan Master Race, ridding it of what they called 'useless eaters' or 'life unworthy of life'. A propaganda campaign followed, using posters and newsreels to attempt to convince the public that these people were a burden on society and even arranging school trips to mental hospitals to show youngsters that the patients were a waste of government money.

Such persecution went further in 1939, under cover of war. Hitler authorized a medically administered euthanasia programme, code-named *Aktion-T4*, after the headquarters of the programme's headquarters at Tiergartenstrasse 4 in Berlin. It was a top-secret operation; not even the victims' relatives were told. Six hospitals across Germany were selected as killing centres. At first, patients were killed by lethal injection or shot. Bodies and belongings were then burned in crematoria and fake death certificates were issued to the relatives. Later, mobile gas vans were used before they were replaced by shower rooms converted to gas chambers.

When stories about these murders began to go public in 1941, rumours that other 'unfit' groups, such as the elderly, wounded soldiers or workers, could be next prompted the Catholic Church to lobby for the action to end. Bowing to pressure, Hitler formally ordered an end to the practice in August that year. However, the killings continued in secret. By the war's end, it is estimated that almost 300,000 people with disabilities had been murdered.

## The great denial

Of course, the greatest denial, a State Secret in Nazi Germany, was the so-called Final Solution to what they called the Jewish Question. The appalling treatment of German Jews began in earnest during *Kristallnacht*, and continued with their segregation into ghettos and then to thousands of camps and other detention sites established across German-occupied Europe. At a secret meeting of senior government officials at Wannsee in Berlin in January 1942, the Nazis developed and launched their plan. Nothing was to be written down; killing orders were to be verbal and on a need-to-know basis only. Any documentation was to be destroyed. No one was to speak about it in public, even in private. Code names and neutral-sounding terms were to be used to describe what is now known to have been mass murder. These euphemisms did much to impede a clear understanding of what the Nazis were doing.

On the battlefields of Eastern Europe, death squads began a campaign of mass shootings and pogroms against Jews, eventually killing some 1.5 million. For the killing of other Jews, death camps were set up outside Germany. Deportations from the ghettos began immediately as thousands of victims were transported to the camps in sealed freight trains, where they were to be gassed, worked or beaten to death, killed by starvation, disease, medical experiments or on death marches. Fearing Jewish resistance if they knew what was really happening, victims were left ignorant of their fate. They wanted to believe that they were being taken for resettlement and so took their valuables with them. They had heard rumours, but they had no real evidence and so went almost willingly.

The bodies of the dead were then burned in huge crematoria by the *Sonderkommandos*. They also cleared the charred remains, which they buried in pits. For their trouble, they lived a few more months than the other inmates before being shot to keep their terrible secrets. There were plenty of others who were forced, or were sometimes willing, to take their places. It is interesting to note that, despite stories of the horrors of the death camps that leaked out, many Germans claimed they had no idea of the functions of these camps.

## Passive resisters

The Nazis clearly failed in their attempt to gain the level of control over the German people that they wanted. As we have seen, they did not get a majority at the ballot box. In the election on 5 March 1933, they received 17,277,180 votes from a total of 44,685,764 voters. Still, they took power and changed the rules, doing away with democracy. But, despite all their efforts, the existence of resisters, both passive and active, provides evidence that German society was never fully indoctrinated by Nazi ideology. This was true even among the youth – without doubt some of the deepest believers, having had little chance to form their own values and beliefs after growing up subject to an unremitting campaign of propaganda and indoctrination at school, in the Hitler Youth and through the media.

As Nazi policies became ever more extreme and the likelihood of war became more certain, resisters from all walks of life began to make their stand. Some acts of 'everyday resistance' were carried out by normal civilians. These may simply have been a refusal to say 'Heil Hitler' or to donate to the Nazi Party, but often it would take the form of absenteeism, malingering, spreading rumours, hoarding and trading on the black market and possibly even telling jokes. Jokes about the Nazis were banned, though some were tolerated. However, others could earn the teller the death sentence. For example, 'What do you get for a new joke? ... Six months in Dachau' might have been art imitating life, but the joke 'Hitler and Göring are standing on top of Berlin's radio tower. Hitler says he wants to do something to cheer up the people of Berlin ... "Why don't you just jump?" suggests Göring', led to the execution of munitions worker Marianne Elise K in 1944. Even so, and even in

Nazi Germany, the power of humour occasionally shone light in the darkness, for example in the description of the Aryan type as 'blond like Hitler, slim like Göring and beautiful like Goebbels'.

There were other, more serious acts of resistance. For example, some factory workers ensured that the explosive shells they made wouldn't work or the piston rings on the truck engines they assembled would crack, screws wouldn't fit, and so on. But these small acts of heroism, the discovery of which would have led to death by shooting, did not present a united front and were of little concern to the authorities.

## Organized resistance

There was more organized resistance from opposing political parties such as the Communists, Social Democrats and even the unions who publicly criticized the Nazis, through leaflets, meetings and collecting money for the relatives of imprisoned party members. However, once again they had little effect on the authorities. After 1939, attempts were made to join these workers' movements together, with groups such as New Beginnings, the Red Shock Troops and the Red Fighters organizing and discussing plans for the time to follow National Socialist rule. A number of Catholic priests opposed and spoke out against Hitler. The most vocal was Archbishop van Galen of Münster, who criticized the concentration camps, the deportation of the Jews, and the Gestapo, and voiced public criticism of the Nazis' euthanasia programme for the disabled. Some Protestant churches were absorbed into the Nazi Reich Church but even among Protestant pastors there was dissent. Dachau had a separate barracks specifically for clergy and kept both Catholics and Protestants along with Evangelical, Greek Orthodox, Old Catholics and Islamic clerics behind its fences.

The Night of the Long Knives had been shocking for many Germans minded to oppose the Nazis but it had little effect on the youths who had grown up in the full glare of Nazism. With membership of the Hitler

Youth made compulsory in December 1936, most were keen to take advantage of the opportunities offered, but some were not interested. Gangs of anti-authority youths had always existed in Germany, but the repressive authority of the Nazis and the growing presence of the Hitler Youth saw a rise in this kind of activity. In the south there were the *Blauen* (blues), a gang of lower-middle class petty criminals. In Munich, the *Blasen* (bubbles) were more politically motivated and committed acts of sabotage. Also politically motivated and taken particularly seriously by the authorities were the *Meuten* (mobs) who formed in Leipzig in 1937, around the time that military conscription was at its peak. They were made up of disaffected youths from former communist neighbourhoods whose main aim was to beat up the 'prigs and snobs' in the Hitler Youth.

*Strongly rejecting the authoritarian nature of the Nazi regime, groups like the Edelweiss Pirates took time and space to be themselves. Of course, this was a criminal act in Nazi Germany. Although apolitical, as the war progressed their activities grew bolder, in the end with deadly consequences.*

In Vienna, the *Schlurfe* (slouches) grew their hair long and wore Teddy Boy-style long jackets and thin ties. They carried knives and knuckle dusters and would hang around the Prater looking for members of the HJ to confront. Other gangs of hostile young working-class men made up the *Edelweisspiraten* (Edelweiss Pirates) group formed in the west, Cologne, Düsseldorf and the Ruhr. They met in cafes and pubs, dressed in checked shirts, red scarves and old hats and were identifiable by their skull-and-crossbones signet rings. The various groups had flamboyant names, such as the 'Kittelbach Pirates', the 'Navajos' and the 'Roving Dudes'. They had a firm hatred towards Nazi rule in general but in particular to how the Hitler Youth had taken over the lives of German youths.

## Pirates and Swingers

At first, the Pirates' activities were pretty harmless – hanging around in the streets and parks and creating their own social spaces to chat and mess about. At weekends, they went hiking and camping, boys and girls together. They'd often meet up with groups from other towns and cities. Inevitably, they'd have encounters with the HJ and fights would start. The Pirates gained a reputation for violence. When the Allied bombing campaign started and blackouts were organized by the HJ, Pirate groups would meet up and ambush them, handing out severe beatings when they could.

As the war progressed, the Pirates grew bolder. They carried out acts of sabotage, such as pouring sugar water into the petrol tanks of Nazi vehicles, and they began to help Jews, army deserters and POWs. They also painted anti-Nazi slogans in public places, posted Allied propaganda leaflets in people's letterboxes, looted Nazi warehouses, derailed freight trains and began to steal and distribute ration cards. The authorities did arrest and punish some members of these groups by shaving their heads, beating them up, torturing them or giving them long prison sentences, but others avoided censure by joining the Wehrmacht when they turned 18. In 1944, however, they raided an army camp in Cologne, stealing arms and explosives for a planned bombing raid on the local Gestapo headquarters. During the raid, a guard and a local Nazi leader were killed. Himmler ordered that the group be rounded up. On 10 November, 13 boys and men, including six Pirates, were publicly hanged for their actions.

Objecting to Nazi conformity in a completely different way were the *Swingjugend* (Swing Youth), who used their love of American swing music as their symbol of rebellion. Formed among upper-middle-class youths in Hamburg in 1939, their extravagant dress, louche behaviour, drinking, loose sexual morals and love of 'negro' music were seen as 'dangerous anglophile tendencies'. The products of rich families, they spoke English and could afford clothes, records and boozy club nights. They had no interest in politics or the Nazis, instead looking westwards for their models of behaviour and individual freedoms. They hid in plain sight, drinking in bars and clubs in their long suits and narrow trousers, or short skirts and black stockings. As a result, they were easy prey for HJ and the police despite offering no threat to the authorities. When the war began, police action against them increased and there were sporadic outbreaks of violence on both sides. Most revealing, however, was that the Nazis were horrified to discover that many of those arrested were actually members of the Hitler Youth. Other middle-class groups existed too; even the old *Wandervögel* movement was revived by former members seeking escape from the repressive regime, which in turn was forced to reiterate its *Gleichschaltung* ban on youth groups in 1936, 1937 and 1939.

## Operation Valkyrie

The most famous dissident groups, however, were the White Rose and the Kreisau Circle. The *Kreisauer Kreis* – formed in 1940 and named after a rural town in Silesia where the group held its meetings – comprised some 20 members, consisting of aristocrats, intellectuals, Protestants, Catholics, military personnel and politicians. They were united in their opposition to Hitler's regime on moral and religious grounds. Convinced that Hitler would lose the war, they planned how they would reorganize the German government following this defeat – aiming to create a society that was democratic, anti-racist and internationalist.

In January 1944, the group's leader, Helmuth James von Moltke, a member of one of Prussia's best-known military families, was arrested and imprisoned by the Gestapo. His crime was one of association with a friend who had been seen at an anti-Nazi salon in Berlin the previous year.

On 20 July that year, Hitler, Himmler, Göring and other senior military officers met at the so-called *Wolfsschanze* (Wolf's Lair) field HQ in Rastenburg, East Prussia, to discuss actions on the Eastern Front. As the meeting began, a huge explosion ripped through the room. The bomb had been placed there by a young German army colonel, Claus von Stauffenberg, as the final act of a conspiracy to kill Hitler. Although he was one of 20 people injured, the Führer survived. A stenographer was killed instantly, and three Nazi officers died later from their wounds. Although Stauffenberg and his aide Werner von Haeften escaped the building and returned to Berlin, he and other conspirators were arrested later that day, tried and executed by firing squad. Investigations revealed the huge scale of Operation Valkyrie, as it was known. Some 7,000 people were arrested in connection with it and nearly 5,000 of them were executed. One of those was Von Moltke, head of the Kreisau Circle, implicated because his cousin, Peter Yorck von Wartenburg, was heavily involved in the plot. Although the assassination attempt failed, it was clear that many people from all walks of German life could see that Hitler's plans were on the point of failure.

# The White Rose

The most affecting story of resistance to the Nazis comes from the most surprising place: a group of ordinary young Germans from a village in Baden-Württemberg, teenagers in the 1930s, enthusiastic members of the Hitler Youth and among those millions who believed that Hitler was leading Germany back to its former glory. However, Hans Scholl and his sister Sophie quickly became disillusioned with Nazi thinking. Hans, three years older than Sophie, was studying medicine at Munich University when war broke out in 1939 and was already involved in producing anti-Nazi literature for the students. Sophie joined him in Munich in 1942, intent on studying biology and philosophy. She met Hans' friends, Christoph Probst, Alexander Schmorell, Willi Graf and their psychology and philosophy professor Kurt Huber. In June 1942, a leaflet entitled 'The White Rose' started doing the rounds of the university. It began: 'Nothing is so unworthy of a civilized nation as allowing itself to be governed without opposition by an irresponsible clique that has yielded to base instinct. It is certain that today every honest German is ashamed of his government?' and called on civilized Germans to rise up 'for the hubris of a sub-human'. The leaflet, secretly written, printed and distributed by Hans, Sophie and their friends, caused a stir among the students. It was soon followed by others, four under the title 'The White Rose' and two labelled 'Leaflets of the Resistance', each essay pointing out the corruption and despotism of the Nazi regime. They addressed the repression of the regime, its racist policies, the euthanasia programme, the atrocities of the *Einsatzgruppen* in Russia and the ugly truth about the death camps.

The friends had to work in the utmost secrecy; they knew what would happen to them if they were caught. The Gestapo grew increasingly alarmed at the widespread distribution of the leaflets that appeared through letterboxes all over Germany and Austria. Early on the morning of 18 February 1943, the group distributed hundreds of copies of their

*Hans and Sophie Scholl, both leaders in the Hitler Youth during their teens, became disillusioned with national socialism and set out to rouse the German people from their slumber and encourage passive resistance to the fascist regime.*

sixth leaflet around Munich University. It was a call to arms: 'The name of Germany is dishonoured for all time if German youth does not finally rise, take revenge, and atone, smash its tormentors, and set up a new Europe of the spirit.' As they were finishing their work, they were spotted by a janitor, Jacob Schmid. Hans, Sophie and Christoph were handed over to the Gestapo, who accused them of treason. Their trial, held four days later, was a farce. The judge, Roland Freisler, spoke only to denounce the defendants, for whom no witnesses were called. Sophie spoke in their defence, explaining to Freisler, 'Somebody, after all, had to make a start. What we wrote and said is also believed by many others. They just don't dare to express themselves as we did.' Later, she asked him, 'You know the war is lost. Why don't you have the courage to face it?'

The judgement was inevitable: guilty of treason. As was their sentence: death. The three – Hans aged 24, Sophie 21 and Christoph

22 – were beheaded by guillotine that afternoon at Stadelheim Prison, apparently facing death with the same dignity they showed in their short lives. Other colleagues, including Schmorell, Graf and Huber, were also arrested and executed in the coming months. Today, the White Rose are remembered in the names of streets, squares and schools all over Germany, as 'enduring symbols of the struggle, universal and timeless, for the freedom of the human spirit wherever and whenever it is threatened.'[139]

# Chapter 12

# The End

Now under new command, that of *Sturmbannführer* Hubert Meyer, in September 1944 the *Hitlerjugend* division travelled back to Germany, to Nienburg in the north-west, for a major refit in terms of equipment, arms and personnel. Time was of the essence, since British and American troops had already crossed the Franco-Belgian border and were heading for Germany. For civilians back home, these were worrying times. Most people understood that Nazi Germany's military defeat was all but certain. They feared defeat, and they feared revenge, particularly for what the Nazis had done to the Jews and Russians. But many ordinary Germans could not imagine a future beyond National Socialism, beyond Hitler.

## The Ardennes Offensive

In late autumn 1944, the advancing Allies had their own problems. Although they took the city of Aachen in the industrial powerhouse of the Ruhr on 21 October, their supply lines were stretched to the limit, making further advances impossible. With this in mind, Hitler had planned a counteroffensive to take advantage of the wintry conditions to come. The refitted 12th Panzer Division, reinforced by volunteers from the Luftwaffe and Kriegsmarine who had little or no infantry training, were selected for the so-called 'Ardennes Offensive' under another new commander, *Standartenführer* Hugo Kraas. Based in the deeply forested Ardennes region between Belgium and Luxembourg, its purpose was to split the Allied forces and their supply lines either side of a corridor from the German border to the Belgian port city of Antwerp. Hitler's thinking was that if his plan succeeded, the Allies, whose generals Montgomery and Bradley were at loggerheads at the time, would argue among themselves and, as a result, be forced to accept a peace treaty. Few of his senior generals agreed with him.

The operation had been planned in considerable secrecy. Since the 20 July plot to assassinate Hitler, tighter security had been imposed. In the build-up to the offensive, radio silence was ordered, and troop movements were undertaken only during bad weather. As a result, the Allies regarded the Ardennes as a 'quiet sector'. The *Hitlerjugend* division, by then attached to the 6th SS Panzer Army, arrived at their rendezvous point in the Schmidtheim forest on 15 December. 'Day O', the start of the offensive, was set for the following day. Despite some fragmentary evidence from eyewitnesses in the area, the Allies were convinced that the Germans were unable to launch any more major operations, and a heavy snowstorm increased their belief. As a result, they were unprepared for the artillery bombardment that began in the early morning and for the scale of the attack that followed as 83,000 inexperienced US troops found themselves up against 200,000 battle-hardened Waffen-SS. With fog, rain and snow keeping Allied air support on the ground and the forest canopy above them covering troop and tank movements, the Germans threw themselves at the US soldiers, breaking through the lines as intended. Thousands of American troops were killed and wounded in savage fighting. In fact, the battle was later renamed the Battle of the Bulge after the bulge that the Germans created in the American lines between Monschau on the German border and Echternach in Luxembourg.

## Battle of the Bulge

Early successes were led by tank commander Joachim Peiper and the 1st SS Panzer Division, while the 12th SS were specially selected to attack the American troops stationed on the Elsenborn Ridge at the northern end of the front. Despite heavy fighting, the *Hitlerjugend* division could not shift the Americans. They were ordered instead to follow Peiper, and the battle formed around the town of Bastogne, a crossroads of all seven main roads running through the Ardennes highlands. The town was critical to the German advance and to the Allies trying to hold it up. American troops got there first, on 18 December, and the paratroopers of the 101st Airborne Division, three artillery battalions with howitzers and the 705th Tank Destroyer with four M18 Hellcat tank destroyers took up defensive positions. They were tasked with holding up the German forces until the arrival of General Patton and the 3rd Army. The *Hitlerjugend* division was sent to capture Hill 510 near the village of Magaret to the east of Bastogne from where observation points could be taken for the German artillery. Despite fierce fighting, they failed to complete their mission in time.

By 22 December, the town was surrounded by the tanks and infantry of the 5th Panzer Army. A contingent of German soldiers, under a flag of truce, handed an ultimatum to Major Alvin Jones. It demanded surrender within two hours or shelling would begin. On reading the note, Brigadier General McAuliffe, commander of the 101st, is reported to have said, 'Aw Nuts!' The message was duly written down and handed to one of the German soldiers, who read it and looked up enquiringly. Colonel H. Harper said, 'If you don't understand what "nuts" means, in plain English it's the same as "Go to Hell".'

The attack began on Christmas Eve when Luftwaffe bombers attacked the town. The following morning, German tanks carrying a battalion of infantry moved in from the north-west, but they were repulsed by the Americans, whose tank destroyers proved invaluable against the attacking Panzers. The German forces were hindered by the terrible weather conditions, the narrow roads and a lack of fuel for their vehicles. On Boxing Day, the first troops from General Patton's 3rd Army arrived to relieve the siege, having smashed a gap in the encircling Panzer forces. Despite Hitler's continued insistence that Bastogne be taken, the fighting ended on 2 January. To the north, the 2nd US Armoured Division stopped enemy tanks short of the River Meuse. During January, Allied troops attacked the sides of the shrinking bulge until they had restored the front, and the Germans began their retreat.

## Defending the homeland

For the youngsters of the *Hitlerjugend* division, however, there was to be little rest. The journey home from Belgium to their new home in Cologne was a long one, with a constant search for enough fuel to get there and many vehicles abandoned en route. Even before some of them made it back to Germany, there was news from the Eastern Front: the Russians had crossed from Poland into Germany and were headed for Berlin.

In the autumn of 1944, following the defeat of the German Army Group Centre in Soviet Byelorussia, Russian troops pushed across into East Prussia. This marked the first time since the perfunctory French raids of 1939 that German soil had come under enemy occupation. With civilian morale in decline, regular Allied bombing raids and growing fears of disruption in German towns and cities, particularly after the news of the assassination attempt on Hitler in July, Hitler and his advisers had to respond. With Allied armies on the Reich's eastern and western borders, they set up the German *Volkssturm*, a compulsory national militia for all men aged 16 to 60, to defend the homeland. It was to be under the control of the NSDAP. In reality, recruits were both younger and older than the required age range and women and girls were included in the ranks of the new People's Militia. The first recruitment drive assembled a motley crew of around 60,000 youngsters, many from the Hitler Youth, alongside old or convalescent soldiers. Unusually, it was the youngsters, with up-to-date military training and accustomed to military discipline, who were put in charge, often of men old enough to be their fathers and even their grandfathers. As more recruits signed up, so the new 'talent pool' became attractive to other organizations, such as the SS and the *Hitlerjugend* division, both still active on the front lines and always in dire need of reinforcements.

*As the invasion of Germany from east and west became ever more likely, the Nazis set up the* Volkssturm, *a compulsory people's militia for all men from 16 to 60. Hitler ordered the recruitment of 6 million men for the task, a number that was never realized.*

## Siege of Breslau

In January 1945, the Russians were approaching the city of Breslau in Lower Silesia. Having voted in support of the Nazis in 1933, it became a model Nazi city during the war years, tucked away from Allied bombing raids and other upheavals of the conflict. As a result, the population swelled to over a million. However, in the autumn of 1944, Hitler had declared the city a 'closed military fortress' that had to be defended at all costs and, as wounded German soldiers flooded the city hospitals, the reality of war came closer.

The city was turned into a fortress, supplies were stockpiled, and two defensive rings were constructed around it. A garrison of 80,000 men was raised and the inhabitants braced themselves for the bloodbath to come. The garrison comprised Hitler Youth, untrained *Volksstürme*, police officers, slave labourers and soldiers from regiments retreating from the front. They were ill-equipped to face the Soviet 6th Army and the First Ukrainian Front. The city's administrators, led by Silesia Gauleiter Karl Hanke, made a disastrous decision to evacuate the civilian population on 19 January after the Soviet artillery had destroyed almost all transport links. In temperatures as low as -15 °C (5 °F), many left the city on foot. Others were trampled to death in the chaos at the railway station. It is estimated that some 100,000 people froze to death during this ill-fated operation.

The situation inside the city was dire, with the remaining civilians in a state of panic. Cut off from the rest of the Reich, supplies could only come in by air. Death squads roamed the city murdering looters and shirkers who were not prepared to do their duty to the Fatherland. The Soviet siege began in the middle of February and lasted for 80 days of brutal slaughter. Starting with an artillery barrage and a huge tank attack, it ended with savage house-to-house street fighting. When the city finally capitulated in early May, it was in ruins, with over 20,000 of its 30,000 buildings reduced to rubble, including all of its hospitals, waterworks and sewers. There was little electricity. Historical figures estimate that 6,000 German troops and 7,000 Russian troops were killed along with 170,000 civilians. One residential area of the city had been levelled to create an airstrip to connect the city with the outside world. At least 13,000 slave workers were killed during the groundworks when the Russians shelled it. In the event, Karl Hanke used it to flee the city before it surrendered. It is said that the rubble that covered the streets at the end of the siege was not finally cleared until the 1960s.

## Mounting casualties

During the early months of 1945, battles like that at Breslau were taking place in both the east and the west as the German Reich began to shrink. Its military was now in full retreat with limited manpower, supplies and equipment. German air defences became increasingly ineffective and the full violence of war was concentrated on what remained of 'Greater Germany'. In January, German casualties reached their peak, with more than 450,000 soldiers losing their lives in a single month. For the three months that followed, the figures reduced slightly but remained at almost 300,000. Among civilians, too, casualty rates were high as millions fled the advancing Red Army, many perishing in freezing winter temperatures. Allied bombers continued their campaign and low-flying fighters, now in range from bases in Belgium and the Netherlands, attacked towns and villages at will. With the walls apparently closing in, discipline among foreign workers and German citizens became hard to maintain and the police, SS and Wehrmacht often responded violently to keep order.

In these circumstances, Himmler's words at a swearing-in ceremony for the *Volkssturm* in East Prussia in October 1944 sounded, to many, like a death sentence. 'Our opponents must know that every kilometre that they want to advance into our country will cost them rivers of blood. They will step onto a field of living mines consisting of fanatical uncompromising fighters. Every block of flats will be defended by men, boys and old men and, if need be, by women and girls. Furthermore, in the territory that they believe they have conquered, the German determination to resist will rise up behind them and, like the werewolves, fearless volunteers will do damage to the enemy and cut off his lifelines.'[140]

Once, when there remained a chance of victory, these words might have roused the faithful. Now, with the military all but defeated, the Nazi vision that civilians armed with anti-tank weapons and a few guns and bullets should face the combined might of the Soviet, US, British and Canadian armies, seemed preposterous. The gulf between the increasingly hysterical military leadership and those who would do its bidding grew wider. Following the failure of the Ardennes Offensive, the war was lost. Despite the Führer's rhetoric that he would not make the same mistakes as those made in 1918, on 1 January he ordered another major operation against the Russians in Hungary and the slaughter of both soldiers and civilians continued.

## Surrender of the 12th Panzers

After a quick refit and complete with new volunteers aged 15 and 16, the *Hitlerjugend* division was sent, along with other divisions of the Waffen-SS, to Hungary with orders to relieve the siege of Budapest, though Hitler was also concerned with protecting the Hungarian oilfields – oil that fed the German war machine – from the Russians. The attack on Russian forces, which surprised the Red Army, began in early February. Panzer and Tiger tanks attacked Russian lines three times in what were known as the 'Konrad Offences'. Despite some German successes, notably the capture of the heavily fortified village of Bart by the 12th Panzers, the Russians repelled each attack and took the city. Once again, the Hitler Youth and other German forces had fought bravely against all odds in order to defend the Fatherland, but once again they were let down by matters over which they had no control.

By now, the German High Command was in open revolt, with Hitler and his loyalists wanting to push on to the inevitable 'glorious' end and others shaken at the prospect of throwing away the lives of German citizens and soldiers in a desperate and pointless last stand. Regrouping one final time, the *Hitlerjugend* division were moved to the area between Lake Balaton and the Danube, where there were valuable oil reserves to be protected. Fierce fighting continued through March with heavy casualties on both sides. However, the Russians had more men, and more and better weapons, petrol and ammunition, all of which were running short for the Germans. Russian progress increased as the German forces retreated towards Vienna. On 8 May, having fought several hopeless rearguard actions and enduring a long forced march to avoid capture and certain death at the hands of the Soviets, the survivors of the once proud and always feared 12th SS Panzerdivision *Hitlerjugend* crossed the River Enns in Austria. After a final parade and inspection by SS-*Brigadeführer* Hugo Kraas, they surrendered to the US 7th Army.

The Wehrmacht, however, had no such choice. Ordered to continue fighting 'to the last man' but with a reduction in manpower, arms, ammunition, food and fuel, particularly with no air support and the railway network supply lines almost completely destroyed by Allied bombing, they fought bravely and effectively, often causing maximum damage on opposing troops. On the Eastern Front, this provoked a furious response from the attacking Soviets already burning with a desire for revenge for the treatment they had suffered at the hands of the Nazis during the first years of the conflict. Towns and cities through which the battles raged were left in total ruin. This explosive situation resulted in huge numbers of casualties on both sides, including among the civilian population. The situation was similar in the west, where

Allied progress through Alsace and over the Rhine was slow, bloody and ruinous.

## No surrender

Of course, Hitler Youths were also found in other military formations and as the war finally reached German soil, this increasingly meant service in home guard units, such as anti-aircraft units, but some also took senior positions in the *Volkssturm*. The use of youngsters in this way provoked objections among some members of the military High Command. General Westphal, for example, pointed out that wasting young lives in this way would 'for future years endanger the reservoir of recruitment to the German armed forces.'[141] His objection was not noted, and *Reichsjugendführer* Artur Axmann repeated Hitler's ever more desperate mantra: 'There is only victory or annihilation.'

*As defeat became more likely so the age of recruits dropped. It is said that the youngest soldiers, sometimes aged 12 or even 10, were often the most fanatical. Fed with romantic notions of 'valour' by everyone they encountered, giving up and admitting defeat was worse than death. With little training and poor weapons, the 'Reich's last defenders' fought on.*

Of all Germans, the youth would be the Reich's last defenders against the 'Anglo-American gangsters' and the 'Bolshevik hordes'. Melita Maschmann explains their unwavering commitment to National Socialism, 'They had been fed with heroes' legends ever since they could remember … They felt that the hour had come, the moment in which they could be counted, in which they would no longer be pushed aside because they were too young … They fed the refugees; they helped the wounded. In the air raids they fought the flames and helped to rescue the sick and the injured. And finally, they confronted the Russians with the *Panzerfaust*.'[142]

But the reality was not always as glorious as this. American troops in the forested areas of the Ruhr pocket reported horrific encounters with units including large numbers of Hitler Youths who would hide when the US armour rolled past and ambush the slower-moving infantry behind. They would inflict maximum casualties then melt back into the forest. If they were cornered, they would fight and die rather than surrender. One lieutenant colonel reported an engagement with a German artillery unit manned by children of 12 and under.

## The Bridge at Remagen

Others had even less chance than that. Following victory in the Ardennes, the US army launched Operation Lumberjack with the intention of reaching and crossing the Rhine. German orders were confusing. Hitler's demand that every foot of territory should be fought for was impossible in the face of the Allied forces. Even with German forces in retreat on the west bank of the river, Hitler ordered that its bridges should be destroyed. In early March, US aerial reconnaissance identified two bridges remaining, but they were both destroyed before US troops could reach them. On the morning of 7 March, however, scouts from the 9th Armoured Division reached the heights overlooking the village of Remagen and were astonished to find that the Ludendorff railway bridge below was still standing and that retreating German forces were still using it.

There had been arguments in the German High Command about where they thought the Allies would try to cross the Rhine. These arguments were compounded by a number of command changes during the first few days of March. On 1 March, *Generalleutnant* Walter Botsch was assigned to the defence of the Bonn-Remagen area. After an inspection of the Ludendorff bridge, he promised to send a battalion of men, labourers, additional explosives, radios, signal equipment and a heavy anti-tank battalion, but it never arrived. On 6 March, Botsch was replaced by *Generalmajor* Richard von Bothmer. He was unable to visit Remagen because he was busy with the defence of Bonn, so he sent a liaison officer to review the situation, but he was arrested by American soldiers after inadvertently crossing their lines. That same day, *Hauptmann* Wilhelm Bratge was replaced as commandant at Remagen by Major Hans Scheller. They too argued about what action to take on hearing of the imminent arrival of the US troops: Bratge wanted the blow up the bridge as soon as possible, whereas Scheller wanted to keep it intact until the last possible moment to allow more German troops to cross to safety.

Because of these circumstances, the defence of the last remaining bridge over the Rhine was left in the hands of a bridge security company of 36 soldiers, a company of 120 engineers, 180 local Hitler Youths, an anti-aircraft battery of 220 men, 120 'volunteers' from Eastern Europe and some 500 badly trained, poorly armed, locally conscripted *Volksstürme* – roughly 1,000 men in all. As German policy did not allow planning for rear-area defence, there were no anti-tank ditches or mines, no barbed wire and no trenches. The roadblocks were insufficient to stop the advancing American tanks. Their defence plan, which consisted of placing inadequate and poor-quality explosives carefully to avoid accidents and explode at exactly the right time, was confused because of new orders from the High Command. A few weeks earlier, another bridge had been destroyed inadvertently by an Allied bomb that ignited defensive explosives that had been placed too early. Hitler was incandescent and ordered that anyone responsible for losing a bridge to the enemy or blowing one up too soon would face the death penalty. Under this serious pressure, the bridge engineers at Remagen attempted to complete the plan before the Americans arrived.

Fearing that the bridge would be blown at any moment, the Americans launched their assault. The 9th Armoured Division's tanks and guns engaged the German forces on the heights across the river, while the 27th Armoured Infantry battalion made their way towards and across the bridge, cutting wires and kicking demolition charges into the river while under heavy fire. The first man over, Sergeant Alexander Drabik from Ohio, remembered, '… it may have been only 250 yards but it seemed like 250 miles to us.' They later discovered that the bridge was set to blow while they were running across it, but the explosives failed because of faulty fuses. By nightfall, scores of tanks and trucks were lining up to cross the river and established a bridgehead. 'The Ludendorff bridge had become a one-way street, east-bound.'[143]

On this and many subsequent occasions during the Allied invasion of Germany, the local civilian *Volkssturm* failed to provide any resistance to the invading forces, hiding in a railway tunnel rather than attempt to defend the bridge. Although the battle at Remagen raged on for a few weeks, as the Germans were determined to destroy it, by the time it collapsed Allied forces had constructed eight new crossings of the river and nothing could hold back the Allied advances into the Ruhr region.

## The Werewolves

As the war progressed, some former members of the Hitler Youth were, as a result of the strength of their belief in Nazi ideology, regularly taking part in crimes against humanity, perhaps working as concentration camp guards or joining the SS *Einsatzgruppen* death squads. Some were given a further opportunity in 1944 with the formation of the *Werwolven* (Werewolf) commandos. The group, a final collaboration between the SS, under Himmler, and the HJ under Artur Axmann, was formed as a sort of Nazi resistance movement dedicated to delaying the advance of the Allied and Soviet invasions in the hope that a prolonged war would be beneficial for the regime.

Prospective members – normally aged between 14 and 17, mainly boys but including some girls – were often asked to commit inhuman acts in order to be complicit in the murderous operations they were going to be tasked with. Some had to shoot recaptured prisoners, or watch a mass execution and help bury the dead, or even kill a deserter from their own flak emplacement. They were fanatics, dedicated to the Führer and ready to sacrifice their lives for him. In all, despite little recorded evidence, it is estimated that the group originally numbered about 5,000 and were mostly recruited from the SS and the Hitler Youth.

With Germany on the verge of defeat and the Allies already on German soil, they operated in small cells of four to six and were dropped behind enemy lines, armed with *Panzerfausts*, grenades, plastic explosives and small arms, and instructed to cause havoc, sniping, ambushing, disrupting traffic, poisoning water and food supplies. They also poured sugar in military vehicle fuel tanks and suspended invisible wires across roads intended to cause decapitation. In addition, they received training in derailing trains and disrupting communication devices.

Set up as a paramilitary organization, they were led by SS-*Obergruppenführer* Hans Prützmann, and fought in uniform. If captured, they would claim the right to be taken as POWs. They had some notable successes. In March 1945, the Americans appointed a German Catholic, Franz Oppenhoff, as the new 'anti-Nazi' mayor of Aachen, the first major German city that fell to their forces. A small group of Werewolves were parachuted in and shot the new mayor in the head, killing him in his own house before escaping, only to be killed by land mines while making their way home. There were other killings reported, too, of Allied soldiers and high-ranking British, American and Russian officers, and of explosions at ammunition dumps and the destruction of buildings being used by occupying forces. There were also regular reports of violent attacks on Germans suspected of collusion with the Allies.

However, because of the clandestine nature of the organization, historians have cast doubt on whether they were actually the perpetrators of all these incidents. In fact, for many historians, the Werewolf movement was a failure because of squabbles among its leadership, inadequate training and equipment and a lack of co-ordination in its activities. The reason it is remembered today is largely because of the effectiveness of Joseph Goebbels' propaganda campaign, championing the idea of Werewolf resistance and urging people to join on his new Werwolf Radio station. Its first broadcast, on 1 April 1945, reported on resistance activity all over Germany, whether true or false, issuing threats to would-be German collaborators and Allied troops or sympathizers. Although they fell on deaf ears among the war-weary German population, such broadcasts and the rumours and stories swirling around about resistance groups caused alarm, particularly among the US military authorities and the press back in the USA. Advice on guerrilla activity was given to the GIs in the form of pamphlets with titles such as 'Combatting the Guerrilla' and 'Don't be a Sucker in Germany', warning them against fraternizing with German women, saying 'German women have been trained to seduce you. Is it worth a knife in the back?' There were newspaper headlines, such as, 'Fury of Nazi "Werewolves" to be unleashed on Invaders'. There were also articles suggesting that 'tens of thousands' of Hitler's fanatical followers would regroup in an Alpine fortress, the 'national redoubt', and conduct a never-ending war on German soil. Some even likened the Werewolves to the Gestapo, stoking fears among the families of GIs in Europe.

In the end, though, the Werewolf's bark was worse than its bite. Estimates of the number of people they killed vary from the hundreds to the thousands – a drop in the ocean in a war costing millions of lives, and causing hundreds of billions of pounds' worth of damage for an economy already in a parlous state. However, the Alpine fortress was just a mirage.

## The end

The *Volkssturm* was set up as a national organization and units were to be arranged in each of Germany's 920 *Gaue* (districts) with hoped-for numbers of about 6 million (a number never achieved). Units mostly comprised members of the Hitler Youth, invalids, the elderly and men who had previously been considered unfit for military service. In February 1945, the Nazis also began to conscript women and girls. A lack of numbers, limited military training and a shortage of weapons meant that they were of little value militarily, though some joined up with Wehrmacht and SS units fighting on the front line. Despite this, on many occasions, they fought with tremendous courage against the overwhelming power of the invading Allies. Indeed, they fought and died at Küstrin, Kolberg, Breslau and Königsberg, where 2,400 members were killed.

Though their actions were not always so heroic, such as at the battle of the bridge at Remagen, many died bravely during the defence of Berlin, the final major offensive of the European theatre of the Second World War. During April and May 1945, the Third Reich was at the end of its own rope since the military chain of command and its administrative organization no longer functioned. The people had begun to welcome invading Allied troops with white flags, while die-hard Nazis tried to dissuade them. In Berlin, Hitler and Goebbels held on to their delusional ideas that the final German defence would hold. On 20 April, the Führer's 56th birthday, those who shared the *Führerbunker* toasted him with champagne. That day, in the garden of the Reich Chancellery, he had handed out medals to some of the city's defenders. Looking haggard and unsteady on his feet, holding a shaky left arm behind his back, the jowly faced Hitler, with nose running, managed a smile as he awarded the Iron Cross, 2nd Class, to various 12-year-old members of the Hitler Youth who had put their military training to good use in the service of their country by knocking out Soviet tanks on Berlin's eastern approaches. The ceremony took place with background sounds of Soviet artillery shells as the Red Army had reached the outskirts of the city centre.

Berlin's defences – comprising the LVI Panzer Corps, about 60,000 *Volksstürme* and some remaining SS and Hitler Youth detachments – were faced by an invasion force of 2.5 million Soviet troops, over 6,000 tanks and 40,000 artillery pieces. On a macro-scale, it was no contest;

*Hitler's last few public appearances took place in the Reich Chancellery garden where he handed out medals to Berlin's young defenders. Here he shakes the hand of Alfred Zech, a member of the* Volkssturm, *after awarding him the Iron Cross for his rescue of twelve German soldiers wounded by a Soviet grenade.*

on a micro-scale, it was the final tragedy of what had become a senseless conflict. German boys, girls, men and women of all ages – from ten to over 60 – were sacrificed at the altar of the Nazi myth in scenes reminiscent of a Hieronymus Bosch painting of hell. Professional soldiers, Hitler Youths, veterans of the First World War, ten-year-old boys with uniforms and helmets too big for them, some armed with rifles and *Panzerfausts* that they were too frightened to fire, some not even armed, defended the bridges and the streets of Berlin from battle-hardened Red Army soldiers and perished in their thousands, lying dead among the rubble of this once great city.

Some time after 2.30 on the afternoon of 30 April, Hitler and his wife of one day, Eva Braun, committed suicide in his study in the *Führerbunker*, she by cyanide pill and he by shooting himself in the temple. They were found side by side on the sofa. The bodies were wrapped in rugs and taken upstairs to the Chancellery garden, where they were doused in petrol and burned.

There was a similar story of capitulation in Munich, whose minimal defences were overrun by US armoured and infantry divisions on 29 April. These same troops also liberated the nearby Dachau concentration camp in the process. The shock of what the soldiers found provoked horror and rage: emaciated survivors, huge piles of rotting cadavers, the stench of death, crematoria filled with ash and more naked bodies piled up ready for burning. Vengeance on any remaining guards was summary though swiftly curtailed. One American soldier, Chaplain Bohnen, recalled: 'We entered the camp itself and saw the living. The Jews were the worst off. Many of them looked worse than the dead. They cried as they saw us. They were emaciated, diseased, beaten, miserable caricatures of human beings. I don't know how they didn't all go mad … I shall never forget what I saw, and in my nightmares the scenes recur. No possible punishment would ever repay the ones who were responsible.'

Dachau was not the first camp liberated by the Americans. Earlier that month, Generals Eisenhower, Patton and Bradley had visited Ohrdruf, a sub-camp of Buchenwald. Shocked and appalled by what they saw, Eisenhower insisted that a film record was taken so that everyone could bear witness to the unbelievable 'cruelty and bestiality' he saw that day in case at some point in the future people might not believe it ever happened. Following Eisenhower's example, a group of frightened youngsters, aged between ten and 14, who the previous day had manned the barricades erected to defend Munich's Maximilian Bridge against American Sherman tanks and taken prisoners of war, were brought to the newly liberated camp at Dachau. They were escorted to a railway siding and ordered to open the door of a freight car. The skeleton of a

*Determined that the German people should 'bear witness' to the atrocities committed in the Nazi deathcamps, a group of Hitler Youths are shown the contents of a freight car that had arrived at Dachau filled with the skeletal bodies of Jews who had been sent there to be killed.*

woman fell out. Peering inside, they saw other skeletal bodies, pressed so close together that they were wedged in tight. They were taken to a red-brick building that smelled acrid. It was filled with furnaces, some with metal stretchers halfway inside bearing the remnants of burned bodies. They walked among the emaciated inmates, dressed in blue-striped suits, who looked at them with blank, uncomprehending and vacant stares. Many of the youngsters could not help but cry.[144]

# Afterword

# The Illusion
# is Shattered

At the end of World War I, the German people faced an uncertain future. The country was in uproar at the punitive terms of the Treaty of Versailles, dealing with skyrocketing unemployment, hyperinflation, political instability and profound social change. Into this crucible stepped Adolf Hitler and the Nazi Party, offering simple solutions to these complex problems. One long-term solution was to introduce children and juveniles to German Nationalist principles and anti-Semitism – the building blocks of Nazi ideology – to help Hitler achieve his ultimate goal of long-term power. For this reason, in 1922, he announced the formation of his party's youth group.

Looking back through the prism of history, the 'success' of the Hitler Youth, perhaps National Socialism's greatest achievement, is almost impossible to comprehend. It was an organization which, at its height, included an entire generation of ten- to 18-year-old German boys and girls – almost 9 million people – more than 90 per cent of the nation's youth. In time, the Nazi regime came to depend on it –

to ensure the future of its much trumpeted 'thousand-year Reich'. For German historian Gerhard Rempel, the HJ acted as the 'social, political and military resiliency of the Third Reich', by constantly 'replenishing the ranks of the dominant party and preventing the growth of mass opposition.'[145] Their duty was to die so that Germany could live. That such a movement could be organized in the West today seems a ridiculous notion but in 1930s Germany these young people were the chosen ones.

Nazi methods of indoctrination, aimed at turning HJ members into disciplined adults who would see the world as the regime intended, were crude, cruel, stifling and enormously effective. By targeting young brains that were not yet fully developed, the incredibly susceptible youth were easily co-opted by powerful authority figures. Hitler's intention was to secure their absolute loyalty. By influencing all aspects of German society, in particular schools, young people were given no room to think for themselves. In her study, 'Propaganda and Children in the Hitler Years', Mary Mills says that, 'No single target of nazification took higher priority than Germany's young.'[146] Nazi messages were presented in schools as scientific fact and were taught and retaught until the messages of Aryan superiority and the 'Jewish problem' were fully digested and adopted with idealistic zeal. Allied to this was a constant propaganda bombardment in the form of newspaper articles, flags, swastikas, uniformed parades, songs, music, films, radio broadcasts, slogans and posters. They all trumpeted simple messages, so simple that even the young could understand them. For many of them, Hitler had even replaced God.

*We all believe on this earth in Adolf Hitler, our Leader. We believe that this God has sent us Adolf Hitler so that Germany should be as a foundation stone in all eternity.*

Hitler Youth poster, 1934

## 'A huge criminal gang'

During the early years of the NSDAP, Hitler used populist ideas and adapted them to his advantage. Following the catastrophe of defeat and revolution in Germany, the 19th-century idea of a truly united nation, free of class, religious and ideological frictions – the so-called *Volksgemeinschaft* (people's community) – became popular once more. Many believed it should be based on the myth of comradeship that grew between soldiers on the front in World War I, when men from all walks of life came together for the sake of the nation. In the 1920s, this community was said to be based on comradeship and friendship, prompting a myriad of youth movements to meet again for conversations, walks, songs and camping as they had done in Germany for so long.

When Hitler took power, the Nazis began to adopt this idea of community for their own purposes. According to German historian Thomas Kühne, the Nazis radicalized the notion in several ways. They made the Hitler Youth the only legal youth movement, they made membership mandatory, and they insisted on the racial purity and ideological conformity of its members. Towards the end of the 1930s the relatively simple military comradeship that had been taught in HJ camps across the country since 1933 took a sinister turn. It became 'community building based on crime' and was in Kühne's view 'barbarously radicalized in the genocide Germany perpetrated from 1941 on. Eventually, the German nation established itself as a huge criminal gang' in which many of the ideologically brainwashed *Hitlerjugend* were complicit.[147]

## HJ: Perpetrators and victims

On 1 September 1939, Germany invaded Poland, marking the beginning of six years of war. Baldur von Schirach's by-then huge organization was put to the test. The effect on the HJ was immediate as more than a million leaders of draft age were called up to fight, a draft that was to occur annually during the conflict that followed. It started in a blaze of glory. Armed with zeal, optimism and purpose, they flooded into all the military units including the Wehrmacht and the Waffen-SS. Later the most ardent of them joined the 'Death's Head Units' that guarded the concentration camps and even the *Einsatzgruppen* death squads.

It ended in mud, blood and death. In the spring of 1945, Russian tanks moving west were met by hastily organized Hitler Youth battalions, often bolstered by former flak helpers – some as young as 13 – posted from elsewhere. Despite stories of their fanaticism and extraordinary bravery when facing overwhelming odds, these inexperienced soldiers were slaughtered in their thousands by the battle-hardened Soviet tank corps. Fighting in occupied territories on the Eastern Front was particularly brutal, with Nazi youngsters brainwashed to show no mercy to the hated Slavic soldiers, and the Russian troops eager for revenge for the atrocities committed by invading German troops earlier in the war. With little military training and often armed with old or substandard weapons that did not work, many of the HJ were killed with unspeakable cruelty. The roads to Berlin were littered with dead bodies, deliberately crushed by tanks, shot in the stomach and left to die or be finished off with knives and clubs, beheaded with bayonets, hung and burned.

Although Nazi policy explicitly excluded German women and girls from combat, as more and more soldiers perished, Hitler's grip on power began to loosen and the country came under threat of invasion, they began to take on military responsibilities. Often called 'helpers', members of the BDM and the RAD (*Reichsarbeitsdienst*) worked with all branches of the German armed forces, as administrators, radio operators, nurses, air raid wardens and the like. But after Stalingrad, as the age of its recruits went down so the likelihood of their taking part in combat increased. Those in the occupied territories were the first to take up arms in the face of the invading Red Army, not only with small arms, but machine guns, grenades and anti-aircraft cannons. German historian Michael Kater says, 'Even after the Reich's capitulation on 8 May 1945, German adolescent females continued to be victimised as the wrath of the conquerors turned against them especially in the eastern provinces, where they were raped, tortured, mutilated, killed or deported to long terms of captivity.'[148]

There are no official figures for how many young German women were killed during these years but it is recorded that some 25,000 of them were deported to do forced labour in Soviet camps. Their journeys east, on forced marches or in cattle trucks, were accompanied by regular beatings and rape. In the camps, the work was brutal, the food was often inedible and disease was rife. Some returned to Germany many years later but most never came back.

On 10 October 1945 the Hitler Youth was officially abolished. A few of its adult leaders were put on trial but harsh punishments were rarely handed out. Some youngsters were suspected of war crimes but not prosecuted due to their age.

Their punishment came from a different source, described by Grainne Feick in her paper 'The Hitler Youth: the "Other" Victims of the Nazi Regime' as 'despair, disillusion, denial, guilt and shame' while coming to terms with the part they played in one of the most heinous political regimes in modern history.[149] Allied soldiers forced captured HJ members who lived in the vicinity to view the piles of emaciated bodies inside liberated death camps. Others were forced to confront directly the atrocities of the Nazi regime by watching films on the subject at local cinemas.

While nothing can compare to the horrors suffered by the Jews and other Nazi 'undesirables' during World War II, Feick points out that members of the HJ were also victims of a brutal regime. For some, acceptance that they had worked for a criminal cause came quickly; for some, like Alfons Heck, it took a year or so. Heck, who had once claimed that he 'belonged to Hitler, body and soul', travelled to Nuremberg in 1946 to hear Baldur von Schirach give evidence at the war crimes trials. At the end of his hearing, Schirach was sentenced to 20 years for crimes against humanity. Heck recalled that at that moment he felt 'an overwhelming sense of betrayal' because Hitler, 'the man that I had adored was, in fact, the biggest monster in human history'.[150] For others coming to terms with their past was a long process, many burdened with feelings of guilt, the knowledge that they had been robbed of their childhood and that they had damaged their souls... for ever.

# Notes

The amount of material available for research into all aspects of the rise and fall of Hitler and the Nazis is immeasurable. A project such as this is as much about what to leave out as it is to decide what to include. There are many good places to start, such as the books written by Ian Kershaw, Richard J. Evans, Richard Bessel, William Shirer and Michael Kater. There are many indispensable websites too: Wikipedia is always good, particularly because of its excellent citations, but other sites used regularly included, in no particular order: www.history.com, www.journals.sagepub.com, www.wandervogel.com, www.historyplace.com, www.imw.org.uk, www.smithsonianmag.com, www.time.com, www.theholocaustexplained.org, www.bbc.co.uk, www.jewishvirtuallibrary.org, www.encyclopedia.ushmm.org, www.britannica. com, www.historylearningsite.co.uk, www.theguardian.com, www.academia.edu, www.nytimes.com, www.alphahistory.com, www.holocaust.org.uk, www.spartacus-educational.com, www.bdmhistory.com, www.academic.oup. com. Specific references are numbered in the text and listed below.

## Introduction

1   www.smithsonianmag.com/revisiting-the-rise-and-fall-of-the-third-reich-20231221/

2   The word 'Aryan' was originally used by 19th-century scholars to describe the ethnicity of peoples speaking related languages in Europe and India. The Nazis, however, linked it to the German word *Ehre*, which means honour, and used it to refer to pure-blooded German people as members of a mythical 'superior race' with classic Nordic (see note [3]) features – pale skin, tall and athletic physiques, blond(e) hair and blue eyes – whose duty was to control the world. This link between Europe and Asia is also behind the Nazi Party's appropriation of the swastika as a symbol of 'Aryan identity'. The motif, a hooked cross, is a Sanskrit symbol first used in Eurasia some 7,000 years ago. Among other things it indicates good luck, the infinity of creation and the unconquered, revolving Sun. Though

now reviled in the West, the *svastika* is still popular in Buddhist and Hindu society.

3 The word Nordic is taken from the French word *nordique*, meaning 'northern' and was used to describe an 'ethic group' of tall, light-haired white people with 'long skulls'. In the 19th century a racist idea developed among anthropologists that these characteristics (phenotype) pointed to the fact that Nordic people (also referred to as Anglo-Saxon) were superior to others. The idea developed that these people were Europeans (Aryans), had originated in Scandinavia and had distinctive physical characteristics of light hair and blue eyes. In 1855, racial theorist Arthur de Gobineau argued that the Germanic people were the finest representatives of the Aryan race. By the 20th century, the theory of an Aryan Master Race with Nordic features was commonly held in Europe and America. One of its greatest proponents was, of course, Adolf Hitler.

## Chapter 1 End of Empire

4 *The Hitler Youth, Origins and Development 1922–1945*, H.W. Koch, Cooper Square Press, New York, 2000.

5 It was later discovered that Princip was not a Serbian nationalist, but a Slav nationalist committed to liberating all locals – whether Croats, Muslims, Slovenes or Serbs – from Austrian occupation, thus undermining the reasons for Vienna's declaration of war on Serbia, which set off four years of world war. historytoday.com

6 *Napoleon the Great*, Andrew Roberts, Penguin Books, London, 2015.

7 *Britain and the Origins of the First World War*, Zara Steiner and Keith Neilson, Palgrave Macmillan, Basingstoke, 2003.

8 Ibid (see note [4]).

9 *The German Youth Movement 1900–1945: An Interpretative and Documentary History*, Peter D. Stachura, Macmillan, London, 1981.

10 *Redemption and Utopia: Libertarian Judaism in Central Europe*, Michael Löwy, Stanford University Press, 1992.

11 'Reconsidering Habermas, Politics, and Gender: The Case of Wilhelmine Germany', Belinda Davis, in Geoff Eley, ed., *Society, Culture, and the State in Germany, 1870–1930*, University of Michigan Press, Ann Arbor, 1996.

12 'The Monarchy versus the Nation: The "Festive Year" 1913 in Wilhemine Germany', Jeffrey R. Smith, 2000, jstor.org

13 'This Day in History, September 29 1918, Allied forces break through the Hindenburg Line', history.com

14 'The Military Collapse of the German Empire: The Reality Behind the

Stab-in-the-Back Myth', Wilhelm Deist (translated by E.J. Feuchtwanger), 1996, jstor.org

## Chapter 2 Blood and Iron

15 Ibid (see note [4]).

16 'The Youth of Nazi Germany', Edward J. Kunzer, 1938, jstor.org

17 'The Rebellion of Youth', Benjamin B. Wolman, Sage Journals, journals.sagepub.com, 1972.

18 *German History in the 19th Century, Vol. 2: Monarchy and Popular Sovereignty*, Franz Schnabel, dtv Verlagsgesellschaft mbH & Co. KG, Munich, 1987.

19 *Bismarck: The Man & the Stateman*, Vol. 2, Otto Von Bismarck, Cosimo Classics, New York, 2013.

20 *The German Empire, 1871–1918*, Hans-Ulrich Wehler, Berg, Leamington Spa, 1985.

21 *Bismarck and the German Empire, 1871–1918*, Lynn Abrams, (Lancaster Pamphlets) Routledge, Abingdon-on-Thames, 2006.

## Chapter 3 Hitler and the Piano Polisher

22 *Hitler: 1889–1936 Hubris*, Ian Kershaw, Allen Lane, The Penguin Press, London, 1998.

23 Ibid (see note [22]).

24 Ibid (see note [22]).

25 Extracts from *Mein Kampf* taken from the Ford translation, der-fueher.org

26 The German Youth Movement is a collective term for a number of youth groups that gathered together to focus on healthy outdoor activities in protest at the country's increasing industrialism and its expanding cities. Beginning in 1896, it included Scout groups, the *Wandervögel* and *Bündische Jugend* among others.

27 Ibid (see note [22]).

28 Quoted in *New York Times*, 3 September 1923, nytimes.com

## Chapter 4 *Kampfzeit!*

29 *The Coming of the Third Reich*, Richard J. Evans, Allen Lane, The Penguin Press, London, 2003.

30    *Hitler Youth: The Hitlerjugend in War and Peace 1933–45*, Brenda Ralph Lewis, Amber Books, London, 2016.

31    Ibid (see note [4]).

32    Ibid (see note [4]).

33    Ibid (see note [25]).

34    The Comintern, short for Communist International, was a Soviet-controlled association of national communist parties formed in 1919 to promote communist doctrine and bring about a world revolution.

35    *The Street as Stage: Protest Marches and Public Rallies since the Nineteenth Century*, ed. Matthias Reiss, OUP, Oxford, 2007.

## Chapter 5 'Deutschland Erwache!'

36    Figure from *Deutsch Zeitung*, quoted in Richard J. Evans, p.310, (see note [29]).

37    Ibid (see note [29]).

38    Quoted in 'The Early Days of Dachau', historyplace.com

39    'Adolph Hitler's Rise to Power', Wikipedia article, en.wikipedia.org

40    'Hitler's "Utopia": An Analysis of Gleichschaltung in the Third Reich 1933–1939', Emma Lichtenberg, *The Expositor*, Trinity University, 2017.

41    *Rethinking the Holocaust*, Yehuda Bauer, Yale University Press, New Haven, Connecticut, 2002

42    *Hitler Youth*, Michael H. Kater, Harvard University Press, Cambridge, Massachusetts, 2004.

43    'Hitler Youth', Spartacus Educational website, spartacus-educational.com

44    *Hitler Youth: Growing up in Hitler's Shadow*, Susan Campbell Bartoletti, Scholastic Focus, New York, 2005.

45    Ibid (see note [42]).

46    'The George Washington of Germany', newspaper article, 1936, facinghistory.org

## Chapter 6 The Nazification of Education

47    Ibid (see note [22]).

48    Ibid (see note [25]).

49    Ibid (see note [25]).

50    'Education in Nazi Germany', I.L. Kandel, 1935, jstor.org

51    *A Social History of the Third Reich*, Richard Grunberger, Orion Publishing Co, London, 2005.

52   Ibid (see note [30]).

53   *The Rise and Fall of the Third Reich*, William L. Shirer, Arrow Books, London, 1991.

54   Ibid (see note [43]).

55   'Six Years Education in Nazi Germany', Anonymous, 1945, taken from (see note [43]).

56   *The Third Reich in Power 1933–1939*, Richard J. Evans, Allen Lane, The Penguin Press, London, 2005.

57   Ibid (see note [50]).

58   Ibid (see note [4]).

59   *Nazi Women: Hitler's Education of a Nation*, Cate Haste, Channel 4 Books, London, 2001.

60   Wilhelm Frick directive, 9 May 1933, taken from (see note [43]).

61   'Nazism in the Classroom', Lisa Pine, historytoday.com

62   Ibid (see note [56]).

63   Ibid (see note [56]).

## Chapter 7 Time is Running Out

64   Ibid (see note [25]).

65   *Hitler Speaks: A Series of Political Conversations with Adolf Hitler on his Real Aims*, Hermann Rauschning, Thornton and Butterworth Ltd, London, 1940. Rauschning, a German politician and author, was appointed as head of parliament in Danzig in 1933. He was a member of the Nazi Party from 1932–34, after which he left the party and defected to the USA. He is chiefly known for this book, also called *Conversations with Hitler*, and claimed that it was the result of his many meetings and conversations with the Führer. Today, the book is considered by historians to be a fraud.

66   Ibid (see note [30]).

67   Ibid (see note [30]).

68   Ibid (see note [30]).

69   Erwin Hammer, quoted in *What We Knew: Terror, Mass Murder and Everyday Life in Nazi Germany*, Eric A. Johnson & Karl-Heinz Redind, Basic Books, 2006.

70   Ibid (see note [69]).

71   Ibid (see note [43]).

72   *Germany Possessed*, Helton Godwin Baynes, Routledge, 1941.

73   'Music in the Hitler Youth', Wolfgang Stumme, 1944.

74  *Hitler's Furies: German Women in the Nazi Killing Fields*, Wendy Lower, Vintage, London, 2014.

75  *Hitler Youth 1922–1945: An Illustrated History*, Jean-Denis G.C. Lepage, McFarland & Company Inc, Jefferson, North Carolina and London, 2009.

76  Ibid (see note [74]).

77  National Holocaust Centre website and museum, holocaust.org.uk

78  Ibid (see note [59]).

79  Ibid (see note [43]).

80  Ibid (see note [75]).

81  Ibid (see note [4]).

82  Ibid (see note [42]).

83  *Frankfurter Zeitung* newspaper, 13 December 1938.

84  Ibid (see note [51]).

85  Ibid (see note [42]).

86  'Hitler Youth: Prelude to War, 1933–1938', History Place website, historyplace.com

87  Ibid (see note [42]).

88  Supreme HQ Allied Expeditionary Force Evaluation and Dissemination Report: The Hitler Jugend (The Hitler Youth Organization), 1944, ibiblio.org

89  Adolf Hitler, 1938, quoted in 'Rulers of the World: The Hitler Youth', Walter S. Zapotoczny, wzaponline.com

90  *My Friend the Enemy: An English Boy in Nazi Germany*, Paul Briscoe with Michael McMahon, Aurum Press, London, 2007.

91  *Heil Hitler: Confessions of a Hitler Youth*, Alfons Heck, film made by HBO, available on Facing History & Ourselves website, facinghistory.org

## Chapter 8 Families in Nazi Germany

92  *The Military, War and Gender in Twentieth-Century Germany*, Karen Hagemann and Stefanie Schüler-Springorum, eds, Chapter 7: 'Body Damage' Sabine Kienitz, Berg, Leamington Spa, 2002.

93  *Women in Nazi Society*, Jill Stephenson, Abingdon-on-Thames, 1975.

94  'But Who Are You', United States Holocaust Memorial Museum website, perspectives.ushmm.org

95  *Gesellschaftsgeschichte, IV, 1914–1949*, Hans-Ulrich Wehler, quoted in 'Coercion and Consent in Nazi Germany', Raleigh Lecture on History given by Richard J. Evans, British Academy, 2007.

96  Ibid (see note [22]).

97   Joseph Goebbels, speech in Munich, March 1933, quoted in 'Women in Nazi Germany', spartacus-educational.com

98   Ibid (see note [59]).

99   Robert Gellately, 'Social Outsiders and the Consolidation of Hitler's Dictatorship', 1933–1939 in Neil Gregor (ed.) *Nazism, War and Genocide. Essays in Honour of Jeremy Noakes*, Exeter, 2005.

100  Ibid (see note [91]).

101  *Through Hell for Hitler*, Henry Metelmann, Spellmount, 1990.

102  *Account Rendered: A Dossier on my Former Self*, Melita Maschmann, Plunkett Lake Press, Lexington, Massachusetts, 2017.

103  Ibid (see note [59]).

104  Hildegard Koch, interviewed by Louis Hagen in his book *Ein Volk, Ein Reich: Nine Lives Under the Nazis*, The History Press, Cheltenham, 2011.

105  Ibid (see note [56]).

106  'The Nazi Capture of Power', Richard Bessel, *Journal of Contemporary History*, No. 39, 2004.

107  Claus Mühlfeld and Friedrich Schönweiss, quoted in *Marriage and Fatherhood in the Nazi SS*, Amy Carney, University of Toronto Press, 2018.

108  Ibid (see note [44]).

109  Text adapted from a page on Dorothy Fleming on The National Holocaust Centre and Museum website, holocaust.org.uk

110  Ibid (see note [44]).

111  *The Gestapo and German Society: Enforcing Racial Policy 1933–1945*, Robert Gellately, Clarendon Press of Oxford University Press, New York, 1990.

112  'The Gestapo: Control Through Fear', Jill Lauerman, article for *Historia*, journal of the History Department of Eastern Illinois University, vol. 9, Charleston, Illinois, 2000, eiu.edu

## Chapter 9 The Fighting Starts

113  Ibid (see note [25]).

114  *The Goebbels Diaries: 1939–1941* (10 October 1939), Putnam Publishing Group, 1983.

115  'Diving Poland and Its People', on website Facing History and Ourselves, facinghistory.org

116  'The War against Poland: Speed and Brutality', ibid (see note [115]).

117  *The Third Reich at War*, Richard J. Evans, Penguin Books, 2009.

118  'The War against Poland: Speed and Brutality', ibid (see note [115]).

119  'Nazi Anti-Jewish Policy During the Polish Campaign: The Case of the Einsatzgruppe von Woyrsch', Alexander B. Rossino, *German Studies Review*, 2001, jstor.org

120  Ibid (see note [119]).

121  Ibid (see note [102]).

122  'Education in Nazi Germany', I.L. Kandel, 1938, jstor.org

123  *A Crack in the Wall: Growing up under Hitler*, Horst Krüger, Fromm International publishers, 1985.

## Chapter 10 Boy Soldiers

124  *People's Century: From the Dawn of the Century to the Start of the Cold War*, Godfrey Hodgson, BBC Books, London, 1995.

125  '30 January 1939, Reichstag speech', en.wikipedia.org

126  *I Was Doctor Mengele's Assistant*, Miklós Nyiszli, Frap Books, Kraków, 2000.

127  Ibid (see note [30]).

128  Ibid (see note [75]).

129  Adapted from an article on military history on website Fandom, 'Emil Dürr', military-history.fandom.com

130  Adapted from an article called 'The Falaise Pocket: Sight of Fanatical German Resistance', Al Hemingway, on Warfare History Network website, warefarehistorynetwork.com

## Chapter 11 Reality and Resistance

131  *If This is a Man*, Primo Levy, Penguin Books, London, 1987.

132  'Teaching the Nazi Dictatorship: Focus on Youth', Stephen Pagaard, Society for History of Education, 2005, jstor.org

133  Text taken from the White Rose pamphlets, 1942–43.

134  *What We Knew: Terror, Mass Murder, and Everyday Life in Nazi Germany: An Oral History*, Eric A. Johnson and Karl-Heinz Reuband, Basic Books, New York, 2005, quoted in 'Coercion and Consent in Nazi Germany', Raleigh Lecture on History given by Richard J. Evans, British Academy, 2007.

135  Fritz Wiedemann, member of Hitler's personal staff quoted in Ibid (see note [132]).

136  Ibid (see note [22]).

137  Joseph Goebbels, extract from speech quoted on 'German History in Documents and Images' website: ghdi-ghi-dc.org

138  Ibid (see note [106]).

139  *A Noble Treason: The Revolt of the Munich Students against Hitler*, Richard Hanser, Putnam, New York, 1979.


## Chapter 12 The End

140  'Himmler's Speeches', 10 October 1944, East Prussia, speech to Members of the Volkssturm, National Archives and Records Administration, www.archives.gov

141  Ibid (see note [4]).

142  Ibid (see note [102]).

143  'Capturing the Bridge at Remagen, 1945', article on Eyewitness to History website, 2008, eyewitnesstohistory.com

144  Ibid (see note [4]).


## Afterword

145  *Hitler's Children: The Hitler Youth and the SS*, Gerhard Rempel, The University of North Carolina Press, 1989.

146  'Propaganda and Children during the Hitler Years', Mary Mills, The Nizkor Project, nizkor.com

147  'Friendship into Comradeship. Gang Culture, Genocide, and Nation-Building in Germany, 1914–1945', Thomas Kühne, Clark University, Worcester, Massachusetts, 2010, academia.edu

148  Ibid (see note [42]).

149  'The Hitler Youth: the "Other" Victims of the Nazi Regime', Grainne Feick, 2013, University of California, Berkeley, academia.edu

150  Ibid (see note [91]).

# Index